CHICAGO PUBLIC LIBRARY
RATURE AND LANGUAGE DIVISION
ERATURE INFORMATION CENTER
400 SOUTH STATE STREET
CHICAGO, ILLINOIS 60605

D1175040

PS
3572
.I9
Z56
1996

Blaeser, Kimberly M.

Gerald Vizenor.

$29.95

DATE			

JAN   1997

BAKER & TAYLOR

Gerald Vizenor

Gerald Vizenor
Writing in the Oral Tradition

By **Kimberly M. Blaeser**

University of Oklahoma Press : Norman and London

Published with the assistance of the National Endowment for the Humanities, a federal agency which supports the study of such fields as history, philosophy, literature, and language.

Library of Congress Cataloging-in-Publication Data

Blaeser, Kimberly M.
    Gerald Vizenor : writing in the oral tradition / by Kimberly M. Blaeser.
        p.   cm.
    Includes bibliographical references (p.) and index.
    ISBN 0-8061-2874-7 (alk. paper)
    1. Vizenor, Gerald Robert, 1934-   —Technique.   2. Oral tradition—United States.   3. Storytelling—United States.
    4. Indians in literature.   5. Narration (Rhetoric).   6. Fiction—Technique.   I. Title.
    PS3572.I9Z56   1996
    813'.54—dc20   96-18188
                                                                              CIP

Text design by Cathy Carney Imboden. Text typeface is Palacio. Display typeface is Oracle II Bold.

The paper in this book meets the guidelines for permanence and durability of the Committee on Production Guidelines for Book Longevity of the Council on Library Resources, Inc. ∞

Copyright © 1996 by the University of Oklahoma Press, Norman, Publishing Division of the University. All rights reserved. Manufactured in the U.S.A.

1 2 3 4 5 6 7 8 9 10

CHICAGO PUBLIC LIBRARY
LITERATURE AND LANGUAGE DIVISION
LITERATURE INFORMATION CENTER
400 SOUTH STATE STREET
CHICAGO, ILLINOIS 60605

R01152 05137

For Marlene and Tony Blaeser,
for Gah-wah-bah-bi-gon-i-kah,
for Lenny

The fine spirit of the Ojibway song has been held in the heart.
—Gerald Vizenor, *Escorts to White Earth*, 1968

Contents

Acknowledgments

T his study could not have been completed without the generous personal support and professional assistance I have received from a variety of sources over the years. I would like to thank the Newberry Library's D'Arcy McNickle Center for the History of the American Indian for the Francis C. Allen Fellowship that allowed me the time to frame this study, and the University of Notre Dame Graduate School for the Zahm Research Travel Grant that gave me the opportunity to undertake extensive interviews with Gerald Vizenor. I would also like to acknowledge the University of Wisconsin-Milwaukee's American Indian Studies program, English and Comparative Literature department, and Center for Twentieth Century Studies, as well as the University of Wisconsin system's Institute for Race and Ethnicity, for the teaching, research, and travel opportunities they have afforded me over the past several years.

I extend sincere gratitude to James Dougherty for guiding this project in its early stages, and offer thanks to my friends and colleagues A. LaVonne Brown Ruoff, Betty Louise Bell, Gordon Henry, Louis Owens, Arnold Krupat, and James Ruppert, all of whom have offered comments on my work, have shared their own research, writing, anecdotes, and ideas on Gerald Vizenor's writings, and have encouraged me throughout this process.

My thanks go as well to Robert and Kay Blaeser for gathering research materials in Minneapolis, to Steven Kirk for editing and research assistance, and to my students over the years for sharing their ideas on Native American literature. I owe a great debt to Gerald Vizenor for his willing and witty participation in interview sessions, for access to materials, for the respect he has given my work, and for his warmth and his valued friendship.

Finally, I express what can only be inadequate thanks to my family, especially my parents, for understanding, love, and encouragement. To my husband, Lenny, I offer the greatest thanks, for without his constancy this work could not have come to fruition. *Miigwech.*

Gerald Vizenor

Introduction

This is one way to tell a story. In this instance it is my way, and it is the
way of my people. When Pohd-lohk told a story he began by being quiet. Then
he said Ah-keah-de, *"They were camping," and he said it every time. I have*
tried to write in the same spirit. Imagine: They were camping.
—N. Scott Momaday, *The Names*

Philosophical Maxims

Gerald Vizenor, mixedblood Anishinaabe, comes from a story-telling people. Of the crane clan, he descends from the orators of that people. Stories form the foundation of his being, words the foundation of his career. In the worst moments of his life, he has survived by the power of these. "You can't understand the world without telling a story," he claims. "There isn't any center to the world but story."[1]

Before he ever conceived of his own power to create, young Vizenor had experienced the liberating power of oral culture, the wonderful imaginative freedom inspired by storytelling. He says, "The thing I remember mostly about stories—whoever was telling them: my grand-mother, my uncles, the kids, even my mother—the thing that I remember most vividly is the idea of being set free."[2] No wonder, then, that Vizenor should attempt in his own literary career to invest the written word with the same liberating power he found in the oral. Vizenor sets forth the goal for his writing when he says:

> To me there is no more profound gesture in communication, or I want to use the word *discourse*...than to set someone free in talk. This is so precious and so gentle and so powerful because so often people don't set us free— they try to control us with language...I think the simplest act of personal liberation is imagination, talk, the play of imagination—in other words, talking so that an idea actually is part of it yet sets you out of it. (Interview)

Over and over again, in every quarter of his work, Vizenor calls for these simple interrelated essentials of writing and life: liberation, imagination, play, and discourse. His writing seeks to function as both the presentation of an idea and as an invitation to discover where that idea might lead, an invitation to engage in a dialogue.

Taken as philosophical maxims underlying Vizenor's work, his seemingly innocuous views on the liberating possibilities of language hardly prepare us for the author's intellectually sophisticated literary theories, his innovative and often tempestuous style, his no-holds-barred attack on the stifling political, social, religious, historical, and educational institutions of society, and his blatant transgression of taboos, both literary and social. Yet this apparent discrepancy between the soft-spoken voice of the contemplative and the raucous voice of the revolutionary actually intimates the multivoiced character of the man and his writing.[3] Vizenor himself, his literary creations, and his philosophy all breathe multiplicity; they refuse to be tied to either end of contrary poles, but take their life from the dialogue between contradictions. "The function of literature," he says in an interview with Neal Bowers and Charles Silet, "ought to be to continually change and upset, to contradict."[4]

Change, upset, contradict—this Vizenor's work does as it refuses to hold still for definition or categorization. His work, his life, and his theory exist in the continuous process of unraveling truth, because the unraveling demands imaginative participation and the freedom to continue growth and discovery. They exist in the process of becoming— which stands in contrast to notions of static being.[5] Vizenor writes of himself: "I am still discovering who I am, the myth in me. . . . I am part crow, part dragonfly, part squirrel, part bear. I kick the sides of boxes out. I will not be pinned down. I am flying home in words and myths."[6]

Biographical Backdrop

Vizenor's life has indeed run the gamut of experience. He has alternately been a member of a large extended tribal family and an abandoned foster child, a delinquent and a corrections agent, a high school dropout and a college professor.[7]

Born October 22, 1934, in Minneapolis to LaVerne Lydia Peterson, a white teenage dropout, and Clement William Vizenor, a twenty-four-year-old house painter, Vizenor is a self-proclaimed mixedblood or "crossblood." Vizenor's father, himself a mixedblood of French and Anishinaabe ancestry, came with other members of his family from White Earth Reservation in Minnesota to the Minneapolis area to find work. The union of his parents Vizenor characterizes as less than successful, and they lived together for only about a year. Then, in late June 1936, when Vizenor was only twenty months old, his father was murdered in what remains an unsolved urban crime. Gerald's care fell to his paternal grandmother and several aunts and uncles with whom he and his father had been living at the time.

His remaining childhood consisted of years living together in a tenement with his paternal relatives, years of loneliness and desperate poverty when his mother would reclaim and try to care for him, and years of abandonment into various foster homes. It was during these years that Vizenor, though never excelling academically, developed the imagination, humor, and independent spirit that would not only see him through his troubled adolescence and early adulthood but would ultimately find voice in a collection of literary works unexceeded in volume by any Native American author to date.

Vizenor remembers and records in his autobiographical accounts his engagement in lively and imaginative adventures with his childhood friends. It was as a boy, he says, that the "little people"—characters present in some of his writing—first came to life in play and imagination. As an adolescent, Vizenor was often truant and involved in petty theft. Then, at the age of thirteen or fourteen, he solemnly decided, "I don't want cops in my life ever again" and became, he says, "pretty much a straight arrow" (Interview).

At eighteen, in his senior year of high school and just months before graduation, Vizenor dropped out of school to join the U.S. Army. Ironically, it was there amid the infamous military strictures that he first experienced a feeling of liberation and promise. Through a standard army intelligence test he was shown to be intellectually gifted, a fact that surprised him so much he insisted the test must be in error. But when a second exam resulted in yet better scores, Vizenor for the first time in his life began to see himself as having potential. He began his first serious reading, delving into the works of authors as varied as Thomas Wolfe and Kahlil Gibran, began to associate with college-educated men and consider the possibilities of education, and began to dream of a writer's life. His stint in the army also exposed him to Japanese culture and Japanese literature, which would have an enduring influence on his style and philosophy of writing.

After an honorable discharge from the military in 1955, Vizenor pursued a college education, eventually earning an undergraduate degree from the University of Minnesota in 1960 in child development and psychology. In 1959 he and Judith Horns were married, and the year of Vizenor's graduation also saw the birth of his son, Robert. After receiving the bachelor's degree, Vizenor went on to earn graduate credits in anthropology, library science, and Asian studies. During this time at the university, encouraged by one of his professors, he also pursued his interest in haiku poetry, and in 1962 *Two Wings the Butterfly*, a collection of his haiku, was privately published. Over the ensuing years, this was to be followed by five more books of haiku: *Raising the Moonvines* and *Seventeen Chirps* in 1964, *Slight Abrasions: A Dialogue in Haiku* (with Jerome Downes) in 1966, *Empty Swings* in 1967, and most recently, *Matsushima: Pine Islands* in 1984.

Vizenor saw great similarities between the haiku form and the Ojibway dream songs, and during the time he was involved in the writing of his early haiku, he also undertook the reexpression of traditional Ojibway songs and stories.[8] The first collection he edited, *Summer in the Spring: Lyric Poems of the Ojibway*, was published in 1965 and reissued in 1970 as *anishinabe nagamon: Songs of the People*. Also published in 1970 was *anishinabe adisokan: Tales of the People*. The songs and stories were published together in 1981 under the title *Summer in the Spring: Ojibwe Lyric Poems and Tribal Stories* and reissued in a revised edition in 1993 by University of Oklahoma Press as *Summer in the Spring: Anishinaabe Lyric Poems and Stories*.

Vizenor's writing received less attention and his graduate career lost significance for him when he became heavily involved with the Native American people and politics of Minneapolis and St. Paul in the mid-1960s. He worked in various capacities in the Twin Cities' Indian community, serving as a social worker for the Waite Settlement House in Minneapolis in 1965 and as executive director of the American Indian Employment and Guidance Center in 1966. He also organized protests aimed at earning Bureau of Indian Affairs (BIA) support for urban Indians. From the people and incidents of these years Vizenor would draw much of the material for his early writing, and the experiences from that decade in his life continue to surface in his current work.

Eventually Vizenor's involvement with tribal politics and his drive to speak out on Indian issues led him back to writing, led to publications in the magazine *Twin Citian* and the *Minneapolis Tribune*, and eventually launched his career as a journalist. He worked first as a general-assignment reporter in 1968 and 1969 and later, in 1974, as an editorial writer for the *Tribune*. Many of the articles and editorials from this period were collected in *Tribal Scenes and Ceremonies*, published in 1976, and reappear in various forms in such later works as *Wordarrows: Indians and Whites in the New Fur Trade* (1978), *The People Named the Chippewa: Narrative Histories* (1984), and most recently, *Crossbloods: Bone Courts, Bingo, and Other Reports* (1990). Another literary work originating at least partly from Vizenor's years of activity in the Indian community and the contacts he made during that time is *The Everlasting Sky: New Voices from the People Named the Chippewa* (1972), in which Vizenor writes of those he calls the "oshki anishinabe," the "new people of the wood-land." This work, much of it built from interviews with contemporary tribal leaders, elders, and youths, uses the voices of real people to chron-icle the blending of change and tradition in the Indian communities.

Although Vizenor held a wide range of other jobs during his early years (everything from meat loader and psychiatric orderly to library assistant, research consultant, and teacher training director), his next major career step took him to the college classroom, where he has remained. His first taste of college teaching came in 1966, when he served as a summer instructor in a special program on tribal cultures at Bemidji State University in Minnesota; but his career in the classroom really began with a one-year appointment at Lake Forest College in Illinois from 1970 to 1971. Vizenor's new career followed a series of personal changes as well. After a long period of separation, Vizenor and Judith Horns were divorced in 1969. He would remain single until 1981, at which time he and British-born Laura Hall would wed. After Vizenor's first academic appointment, he would eventually teach in various capacities at several Twin Cities campuses (including Augsburg, Macalaster, Hamline, and the University of Minnesota), serve a term as director of Indian studies at Bemidji State University in Minnesota, and teach at universities as far-flung as Tianjin University in China, the University of Oklahoma, and the University of California at Berkeley and at Santa Cruz.

During these years of teaching, Vizenor began publishing his first fiction. *Darkness in Saint Louis Bearheart* (1978),[9] a futuristic novel and satire, introduced many of the themes, methods, and metaphors that Vizenor would develop in his later works: the spiritual pilgrimage; the political confrontation carried out with wit, not weapons; the challenge of romantic Indian stereotypes; the deliberate transgression of "polite" sexual limits; the theories on the power, as well as on the misuse, of words; and the use of tribal myths, images of transformation, and dream vision experiences. In the works to come, this collection of ideas was expanded to include challenges of history and historical method, as well as attacks on social science methodology (perhaps most apparent in *The People Named the Chippewa: Narrative Histories*). Vizenor's work also began to emphasize the identity and role of the mixedblood, creating images of urban and academic tribal encounters. The working out of these themes can be seen clearly in *Earthdivers: Tribal Narratives on Mixed Descent* (1981), a collection of short works that blend fiction and autobiography.

Earthdivers also showcases what is perhaps the single most significant aspect of Vizenor's writing to date: his use of the Native American trickster figure. This trickster persona again takes prominence in Vizenor's next four novels: *Griever: An American Monkey King in China* (1987), *The Trickster of Liberty* (1988), *The Heirs of Columbus* (1991), and *Dead Voices: Natural Agonies in the New World* (1992), as well as in his short fiction collection *Landfill Meditation: Crossblood Stories* (1991). Clear parallels can also be drawn between the methods and perspective of the Ojibway trickster figure Naanabozho and that of the autobiographical Vizenor we meet in *Interior Landscapes: Autobiographical Myths and Metaphors*. In this 1990 autobiography, Vizenor leads us through a series of odd, touching, sometimes maddening, and frequently hilarious adventures and misadventures that have made up his life.

Read the endorsements on Vizenor's book jackets, note the publications that review his work, and you get some sense of the reputation he has earned and the arenas to which his writing play is directed. N. Scott Momaday, Ishmael Reed, and James Welch are among those whose quick takes adorn Vizenor's book covers. Momaday, for example, says of Vizenor, "He is perhaps the supreme ironist among American Indian writers of the twentieth century."[10] For his novel *Griever* Vizenor won the Fiction Collective Award in 1987 and the American Book Award in 1990. He was the 1989 recipient of the California Arts Council Literature Award and received the PEN Oakland Book Award for his 1990 *Interior Landscapes*. His work has received a great deal of attention by international scholars, with various of his works translated, for example, into Italian, German, and French.[11] Vizenor held the James J. Hill Professorship at the University of Minnesota, was honored with the David Burr Chair at the University of Oklahoma, chairs the selection committee for the University of Nebraska Native American Prose Award, and now edits the American Indian Literature and Critical Studies Series for the University of Oklahoma Press. The most recent addition to the Vizenor canon of works, a Vizenor reader, itself illustrates the author's reputation. The book, *Shadow Distance*, collects excerpts from the author's autobiography, novels, short fiction, and essays, and includes the first published version of his screenplay *Harold of Orange*. Vizenor is also the subject of one of a series of recent films on Native American novelists. But whatever the accolades, Vizenor's work draws the most attention for its radical intellectualism and experimental nature.

Ishmael Reed, for example, writes, "Gerald Vizenor combines ancient American storytelling with space-age techniques. I don't know of anybody else who is doing this."[12]

Critical Intersections

With Vizenor's works spanning over a thirty-year period from 1962 to the present, naturally his writing admits many variants in genre, style, purpose, and quality. He has given his voice to poetry, journalism, short and long fiction, "reexpressions" of traditional works, genealogy, autobiography, editorials, essays, literary journalism, screenplays, and to what he calls "narrative histories." In addition, since Vizenor is widely read in history, literature, critical theory, and the social sciences, the possible influences on his writing are multiple. Key among these influences are the reader-response theories of such scholars as Wolfgang Iser and Umberto Eco, the explorations of the oral tradition by Walter J. Ong, the language theories of Mikhail Bakhtin and Jacques Derrida, and cultural studies theories such as that of Jean Baudrillard. Vizenor's interest in contemporary theory resulted, for example, in his editing of the collection *Narrative Chance: Postmodern Discourse on Native American Indian Literatures* (1989, reprint 1993), which includes his own essay "Trickster Discourse." In a recent collection of essays, *Manifest Manners: Postindian Warriors of Survivance* (1994), he employs various theoretical stances to offer commentary on the historical and contemporary situation of Native America.

Innumerable other names can, of course, be added to the list of literary and theoretical influences on Vizenor—George Steiner, N. Scott Momaday, Michel Foucault, Basho, Roland Barthes, and so on. My purpose, however, is not to catalogue or categorize Vizenor's work, nor to trace out all similar strains of thought or method.[13] Instead, I look at Vizenor's ideas about language, written and performed, try to understand his own view of his vocation as a tribal storyteller-cum-writer, explore the manifestations of the tension between the oral and the written in his work, and shed some light on his place in the expanding canons of Native American, American, and world literature. I look both at his philosophy and his work to discover if indeed he has found a way to write in the oral tradition of the Ojibway.

My first chapter explores both the ideals of tribal oral tradition and the contemporary theories Vizenor has found compatible in striving for a sense of cultural continuity in his writing. Within the rhetoric and theory of Native American writers such as N. Scott Momaday and Simon Ortiz and the analysis of scholars such as A. LaVonne Brown Ruoff and Larry Evers, I place Vizenor's own ideas about tribal oral tradition. Within the framework of these centuries-old tribal traditions, I place contemporary critical theories, such as those of Ong and Bakhtin, that Vizenor has used both to explain the dynamics of the oral and to identify the possibilities that exist for sustaining aspects of orality in the written tradition.

The ideological struggles to maintain tribal culture, Vizenor's accounts of the "cultural word wars," become the topic of the second chapter. Once actively involved in tribal reform movements, Vizenor now carries on his efforts in intellectual and verbal politicking. I look at his works in cultural studies which analyze the origins of stereotypes and the effects of popular stereotypic expectations on Native Americans. Using real-life incidents from tribal life, he writes of the continuing tragedies wrought by the systematic abuse of word power, identifies the contemporary rhetorical disguises of manifest destiny (which he labels "manifest manners"), and unmasks tribal simulations and other unlikely threats to tribal continuance. Among the particular examples I explore are Vizenor's essays and journalistic writings on Ishi, The American Indian Movement (AIM), and Thomas James White Hawk in works such as *Manifest Manners*, *Crossbloods*, and *Wordarrows*, as well as his fictional commentaries on the cultural word wars in *Bearheart*, *Trickster of Liberty*, and *Landfill Meditation*. In these and other works, although Vizenor clearly identifies the threats to tribal integrity, he ultimately upholds the possibility of survival for tribal people through trickster consciousness and imagination, and through the efforts of "postindian warriors" who create new narratives of "survivance."

How Vizenor, as himself one of the tribal survivors, attempts to embody the essence of oral culture in the written word becomes the topic of Chapter 3, where I use as examples "Sand Creek Survivors," "Shadows at LaPointe," *Heirs of Columbus*, and *Interior Landscapes*. Here I specifically examine Vizenor's dissatisfaction with conventional methods of history and journalism (and with the inherent possession of story they enact), and I examine his critique of the conventional claims and methods of autobiography. I look at Vizenor's efforts to break out of these and other literary conventions in his own writing, and at his attempts to challenge and undermine their dominance. By working in a narrative form, creating a context of contested visions, and imbuing his writing with the understanding of oral and mythic traditions, of cultural continuity and historical continuum, and with the richness of what he calls "shadows," Vizenor is able to present a more complete vision of reality than those accounts normally recognized as realistic or factual.

Yet never in his work does Vizenor allow his readers to find complete fulfillment within the text itself. Instead he demands their involvement in the search for truth, for meaning; he demands their involvement in experience, in life. His writing sends out a call for imaginative re-creation of our reality, and he delineates the role his reader must play to find the "spaces between" his words.[14] Vizenor's simultaneous involvement with tribal oral tradition and reader-response aesthetics, and how this manifests itself in his writing, becomes the focus of the last three chapters in this study.

First, in Chapter 4, I look at the similarities in Vizenor's understanding of tribal dream songs and his philosophy of haiku. I examine the way both forms engage the reader in the process of discovery and allude to a meaning the reader must imagine, the way they work to propel the reader beyond mere words toward the imaginative dream vision experience. This haiku method becomes a recognizable part of Vizenor's style, manifested not only in his poetry but in the various other forms his writing takes.

What Vizenor calls "trickster consciousness" likewise informs the great majority of his writing, and like haiku, it both places demands on the reader in the making of the text and ultimately liberates the active reader from the text. Chapter 5 traces the topsy-turvy dynamics of Vizenor's trickster fiction and social satire, using as examples his screenplay *Harold of Orange* and the short story "Almost Browne." It explores the connections in Vizenor between the trickster and the mixedblood and considers his use of trickster fiction as mediation.[15]

Both Vizenor's haiku method and his trickster consciousness are part of a broader, self-conscious strategy. Chapter 6 analyzes various elements of Vizenor's style, their literary and social implications, and the problems this sometimes difficult style poses for uninitiated readers. It examines the ways in which Vizenor's work runs counter to the dominant literary aesthetic and why it might consciously seek this breach. It looks at works like *Dead Voices*, for example, to illustrate how Vizenor purposefully exposes the artifice of written language, how he attempts to write in a way that requires, by way of response, more than the consumption of a text. Vizenor immerses his own text in a network of literary, social, and critical subtexts that essentially encourage and enact a multilevel discourse, and he employs various recognizable rhetorical strategies to create an "open text." Through multiple forms of ambiguity or indeterminancy, for example, Vizenor strives to compensate for the inadequacies of written language by involving the active imagination of the reader in discovering the unwritten elements of his work. Through employment of metaphor he attempts to move the reader beyond the words to an experiential reality.

But in these and other moves to challenge the reader, Vizenor runs the risk of asking too much. He essentially pulls the text out from under complacent readers. By his exposure of literary artifice, he attempts to give his readers a nudge that will allow them to transcend language and gain access to a primal, spiritual, or at least experiential, realm.

Indeed, throughout Vizenor's literary works to date, the words on the page have seldom seemed as weighty as their unstated implications. Though enormously varied in nature and scope, Vizenor's writing shares certain essential characteristics, but none more significant than its tendency to gesture broadly beyond itself. This allusiveness sets him apart in some ways from most other contemporary Native American authors. His stories seldom progress in smooth plot lines. His characters often speak in puzzling and convoluted ways. Very little is resolved in the works of Vizenor. He refuses to grant his reader certain satisfactions in the text because they would close off other possibilities he deems more essential: the possibilities of reader participation and discovery, the possibility that the story has life beyond the page, the possibility of a new kind of "survivance."

As an examination of an author of a prodigious collection of works and of an author who continues (seemingly tirelessly) to write in various genres, this critical analysis cannot hope to give attention to each of Vizenor's literary creations nor to trace the various nuances of development in his career. I do believe, however, that an understanding of the essential participatory quality of his writing, a mapping of the dynamics of his method, will prove invaluable in analyzing any of his texts. At the most fundamental level, Vizenor's writing is invitation. As with any invitation, the summons is not the event, but it is the ticket to getting there. Likewise, Vizenor's texts are not the end, but the means. They invite the reader to become a party to discovery.

1

Intersections with the Oral Tradition

It's like a story being told when it's not only being told. The storyteller doesn't just tell the characters, what they did or said, what happens in the story and so on. No, he participates in the story with those who are listening. The listeners in the same way are taking part in the story. The story includes them in. You see, it's more like an event, the story telling. The story is not just a story then—it's occurring, coming into being.
—Simon Ortiz, "What Indians Do"

The events of oral tradition, the occurrences, the comings into being, the community of story, these are the elements of tribal telling that Vizenor attempts to incorporate into his written works. His goal, ultimately, is to destroy the closure of his own texts by making them perform as "word cinemas," turning them into a dialogue, releasing them into the place of imagination.[1]

Most scholars agree that the oral can never be fully expressed in the written, experience cannot be duplicated in text. Context, Native language, and Native culture ultimately cannot be translated.[2] While conceding these points, Vizenor still believes in the importance of the attempt and in the possibilities for vivifying the text. When asked by interviewers Neal Bowers and Charles Silet about translating oral tradition, he responds: "Well I don't think it's possible, but I think people ought to interest themselves in trying to translate it. . . .I think it can be reimagined and reexpressed and that's my interest."[3] What this interest has meant in Vizenor's work is involvement, not only in the reexpression and reimagination of traditional stories, songs, and ceremonies, but also in the attempt to invest the written form and his own creative works with the qualities and the power of the oral. Vizenor seems to have an idea of himself as one of the "wordmakers" he writes of in *Wordarrows* who "shapes his words in the oral tradition" (vii).[4]

He did not come to this philosophy nor develop a method for his writing in an instant and then hold to his beliefs and form like one of the "terminal believers" he criticizes so strongly in his writing.[5] Rather, the role of "wordmaker" is one Vizenor continues to grow into, much as tribal initiates once spent their lives discovering the meaning of their dream visions.[6] At first he had many misgivings about the title of "writer" because he saw the power of language, especially the written word, repeatedly abused (Interview).[7] This early mistrust, which has kept him vigilant and wary in his own literary pursuits, has also greatly influenced his direction, and he has sought in various ways to avoid the static, monologic quality which too often characterizes the written mode.

In order to mirror the functioning of orality and to imbue his writing with dialogic qualities, and thus to relocate it for potential readers from the passive to the active realm of experience, Vizenor has turned to traditional and contemporary Native American sources, as well as to multiple critical and cultural theories. He finds inspiration for his work of personal and communal liberation in traditional Ojibway tales, ceremonies, and dream songs, and in the pantribal milieu of oral and mythic tradition. He finds theoretical alliances in the work of other Native American writers such as N. Scott Momaday, Leslie Silko, and Simon Ortiz, as well as in the work of past and present scholars of tribal literatures such as Frances Densmore, Dennis Tedlock, and Arnold Krupat. Less expected, but still characteristic of the revolutionary and eclectic Vizenor, he also leads the way among scholars of Native American literature and champions of oral tradition in finding inspiration and allies in the works of such contemporary critical theorists as

Walter J. Ong, Mikhail Bakhtin, Valentine Vološinov, and Jacques Derrida. Looking in each of these four directions—oral tradition, contemporary tribal literature, scholarship in Native American studies, and movements in critical theory—Vizenor strives in his own philosophy and in his enactment of his vocation as a tribal "wordmaker" to bring together the potential of each. In so doing he has taken Native American literature in a new and uncharted direction. What follows in this chapter is a brief examination of certain ideas key to these four elements and to their interconnections in Vizenor's work.

"It's Life, It's Juice, It's Energy!"

With these words—life, juice, energy—Vizenor describes Native American trickster tales (Interview); he could as well be describing the qualities he most admires in the more encompassing tribal oral tradition and the qualities he seeks to emulate in his writing. A. LaVonne Ruoff calls "Indian oral literatures" a "vibrant force." *Studies in American Indian Literature*, the collection edited by Paula Gunn Allen, refers to oral literature as "a living reality." Brian Swann calls "the Word" in Native American tradition "a sacrament, a vital force." Simon Ortiz, speaking of the oral tradition, says, "The stories come from the source and nature of all life."[8] And in *The People Named the Chippewa*, Vizenor himself writes, "Tribal words have power in the oral tradition, the sounds express the spiritual energies" (24). Spiritual energies, life, vibrancy, force, vitality, power—these are the kinds of words used by indigenous people and scholars alike to characterize the Native American oral tradition.[9] This vitality originates in the word itself, as well as in the expansive nature, the communal quality, and the generative character of the oral tradition.

Most tribal cultures have great reverence for language, believing in the power of words to affect their reality, to bring about change, to create. "Language to me was magic," writes Ortiz, "magic in its purest essence, magic that can create, change, rebuild."[10] Words are also often identified as the ultimate source of being. In her 1946 study of Native American oral literature, for example, Margot Astrov acknowledges this belief and speaks of the "Creative Potency" of the word: "The word, indeed, is power. It is life, substance, reality. The word lived before earth, sun, or moon came into existence. Whenever the Indian ponders over the mystery of origin, he shows a tendency to ascribe to the word a creative power all its own. The word is conceived of as an independent entity, superior even to the gods."[11]

Among those contemporary Indian authors who have spoken of words as origin, N. Scott Momaday has perhaps addressed the topic most directly and is frequently quoted on the subject. In *The Way to Rainy Mountain*, for example, he claims, "A word has power in and of itself. It comes from nothing into sound and meaning; it gives origin to all things." And in his novel *House Made of Dawn* he writes of the primacy of the word through the voice of Tosamah, the Priest of the Sun, who says, "The Word did not come into being, but *it was*. It did not break upon the silence, but *it was older than the silence and the silence was made of it*."[12] In *Wordarrows: Indians and Whites in the New Fur Trade*, Vizenor himself quotes this latter passage from Momaday and, through the character of Matchi Makwa, offers his own statement about the word as origin: "The speaker is not the center of the word world because words were on the earth before the talkers and tellers" (94).

Vizenor's statement acknowledges not only the primacy of the word but also its place in the relationships that constitute an oral tradition. Storytellers (and, by extension, writers) are merely vehicles or voices for the words that have always existed. "Creative writers," he claims in the 1978 *Wordarrows*, "find words in colors, soaring birds, flowers in the sun, wine at night" (94); and in the 1991 short story "Almost Browne," he returns to these ideas about words as origin and as presence within creation: "Listen, there are words almost everywhere. I realized that in a chance moment. Words are in the air, in our blood, words were always there. . . . Words are in the snow, trees, leaves, wind, birds, beaver, the sound of ice cracking; words are in fish and mongrels, where they've been since we came to this place with the animals" (*Landfill Meditation*, 8).

Implied in Vizenor's comments is the act of connection, the recognition or discovery necessary for the creation that comes from verbalization. The understanding of word as origin is intricately linked to the power of thought. So thought realized in words becomes creator of our reality. "We are touched into tribal being with words," writes Vizenor, "made whole in the world with words and oratorical gestures" (*Wordarrows*, vii). Both Leslie Silko and Paula Gunn Allen dramatize this Native American understanding of origin as arising out of the union of thought and words. In their contemporary novels, each begins with a retelling of the mythic origin of the world. In *Ceremony* Silko begins with the story of Ts'its'tsi'nako, Thought-Woman, who thinks and speaks the world into being. "Whatever she thinks about / appears," writes Silko, and "Thought-Woman, the spider, / named things and / as she named them / they appeared."[13] Allen begins *The Woman Who Owned the Shadows* with Spiderwoman's creation, which also involves both thought and verbalization: "Thinking thus she made the world." And, "Thus sang the Spider. Thus she thought."[14]

The originating force spoken of by Vizenor and dramatized in the opening passages of these novels is not a thing of the past. Words and thoughts retain their capacity to create, to cause, and to change. As Allen claims in *Studies in American Indian Literature*, "The oral tradition is alive and well, moving and changing."[15]

The larger stories of Silko and Allen's novels both dramatize the contemporary power of language. Silko, for example, invests her story with great immediacy and a sense of present creation by concluding the opening passage with: "She is sitting in her room / thinking of a story now / I am telling you the story / she is thinking."[16] Thus, as Ruoff notes, Silko's story of Thought-Woman enacts not only the mythic origin but "the continuum of the oral tradition from the mythic past of the Lagunas to the present."[17] Later in the novel, Silko's account of the evil "set in motion" by the witch's telling of a story that "can't be called back" dramatically illustrates the still extant power of language and thought.[18]

Vizenor's own works frequently employ a contemporary setting to illustrate the embedded force of language. In his novel *Dead Voices*, for example, he writes of a woman who "had the power of stories," who "could do things with stories, real things" like "start fires," "change the direction of the wind," and "heal people on the reservation" (120). Chivaree, the woman's granddaughter, a contemporary crossblood, likewise "has the power of stories." She has learned from her grandmother the stories that will make the birch tree create environmentally friendly paper products.

As these statements and examples illustrate, in Native belief systems and literary accounts the creative power of words and thought is not confined to mythic time. Past and present, words and thought are believed to have a certain power, and this power is enlisted to order all manner of things in American Indian life. According to Ruoff: "The power of thought and word enables native people to achieve harmony with the physical and spiritual universe: to bring rain, enrich the harvest, provide good hunting, heal physical and mental sickness, maintain good relations within the group, bring victory against an enemy, win a loved one, or ward off evil spirits."[19]

Because of the power of words in speech and thought, they are held in reverence in tribal cultures, awarded great attention, and used carefully and, often, sparingly. Their use is ritualized to varying degrees among the tribes and made subject to certain taboos. Stories, for example, are often framed by ritual openings and closings, and the telling of certain stories is restricted by season. Some tribal cultures forbid the mention of the names of the dead, believing that speaking their names could call the spirits of the dead, disturb their rest, or prevent them from finding their place in the spirit world. There are also appropriate and inappropriate uses of language dictated not by tribal taboos but by a notion of what is proper in a specific relationship.

Words must be used in a certain way, in a certain spirit, spoken with the proper understanding. Part of this understanding is a recognition of their source and the inherent meanings of the words. The same word may be spoken well or poorly depending on the disposition of the speaker and the occasion of the word's pronouncement. For example, the appropriate name by which to address an Indian person involves, not only the relationship of the speaker to the person being addressed, but also things like the occasion, the place of the encounter, the demeanor of both speaker and addressee, and who else is present at the time. The right name can also be improperly spoken if modulations of intonation, sequence, or gesture are not followed.

The subtleties involved in these distinctions are many, but on these kind of subtleties Vizenor builds much of his commentary on language use and his criticism of inappropriate use. He writes, for example, in *Wordarrows* of words spoken without proper awareness: "Silence and wind and water sounds were here before birds and fish. The birds knew how to sing from the wind that shaped their wings in flight. Like fish out of water, white people speak words out of meaning"(94). For Vizenor, words in the oral tradition reflect and enact relationships: "Words are rituals in the oral tradition, from the sound of creation, the wisps of visions on the wind . . . not cold pages or electronic beats that separate the tellers from the listeners" (*Landfill Meditation*, 99). If words are used in isolation they lose their life, their connection with origin, they cease to be the "real words" he speaks of in "Almost Browne" (8) and become instead the "dead voices" of his novel by that name.

In developing an understanding of what is proper within the tribal oral tradition, we must recognize that often speech itself is inappropriate; silence in these instances becomes the vehicle of communication or connection, and silence too has inherent power. It is, as Astrov notes, "esteemed as a reservoir of spiritual strength;" or, as Momaday writes in *House Made of Dawn*, "the older and better part of custom still."[20] We see silence as sacred presence and as active communication in a scene from Momaday's novel in which Francisco remembers an encounter with a bear during a hunt: "He did not want to break the stillness of the night, for it was holy and profound and it was rest and restoration, . . . the silence was essential to them both, and it lay out like a bond between them, ancient and inviolable."[21] Francisco sees silence not as one optional response here, but as necessary, "essential" and "inviolable," and as the very fiber of communication between himself and the bear.

In Vizenor's writing, too, silence may work as a dramatic device in story or as a philosophical maxim and, like words, it is of two qualities. In "Laurel Hole In The Day" from *Wordarrows*, for example, Laurel's silence is portrayed as a kind of voicelessness (similar to Abel's in Momaday's *House Made of Dawn*):

Laurel Hole In The Day opened her mouth to speak, her lips moved to shape the first words, but she could not tell her impossible dream. She stood in silence in the Waite Neighborhood House kitchen, dressed in a new colorful print dress. Tears were dripping down her plump brown cheeks.

Laurel could hear her voice inside, but when the words took shape on her lips her throat tightened and she could not speak. She knew that if she forced but one word, a single word into sound, it would burst with all the dreams and emotional pain and loneliness from her heart like a bird at dusk against a window. (47)

Here her inability to speak, her silence, illustrates her powerlessness and the extent to which she is cut off from the community. In the "Tricksters" chapter of *Dead Voices*, however, when the character Chivaree refuses to reveal the stories told her by her grandmother, stories that have certain powers, her silence demonstrates her strength and her connection to tradition. "The minute the stories are told," she claims, "they lose their power" (122). Holding silence in this instance is the appropriate response.

But Vizenor does more than employ silence dramatically or philo-sophically in story; it also becomes a dialogic device to engage the reader. In pieces like "Natural Tilts" and "The Sociodowser" from *Earthdivers*, in which he uses the word "silence" itself repeatedly, the reader is required to imagine the scene, the heavy silence and its significance (88–89, 153). In other places in his work, the silence is not that of a character in the story; it is the author's own. Vizenor resists commentary, he omits connective phrases, he juxtaposes unrelated scenes, he employs ellipses. These and other techniques, forms of literary restraint or silence (which I take up later in greater detail), require active participation. They become a part of the interaction with the reader, one of the ways in which Vizenor's writing attempts to retain both the immediacy of oral story and the power of silence.

Another important means of communication—like silence an integral part of the tribal oral tradition—is nonlinguistic sound: vocables in song, the sound of drum and rattle, the sounds made in the voice of other beings, the sounds of spirit voices, and so on. Note, for example, how the following three translations of Anishinaabeg *midé* songs have nonlinguistic sound as their inspiration: "All around the circle of the sky I hear the Spirit's voice." "There comes a sound / From my medicine bag." "The sound is fading away. / It is of five sounds. / Freedom. / The sound is fading away. / It is of five sounds."[22] Clearly the sounds referred to by these singers carried meaning for them. In the intro-duction to his own "reexpressions" of Anishinaabeg songs, Vizenor explains: "The Anishinaabeg hear music not only in the human voice but in the sounds of animals and trees and in ice cracking on the lakes" (*Summer in the Spring*, 11). In Momaday's *House Made of Dawn*, too, we see sound functioning directly as communication in the scene in which

Abel recalls hearing his grandfather at prayer with the old men. Abel "remembered the prayer, and he knew what it meant—not the words, which he had never really heard, but the low sound itself, rising and falling far away in his mind, unmistakable and unbroken."[23] Even though Abel does not hear words, he understands the meaning; the very sound is "unmistakable."

Vizenor, like the early Anishinaabe song makers, like Momaday and many other tribal authors, uses sound as a recognizable means of communication. In *Dead Voices*, for example, the character Chivaree, like Abel in the above passage, remembers the sound of her grandmother's voice: "I just listened, and in my head practiced the exact sound, the rise and fall of the voice, the way my grandmother spoke to the birch" (121). In the story, Chivaree cannot translate the sounds into meaning in English, but the remembered sounds themselves have power: they cause a reaction in the birch.

Nonlinguistic sound plays a significant role in placing Vizenor's work within the context of tribal tradition and contributes to the referential character of his writing. Note, for example, how in *Bearheart*, in stories such as "Mother Earth Man and Paradise Flies" and "Spacious Treeline in Words," and in various other accounts of transformational experiences involving the bear, Vizenor uses sounds rendered either "ho ho ho ho" or "ha ha ha haaaa" (*Bearheart*, vii and throughout; *Wordarrows*, 90; *Earthdivers*, 183). Densmore has explained the significance of these sounds in *midé* tradition in the same way Vizenor does in a note to one of the Anishinaabe songs he includes in *Summer in the Spring*, a song which also makes use of sounds. He writes, "The expression *he hi hi hi* is the sound of the feeling of the power of the sacred spirit of the *midewiwin*. A *midewiwin* song is completed with the syllables *ho ho ho ho*" (147). His use of these kinds of vocables, then, works to place his own writing in the oral tradition of the *midéwiwin* songs and alludes in a broader sense to the belief system inherent in that religious society.

The allusiveness of Vizenor's writing can itself be seen to arise out of the allusiveness inherent in a tribal oral tradition that sees itself partly as a means of access to the sacred reality from which it originated. Vizenor notes, for example, in speaking of the Anishinaabe songs: "The songs of the people are the energy of life and the words are the sounds and pictures of spiritual power" ("Tribal People and the Poetic Image," 20). The exact understanding of the relationship between the oral tradition and a primal or spiritual realm varies from tribe to tribe, but many tribes understand the purposes of speech and song to be embodiment or translation and a means of access, giving form or voice to the ultimate core of being, or bringing the singer/listener into the presence of the spiritual reality. In *Language and Art in the Navajo Universe*, for example, Gary Witherspoon describes the Navajo belief that the gods make their thoughts and voices known through human song, prayer, and speech; and in *Yaqui Deer Songs* Larry Evers and Felipe Molina speak of the "enchanted talk" of deer songs, describing them as "verbal equations" between this world and that "mythic, primeval place called...sea ania, flower world." They explain: "It is through song that experience with other living things in the wilderness world is made intelligible and accessible to the human community."[24] Vizenor himself describes "words" as "rituals in the oral tradition, from the knowledge of creation, little visions on the winds,"[25] and Paula Gunn Allen comments on the pantribal understanding of the referential quality of the oral tradition in "The Sacred Hoop":

> The tribes seek—through song, ceremony, legend, sacred stories (myths) and tales—to embody, articulate, and share reality, to bring the isolated private self into harmony and balance with this reality, to verbalize the sense of the majesty and reverent mystery of all things, and to actualize, in language, those truths that give to humanity its greatest significance and dignity. To a large extent, ceremonial literature serves to redirect private emotion and integrate the energy generated by emotion within a cosmic framework.[26]

The connection to what Allen calls a "cosmic framework," what Evers and Molina call a "mythic, primeval place," and what Vizenor calls "spiritual power," "the energy of life," and "visions on the winds" depends not only on the words of songs and ceremonies but also on the active performance and reception of those songs and ceremonies. It depends on the active engagement and participation of the singers, storytellers, and listeners. "A story," Simon Ortiz explains, "is not only told but it is also listened to; it becomes whole in its expression and perception."[27] Momaday, too, has given a great deal of attention to this notion of perception or reception in oral tradition. In *House Made of Dawn*, through the Priest of the Sun's remembrances of his grandmother, he, like Ortiz, comments directly on listening as an important element of oral tradition. Storytelling involves more than speech; according to the old woman, it is both "to utter" and "to hear," "to listen" and "to delight."[28]

This notion of reception and participation is key as well to Vizenor's understanding of oral tradition and becomes a major thematic and stylistic element in his writing. In describing the stories of the "oshki [contemporary] anishinabe" in *The Everlasting Sky*, for example, he explains: "The tension only suggests the pathos and humor, leaving the listener to complete the story" (72). And in discussing the process of storytelling, he notes the importance of active listening: "There has to be a participant and someone has to listen. I don't mean listening in the passive sense." He characterizes this active listening in various ways—as "discourse," as "dialogue," as "engagement"; he calls it "agonistic," "active," "play in language," "communal"; and he describes the storytelling as a process or relationship:

> The one thing it's not is passive. . . .The oral tradition is active. The listener
> is active, not passive. The listener makes the story, but the story is also
> set up in a way that it can be personal and recognizable, too. It has its
> own energy. . . . All of this I am suggesting is discourse. It's a discourse
> between the listener, the implied author, the narrator, and the events that
> took place (that are called upon), the characters. . . . We imagine it by telling
> and by listening. (Interview)

The reception, or perception, involved in the give-and-take relationship of oral tradition requires more than simple listening. Ortiz says we must "listen for more than just the sounds, listen for more than just the words and phrases"; we must "try to perceive the context, meaning, purpose."[29] The particular kind of engagement described requires that we add something to the exchange, something not directly named in the language. Vizenor's comments on one Anishinaabeg oral form in *Summer in the Spring* give some indication of how and where the required ingredients may arise: "The song poems of the Anishinaabeg are imaginative events, magical and spiritual flights, and intuitive lyric images of woodland life" (11). Vizenor suggests that it

Intersections with the Oral Tradition / 25

is through the powers of imagination and intuition that the listener can get beyond the words, can help bring story and song into being, and can experience them as events in the oral tradition.

Vizenor has frequently extolled the crucial role imagination plays in our personal and literary acts of creation, and often employs Momaday's well-known statements on the subject, including the following from "Man Made of Words": "We are what we imagine. Our very existence consists in our imagination of ourselves. Our best destiny is to imagine, at least, completely, who and what and *that* we are. The greatest tragedy that can befall us is to go unimagined." How imagination empowers us becomes clear in Momaday's comments in "Native American Attitudes to the Environment," which identify the imaginative as a link to a reality more real or more true than the physical one and as a whole way of seeing. Momaday distinguishes between what he calls the two "planes of vision," identifying one as "physical," the other as "imaginative." "The Indian," he claims, "has achieved a particularly effective alignment of those two planes of vision" and thus perceives both with "the physical eye" and with "the eye of the mind." The goal, which he says takes on a moral dimension, is to achieve "perfect alignment" of the two planes of vision: "The appropriation of both images into one reality is what the Indian is concerned to do: to see what is really there, but also to see what is *really* there."[30]

Both Barre Toelken and Matthias Schubnell also comment on this important aspect of a Native worldview. Toelken discusses the sites or sources of meaning for different peoples in "Seeing with a Native Eye": "Many tribes feel the real world is not the one that is most easily seen, while the Western technological culture thinks of this as the real world, the one that can be seen and touched easily. To many native Americans the world that is real is the one we reach through special religious means, the one we are taught to 'see' and experience via ritual and sacred patterning." Schubnell comments on the notion of a dual plane of vision and claims: "Virtually all tribal philosophies maintain a fluid line between what's natural and supernatural, material and spiritual, conscious and unconscious."[31] Many other writers and scholars, including Vizenor, have recognized the fluent passage in Native cultures between these supposedly separate realms of being, a passage fashioned and enacted in ritual, chant, story, song—in the whole of the Native oral culture.[32]

If we understand the oral tradition as being allusive or referential, attempting to embody or translate the spiritual or to engender access to the spiritual realm, then the imaginative response becomes the means of appropriation, the action taken on the part of the listener (or reader) to get beyond the static physical reality of the words to the generative, larger reality, to "life," "juice," and "energy." Oral culture thus owes its vitality, at least in part, to the relational contexts of language. The "structure and texture" of language, says Toelken in his essay on Navajo narratives, "unite to provide an excitement of meaning which already exists elsewhere." In tribal tradition, he explains, "the stories act like 'surface structure' in language: by their articulation they touch off a deeper accumulated sense of reality," they "excite perspectives on truth," and they "provide . . . correlatives to a body of thought" he describes as "complicated and profound."[33]

The energy in orality is dialogic. It draws its life, as the above discussion has shown, from the movement between words and implied realities, and because language bears vast connective threads, the arenas of discourse are many. As crucial to a concept of Native oral traditions as the "verbal equations" of spirituality are the discourses enacted between speaker and listener. "The poetic of oral cultures," says Walter J. Ong, "is participatory. Speaker, audience and subject form a kind of continuum." This dialogic quality of oral tradition bears responsibility for more than mere verbal understanding; it bears responsibility for the formation and the sustenance of community. As Vizenor claims, "Language determines culture and the dimensions of consciousness" (*Wordarrows*, x). "The spoken word," says Ong, "forms human beings into close-knit groups." Toelken speaks of the way language references and reinforces the "shared ideas and customs of people raised in an intensely traditional society."[34] The identification wrought by participatory oral culture is illustrated in the slang expression sometimes used to describe a person or group that shares our perspective: "we speak the same language." Language defines, language creates our sense of self, but only through dialogic relationship.

Mikhail Bakhtin's theory of discourse offers a helpful analysis of this relationship.[35] First Bakhtin, like Native traditions, acknowledges the primacy of language: only through language (thought and words) do we come to understand experience. But language, in order to have power, must be understood, must carry meaning in a relationship. Bakhtin makes an important distinction between mere words or sentences and what he calls "utterances." Static words and sentences exist in isolation or in a social void and therefore lack purposeful reality, whereas "utterances" come into existence only by means of an intrinsic awareness of connection: they originate from, and therefore exist in, the context of dialogic reciprocity. We "have voice" only if we both speak and are heard. A statement made by the Native author Joseph Bruchac offers a fine illustration of Bakhtin's concept of utterance. Speaking about the power of story, Bruchac recognizes how "a person can be burdened by a story when that story can't be told because the participant audience has disappeared."[36] In an almost symbiotic relationship, Native voice and story require, exist within at the same time that they sustain, a sense of community. Our words, then, truly "mean" only in their active state.

This alive quality of language, Ong explains, belongs naturally to the spoken rather than to the written: "The spoken word is always an event, a movement in time, completely lacking in the thing-like repose of the written or printed word."[37] He offers an analysis of the difference between the spoken and the written based on our sensory reception of each, an analysis that becomes particularly important in Vizenor's own philosophy and literary works. Ong's primary contention is this: "Sight isolates, sound incorporates." He bases this conclusion on actual physical as well as psychic positioning. "Sight," he explains, "situates the observer outside of what he views, at a distance." "Vision," he continues, "dissects. . . . Vision comes to a human being from one direction at a time." "Sound," however, he claims, "pours into the hearer": "When I hear . . . I garner sound simultaneously from every direction at once: I am at the center of my auditory world which envelops me, establishing me at a kind of core of sensation and existence. . . . Sound is thus a unifying sense." He identifies the visual ideal as "clarity and distinctness, a taking apart," the auditory as "harmony, a putting together."[38]

Ong's distinctions here between sight and sound are similar to those Vizenor makes, particularly in *Dead Voices*, between the eye and the ear. Through the novel's character of Bagese, for example, Vizenor insists that "stories be heard through the ear and not the eye" (6); and that "printed books are the habits of dead voices. . . . The ear not the eye sees the stories" (18). The stated preference in the novel for the oral really involves most of the qualities of orality previously taken up in this discussion: the power of words, the proper and improper use of language, the multidirectional referential quality of oral tradition, the dialogic nature that forms and sustains community, and the vitality of oral culture. The book contains innumerable discussions of all of these subjects. Vizenor's awareness of the allusiveness of tribal stories, for example, is shown in such statements by the character Laundry as "She taught me how to hear and see the animals in stories" (16) and "The secret, she told me, was . . . to see and hear the real stories behind the words, the voices of the animals in me" (7). An awareness of communal discourse and the transformative quality of language can be read in the narrator's insistence on the use of "we" rather than "I": "There is a trickster in the use of words that includes the natural world, a world according to the we" (39). Vizenor's novel recognizes the power of words when he writes of "the healers" who "touched an inner sound in their stories" (127) and of "the stories that liberated shadows and the mind" (16).

Finally, the novel's plot itself enacts Vizenor's beliefs regarding oral culture: The young protagonist Laundry passes on the story of his encounters with an old tribal woman in the city, Bagese Bear. Her instructions to him about trickster liberation, stories in the blood, the transformative power of story, and surviving through story, become Vizenor's instructions to us. The penultimate statement in the novel is about the possibility of tribal stories' surviving the dead voices of the "wordies," the real enduring beyond the published versions. The survival, the ability to "go on," comes through written words, but like the oral stories of Bagese, they are written to bear allusive "traces" of the real.

"Raising the Word from the Page"

Recognizing the vitality of the oral, Vizenor's effort is to write in the oral tradition, to invite or require an imaginative response similar to that required in the oral exchange, one that will move the reader beyond the "dead voices" on the page: "I have never overcome my wearisome want to raise the word from the page" (*Interior Landscapes*, 144). If writing implies closure, Vizenor is working for what Ong calls "opened closure." He wants to cross the boundaries of the printed word, make his writing what Jahner calls a "specific kind of mythic 'breakthrough into performance,'" and place his writing in an oral tribal context.[39] The methods he employs to accomplish these goals have connections with both Native literary traditions and contemporary critical theory. In fact, according to Vizenor, the two ultimately converge in important ways.

Like many other contemporary storytellers, Vizenor underscores the connections between his written works and the body of tribal oral literature by including segments from, allusions to, or a new version of, tribal songs, legends, and tales in his writing, such as he does with the various Naanabozho stories in *The People Named the Chippewa*, *Earthdivers*, *Wordarrows*, and *Dead Voices*. In addition, Vizenor's works in the various genres tend to depict voice dramatically. They include several screenplays, which naturally center on the verbal exchange. But his other writings, too, are often formed of the oral. They include, for example, spoken testimony, both actual legal testimony taken from contemporary incidents or historical documents, and fictional accounts of legal proceedings. They include interview scenes (fictional and actual), segments from a fictional radio talk show, and innumerable other incidents and techniques that emphasize sound, conversation, telling. Indeed, the human voice is everywhere prevalent in monologues, dialogues, letters, and first-person narratives; dramatized in storytelling scenes, classroom scenes, lectures, and political speeches; and highlighted in jokes, puns, and other verbal play. Finally, the works in the Vizenor canon demonstrate less obvious stylistic and philosophical connections with the traditions of oral literature.

Many scholars have identified notable stylistic characteristics of orality, including Ong, who makes a comparison between the oral tradition, which he describes as "mnemonic, . . . aggregative, redundant, copious, traditionalist, warmly human, participatory" and the "antipathetic" written tradition, which he describes as "analytic, sparse, exact, abstract, visualist, immobile."[40] Vizenor has spoken of Ong's *Orality and Literacy* as being "very helpful to me as a teacher and a writer," identifying as it does characteristics Vizenor himself recognized in the Ojibway dream songs and stories. Vizenor mentions particularly the agonistic and aggregative qualities, and the use of repetition and memory devices (Interview).

Other characteristics from the literature of oral cultures also seem significant in this discussion. A longer and somewhat more specific list by Linda Ching Sledge of what she calls "those persistent, unchangeable forms common to all oral cultures" names the following: "formulaic diction; a fixed 'grammar' of repetitive themes, or topoi; a spectrum of stock characters; ceremonial and heroic reappropriation of history; symmetrical structures, including balanced oppositions (verbal or physical contests, antithetical characters, dialectical or casuistical discourse such as question and answer forms, riddles, and so on); copia and repetition." Ong compiles a similar list in *Orality and Literacy* which he calls the "psychodynamics of orality."[41]

A good many of the characteristics identified by Vizenor, Sledge, and Ong are readily apparent in Vizenor's work: a fixed grammar of themes such as the invented Indian, the new urban reservation, and trickster liberation; a spectrum of stock characters such as the various rein- carnations of the evil gambler, the tribal entrepreneur, and Naanabozho, the tribal trickster; dialectical discourse such as the numerous question- and-answer scenes between a Vizenor persona and a representative of the social sciences, or between reincarnated historical figures and a contemporary trickster figure; and riddles in the form of neologisms, or English words written backward. We even find, for example, Vizenor's own special brand of formulaic diction, repetitive phrases, and epithets (used in oral cultures to aid in memory and for amplification). In Vizenor's work, phrases like "lost and lonesome," "at the treeline," and "summer in the spring" reappear again and again in new contexts; characters are often described as having "outsized" noses or "toothless" mouths; and various gestures and other identifying qualities are repeated from story to story, attached to new characters. Characters themselves migrate from one book to another; in fact, over time whole scenes have been repeated in new plots. Alan Velie has described Vizenor's works as "one huge moebius [Möbius] strip" because "the same characters scuttle in and out, often telling the same stories."[42] I do not propose to debate which of these (and other) stylistic qualities of Vizenor's work show a conscious, which an unconscious, connection to the literature of a tribal oral culture; I merely suggest a stylistic influence to which I will continue to give attention throughout this study.

One critical study that discusses the methods specific to traditional Indian literatures, methods also extremely pertinent in examining Vizenor's own style, is Jarold Ramsey's *Reading the Fire*. Ramsey, for example, comments on the minimalism of the texts and how this minimalism necessitates active reader participation: "One universal characteristic of the printed texts of the traditional Indian literatures is their tacit, economical texture...typically, more is suggested in the withholding of narrative and descriptive details than in the outright rendering of them." To explain one of the reasons for this minimalism, Ramsey uses the example of an encounter by the ethnographer Ruth Underhill with a Papago woman who, before providing Underhill with a version of a tribal song, explains, "The song is very short because we understand so much." Tribal telling assumes an acquaintance with and understanding of the tribal world view in which, as Ramsey says, "so much [is] tacitly understood."[43]

But Ramsey and other scholars of Native literature claim that this minimalistic writing stems from more than the sense of "cultural homogeneity." The method is, in Ramsey's words, "a deeply ingrained habit of the native imagination, with enormous implication for what modern Indian writers do with the stories they tell." Native storytelling often self-consciously and purposefully proceeds by suggestion and implication because it thus becomes a dialogue or pluralistic creation. "One is compelled," Ramsey writes, "to participate in the story, eking it out of what the characters say and what they do."[44]

Among the other literary scholars and tribal "lay persons" who have noted the minimalistic methods of traditional literatures are John (Fire) Lame Deer, William Smith, Lester Standiford, and Kenneth Lincoln. Lame Deer, in *Lame Deer: Seeker of Visions*, speaks of symbols and imagery in tribal life and notes, "We need no more than a hint to give us the meaning." Swampy Cree tribesman William Smith Smith reveals much about both method and purpose in tribal storytelling with his comment: "Maybe it won't be easy to hear, inside the story, but it's there. Too easy to find you might think it too easy to do." Smith's statement also, of course, implies audience engagement. Like Ramsey, Lester Standiford draws a parallel between the "dense holophrastic nature" of tribal language, the "compactness of the literature," and the "embedding technique" and "cryptic nature" that characterize contemporary Native American literature. He claims that this "nondirective approach—allows a reader the feeling and the meaning of the experience in his or her own turn." Lincoln, too, discusses the tribal method of telling, saying: "In general, a storyteller does not interpret or gloss the tale too much. Listeners imagine their participatory places in the story."[45]

Vizenor strengthens his link with the oral by subscribing to the storytelling techniques and intentions of tribal predecessors, including, for example, this technique of minimalism. In the writings of Vizenor, as in traditional oral tales, audience participation is elicited through the method of telling: specifically, through implication, absence, contradiction, and ambiguity, and by making use of allegory, metaphor, satire, shock, and humor. In addition, Vizenor tries to offset some of the losses inevitable in the transition from oral to written (like context, performance quality, and spontaneity) by employing various literary stylistic techniques. Notable among these techniques are abrupt transitions, unusual juxtapositions, pronoun shifts, repetitions, self-conscious or metaliterary devices, understatement, and lack of closure.

While in early works Vizenor seemed aware only of the tribal impetus for and significance of such audience engagement, his later writings self-consciously practice the postmodern as well as the tribal ideas of dialogue and offer critical comments on the theories of both. Arnold Krupat has commented on the similarities between elements of Native American oral tradition and contemporary critical theories involving the text in flux in *For Those Who Come After* and "Post-Structuralism and Oral Literature," and Elaine Jahner addresses Vizenor's eclectic movement between the two in "Allies in the Word Wars: Vizenor's Uses of Contemporary Critical Theory."[46]

To apply Jarold Ramsey's generalized comments about Native American writers to Vizenor, we can look at his writing both as "an expression of the author's grasp of his or her people's traditions and, in a real sense, as an extension of those traditions; and . . . as the work of a contemporary American writer, certifiably an Indian, but who probably reads *Newsweek*, Lewis Thomas, and an indifferent newspaper like the rest of us, and must likewise make poems out of the available words and the interplay of imagination and tradition." In Vizenor's case, he has found ways to imaginatively blend tribal tradition with significant contemporary situations, events, and, the object of my discussion here, literary and critical theories and methods. Jahner points to Vizenor as one of a group of "minority intellectuals" who are "borrowing phrases from developing metalanguages to defend and clarify the continuity at the heart of their own traditions, a task that involves demonstrating the philosophical assumptions implicit in tribal mythologies and showing how they might function today in an urban technological setting."[47] Vizenor has discovered in contemporary theories about metaphor, the play of difference, the utterance, and reader response, philosophies and intentions similar to his own tribally based ideas and has imaginatively incorporated the theories and methods into his own chameleonlike (or tricksterlike) creations.

Because Vizenor's overriding intention is always to imaginatively involve the reader in the words on the page to the extent that the ultimate experience surpasses that of mere words and stems from co-creation, the theories that most widely influence his writing all reflect in some way reader-response criticism. The modes employed to attain this audience engagement stem from or relate to a multitude of other sophisticated theories.[48] I intend to confine this discussion to some generalizations about reception theories and to identifying their major characteristics in order to show how Vizenor's writing reflects his involvement with these ideas.

As the name suggests, the element that differentiates reader-response theories from other types of critical theories is the emphasis on the role of the reader in the literary process. Literature, according to Terry Eagleton, "may be at least as much a question of what people do to writing as of what writing does to them."[49] Although those who espouse reception theories differ on the degree to which they think the text limits reader response and on whether or not they think "open" texts also inherently allow for "misreading," they do agree that the literary process comes to fruition only through dynamic reading and involves much more than the previously accepted notion that a reader reads simply to discover a fixed meaning provided by the author. According to the prominent reader-response proponent Wolfgang Iser:

> The work is more than the text, for the text only takes on life when it is realized, and furthermore the realization is by no means independent of the individual disposition of the reader—though this in turn is acted upon by the different patterns of the text. The convergence of text and reader brings the literary work into existence. . . . As the reader uses the various perspectives offered him by the text in order to relate the patterns and the "schematized views" to one another, he sets the work in motion, and this very process results ultimately in the awakening of responses within himself. Thus, reading causes the literary work to unfold its inherently dynamic character.[50]

The theorists agree that indeterminacy or suggestiveness works to draw the reader in, although the ways the text engages the reader obviously vary with each writer. Several common methods for achieving an "open" text include intentional gaps, paginal and typographical layout, implication through juxtaposition, concreteness and dramatization without generalization (signifiers without the signified), a rhetoric of process (writing as if the ideas are only that moment being formed), self-contradiction, tentative statements, stated or implied questions, transgression of literary conventions, self-conscious prose or metafictive techniques, and abandonment of the guise of author/creator.[51] How readers interact with the text obviously depends on the nature of the text and which, if any, of the above-noted stylistic devices it contains. Eagleton, however, offers this generalization about the process of reading:

> Although we rarely notice it, we are all the time engaged in constructing hypotheses about the meaning of the text. The reader makes implicit connections, fills in gaps, draws inferences and tests out hunches; and to do this means drawing on a tacit knowledge of the world in general and of literary conventions in particular. The text itself is really no more than a series of "cues" to the reader, invitations to construct a piece of language into meaning. In the terminology of reception theory, the reader "concretizes" the literary work, which is in itself no more than a chain of

organized black marks on a page. Without this continuous active participation on the reader's part, there would be no literary work at all. However solid it may seem, any work for reception theory is actually made up of "gaps." . . . The work is full of "indeterminacies," elements which depend for their effect on the reader's interpretation.[52]

Not all reader-response theories originated with or can be classified with the same critical school of thought. Reception theory, however, especially as it is manifested in the works of Vizenor, aligns most clearly with poststructuralist and postmodern criticism, having most in common with the intentions of these two related theories. For instance, in Ihab Hassan's essay on postmodern concepts, which lists the contrasting characteristics of modernism and postmodernism, reception aesthetics lines up more clearly with the identified postmodern intentions in the following excerpted items:

Modernism	Postmodernism
Form (conjunctive, closed)	Antiform (disjunctive, open)
Purpose	Play
Design	Chance
Art Object/Finished Work	Process/Performance/Happening
Distance	Participation
Hypotaxis	Parataxis
Presence	Absence
Origin/Cause	Difference-Differance/Trace
Determinacy	Indeterminacy[53]

Eagleton also comments on the differences between structuralism and poststructuralism and illustrates the similarities between reception theories and the latter critical school: "The movement from structuralism to post-structuralism is in part . . . a shift from seeing the poem or novel as a closed entity, equipped with definite meanings which it is the critic's task to decipher, to seeing it as irreducibly plural, an endless play of signifiers, which can never be finally nailed down to a single center, essence or meaning." Eagleton further enforces the connection between poststructuralist ideas and the reader-response critics by noting, "If there is any place where this seething multiplicity of the text is momentarily focused, it is not the author but the *reader*."[54]

Although Vizenor's critical ideas have gradually developed more sophistication, throughout his career they have had many points of intersection with postmodern and poststructuralist theories and have particularly significant parallels to reception aesthetics. Like other proponents of reader-response criticism, Vizenor espouses a belief in the necessity of the reader's participation to fulfill the literary intentions of the writer. He says, for example:

> Our experience we give to the page. . . . For the purposes of reading, there isn't anything there [on the page]; we have to give it something. I mean, the page is not sacred. It's what we send to the page that is sacred. . . . You have to go get it, find it, put it on the page. It has to be active. It [reading] is not a passive business. The reader has to be engaged. The reader has to act. . . . It comes back to the general idea that it's a discourse. It is active. And you have to put into that. If you don't put into that, it's nothing. (Interview)

This understanding of the role of the reader is clearly evident in Vizenor's writing, which has much in common with the professed philosophies of the reader-response theorists and displays many of the stylistic devices they have noted. In the critical intersections of Native American oral tradition and postmodern response aesthetics, the wordmaker positions his literary craft.

2
Surviving the Word Wars

The old Indian had been defeated, but not vanquished. His way of thought had been submerged, not destroyed. In the aftermath of World War II, when the society of his conquerors had been so badly shaken up and disorganized, the old ways began to surface in modern forms.
A new harmony emerged out of the old.
—Stan Steiner, *The New Indians*

Survival Writing

Asked in 1980 whether there is "ultimately any hope that tribal traditions will survive in any way other than as artifacts," Gerald Vizenor's response was unfaltering: "I am certain of it."[1] If there is a single note intoned more loudly throughout Vizenor's work than any other, that note is survival. Writing about the "Now Day Indi'ns," Kenneth Lincoln has said, "The new Indian poets are children of the old ways, students of historical transitions, teachers of contemporary survival."[2] The phrase could not more aptly describe Vizenor and his writing. As one of the "Now Day Indi'ns," Vizenor endeavors to salvage the truly timeless elements of the tribal, to relinquish to history the nonessential accoutrements of the past, and to teach the ways of survival in the new Indian wars—those media-driven, intellectual and verbal skirmishes he calls the "cultural word wars."

Survival, in Vizenor's view, is keenly dependent on identity; identity is formed through language and literature; language and literature are driven by money and politics. A mixedblood intellectual with an incredible capacity for exposing the subtle finesses in identity politics, Vizenor fills his work with dramatization and critique of the complicated moves surrounding the status of the contemporary Indian in America. In his depictions of what he calls the "Cultural Word Wars between Whites and Indians in the New Fur Trade" (*Wordarrows*, viii), Vizenor offers portraits of those he sees as victims and those he sees as survivors. With his own writing he has also entered into the midst of the conflict. His primary goal, in fact, seems to center on preserving or creating a space of survival. Oddly, that space of survival may be more imaginative than physical.

With the contemporary conflicts about treaty rights, trust status, and tribal sovereignty, the general public may well believe that "the Indian problem" continues to situate itself around land rights. Vizenor knows otherwise. The destiny of the American Indian rests with language. The Indian will survive or will "vanish" through the merits of language: survive through tribal oral tradition, or be made to vanish through popular, scientific, literary, and political rhetoric. For even should the literary sign "Indian" survive, Native cultures can survive in fact only by the power of tribal traditions. Indeed, Vizenor has gone so far as to suggest that if the sign "Indian" does survive, it will be at the expense of Native people themselves, that Native peoples can actually survive only if they dissociate themselves from "Indianness" as it now exists. "Vizenor's aim," claims the Choctaw/Cherokee scholar Louis Owens, "is to . . . liberate 'Indianness,' and in so doing, to free Indian identity from the epic, absolute past that insists upon stasis and tragedy for Native Americans." Or as the British scholar A. Robert Lee notes, Vizenor, recognizing the popular "invention" of Indianness, undertakes by "appointed flights of language and image" to "re-invent the invention."[3] Indeed, throughout the Vizenor canon we find his efforts to expose, remove, relocate, and rewrite the sign "Indian." He has often, to fine effect, replaced it with other words—"oshki anishinabe," "new earthdivers," "postindian warriors"—or linked it with new signification—liberation and comic "survivance."

"Survival," writes Vizenor, "is determined by the stories" we "remember at the treeline" (*Dead Voices*, 62–63). Much of Vizenor's writing is offered as a corrective to the popular romantic stories about Indian people, as encouragement to remember or imagine the real stories. As Ruoff claims, "Vizenor sees his literary role as that of illuminating both the sham of contemporary 'Indianness' and the power of vision and dream to restore tribal values."[4] Vizenor explains his intentions and aligns them with those of traditional tribal visionaries and storytellers, claiming: "Some personal visions and stories have the power to liberate and heal, and there are similar encounters that liberate readers in the novels and poems of contemporary postindian authors" (*Manifest Manners*, 104).

This chapter examines Vizenor's attempts to bring liberation by deconstructing the false rhetoric surrounding "Indianness." His analyses of the cultural "word wars" have been framed in virtually every genre, but have drawn heavily from personal experience, from historic encounters in the contemporary era, and from popular figures and accounts in history. Among those works that most clearly illustrate Vizenor's understanding of the word wars are those involving the American Indian Movement (AIM) leaders, Ishi, and Thomas James White Hawk. I give particular attention here to several literary journalistic works based on actual encounters Vizenor had while serving either as executive director of the American Indian Employment and Guidance Center in Minneapolis or as a writer for the *Minneapolis Tribune*, works published in *Earthdivers*, *Wordarrows*, and *Crossbloods*. Much of the material he has fictionalized and most he has "toned down" because the actuality "was unbelievable." He says, "It exceeds fiction. People wouldn't believe that if it were fiction" (Interview). I draw as well on various scholarly essays, especially those in *Crossbloods* and *Manifest Manners*, that reflect Vizenor's theoretical preoccupations in his second career as a professor in American Indian studies at various universities around the country. And finally, I give attention to sections from his novels *Bearheart* and *The Trickster of Liberty*, both of which can be characterized, to use Vizenor's own term, as "trickster literature." In my examination of these works from various eras and genres, I discuss Vizenor's satiric and theoretical attempts to expose "invented Indians," "terminal creeds," and "tribal simulations"; his efforts to contest "cultural schizophrenia," the "literature of dominance," and "manifest manners"; and his moves to characterize the "Now Day Indi'ns" and their self-conscious tactics as "postindian warriors of survivance."

The Victims in the Word Wars

In Vizenor's depiction, victims are those people who relinquish or have stolen from them the responsibility for their own lives. Though the circumstances of their stories vary, in every instance we can detect the negative presence of stasis. Vizenor identifies the most dangerous threat to the survival of tribal people as the gradual insinuation into their lives of Indian stereotypes. "The 'Indian' of American history," Linda Ainsworth explains, is "largely a creation of the colonists" and has had "a damaging effect on the Native population itself." A great deal of space in Vizenor's writing is given to examining the negative effects the "invented Indian" has had and continues to have on the lives of Native Americans. The victims in Vizenor's accounts seem to have been captured as "Indians" in the word wars. Like specimens preserved in amber, they become objects, artifacts, readily illustrating Leslie M. Silko's claim in *Ceremony*: "Things which don't shift and grow are dead things."[5]

The enshrined Indian stereotype dictates a static identity that precludes growth, change, and adaptation, as well as individual tribal characteristics. It permanently restricts Native Americans to second-class status as the marginal exotic other. But most significantly, it replaces and therefore threatens the survival of an authentic tribal reality, threatens the continuation of tribal traditions. "In Vizenor's view," claims Ruoff, "whites invented 'Indian' as a new identity for tribal people in order to separate them from their ancient tribal traditions."[6]

Vizenor demonstrates how the substitution of the invented identity for the real proceeds by means of our educational system and academic institutions, popular media, social service agencies, political and legal machinery, and religious organizations. He labels various bureaucracies as among the agents of the word wars or as "factors in the urban fur trade" (*Wordarrows*, 25). These include the Bureau of Indian Affairs (BIA), the nearly all-white boards appointed to run Indian agencies (such as the Minneapolis Guidance Center), as well as numerous social service organizations like welfare agencies, alcohol treatment centers, and law enforcement bureaus. But Vizenor does not level his attack at the agencies per se nor merely against white society in general. "My opposite," he says, "is not the white man. My opposite is the methodology that separates" (Interview). As Edward Said does in *Orientalism*, as Bill Ashcroft, Gareth Griffiths, and Helen Tiffin do in *The Empire Writes Back*, Vizenor sees not only racism but "political intent" behind the classic rhetoric about Native peoples.

Said has described the West's interaction with the Orient as "dealing with it by making statements about it, authorizing views of it, describing it, by teaching it, settling it, ruling over it: in short, Orientalism is a Western style for dominating, restructuring, and having authority over the Orient."[7] Vizenor offers similar analyses of the discourse and politics surrounding American Indians. For example, alluding to Roy Harvey Pearce's famous study *Savagism and Civilization*, which traces and explicates the moves involved in American culture's eventual classification of Indians as "morally inferior to civilized society,"[8] Vizenor says, "It is clearly in the interests of neocolonialists to carry out the idea of 'savages and then civilization'" (Interview).

Story is often the vehicle for Vizenor's own explication of the complicated twists in the word wars. In *Wordarrows*, for example, he presents the character of Marlene American Horse as a dramatic embodiment of the fallout the "savage" epithet of the word wars can produce.[9] American Horse comes to Minneapolis when her home and birthplace, Elbowoods, is flooded to create a potential resort area, Lake Sakakawea. She marries a white man, suffers physical abuse, turns to alcohol, has her children taken by welfare workers, and is evicted from her apartment. When Vizenor's persona Clement Beaulieu meets American Horse, she has accepted the white definition of her problem—Indian alcoholic—and therefore seeks the assistance of a white agency to overcome it. But, alas, all the agencies have what Chief Joseph disparagingly called "good words" to explain, justify or, Vizenor writes, "excuse" their inability to help.[10] The story's thematic core, though, centers not on the failure of helping agencies to help but on words that imprison.

Vizenor, through the persona of the "tribal advocate," attempts to show American Horse that she has allowed herself to become trapped by the words of white society, that she derives her self-image from the words used to label her. She has "become a white problem. . . . Drunken Indian" and therefore become dependent on a white solution (*Wordarrows*, 43). But according to Vizenor, her only true salvation lies in being able to "unwind the tribe from the white words we have become" (41). Tribal identities, he claims, have become entangled in stereotypes and negative expectations. White America has a stake in keeping Indians in their assigned roles: to safeguard their position of power, they must preserve the status quo. The white agencies' raison d'être relies on Indians' fulfilling their stereotypical "savage" roles. As Vizenor's persona explains:

> White words have become part of the problem, white expectations, because we are held down, stuck in our own problems, through the language of white people. . . . We are taught to be failures for the winners and then we must be grateful to those who are pledged to help us through the problems defined in white words. . . . We are treated like children in a new school on the first morning of classes, words are like prisons then, new controls, learning the definitions of tribute to the teachers. And we are taught to praise those who detain and define us in simple words, disagreement is defined as being a loser. (*Wordarrows*, 42)

Even should one of the helping agencies wend its way through the verbal maze of restrictions and find that American Horse meets all the requirements to receive alcohol treatment, the tribal advocate believes, they will succeed only in reinforcing her verbal prison by adding one more negative label to her already heavy identity baggage. He warns her against accepting the "worst words" and becoming "dependent on the definitions" and "dependent on the word cures" (42). The programs, he claims, teach mere recitations, shallow words that separate experience into neat verbal categories but lack power to heal because they remain one-dimensional. The tribal advocate tells American Horse:

> This is no cure in words, answers are not cures, words are not cures, ceremonies are cures, but not oaths and promises and the bullshit language of cures. . . . These are dependencies. Word cures are like eating menus for dinner and wondering why our children are still hungry. . . . Words cause internal word wars. . . . Words have power when words are not over the counter cures. (43–44)

Here the tribal advocate's claim that "words are not cures" seems to belie or run counter to the tribal belief in the potency of language. But he also says that "ceremonies are cures" and that "words have power when words are not over the counter cures" (43), thus making a clear distinction between two ways of understanding and interacting with words. The language of the social services, he suggests, does not stem from or operate within the consciousness of interconnected and interdependent planes of reality. The institutions isolate and treat the "problem" that, in a tribal view, is only a symptom of a more significant imbalance. Institutionalized words, "white words," cannot initiate the kind of healing achieved through tribal rituals; they cannot, as Barre Toelken says of Navajo healing ritual, reestablish a person's "relationship with the rhythms of nature" or "put you back in step with things, back in the natural cycles," primarily because they do not recognize how the deeper harmony has been destroyed.[11]

What American Horse needs is not only to stop drinking. She needs to break loose from stereotypical labels, to reclaim creative responsibility for herself, and to reimagine her identity as something other than a problem (Indian problem, welfare problem, alcoholic problem).

The struggle with cultural labeling, the pressure to fulfill expectations, and the complicated tensions that shape contemporary Native American identity lead, in American Horse's case, to what Vizenor labels "dependencies." They lead, in the case of a young Dakota man, to what Vizenor characterizes as "cultural schizophrenia." In the factually based accounts of Thomas James White Hawk, in which Vizenor tells the story of another victim of the word wars, he depicts the process as well as the effects of indoctrination. The White Hawk saga records a fall from favor, a gripping tale of a pre-med student turned rapist and murderer.

The tragedy of White Hawk seems to symbolize for Vizenor the confusion bred by internalized cultural conflicts, the negative effect of the good Indian/bad Indian propaganda used to propel the assimilation machine of white society, the causes and the consequences of what he calls "cultural schizophrenia":

> Tom was involved in a conflict of his own identity, his own unconscious life of Indian identity and his pursuit and involvement in the demands and expectations of the dominant white society. . . . I saw it in myself. I saw it in many other Indian people. . . . I wanted to make a statement that a great many Indian people in this country suffer from this same conflict . . . cultural schizophrenia. (*Wordarrows*, 154)

White Hawk's story has haunted Vizenor over the years. He has continued to follow the young man's case, keeping abreast of appeals and parole hearings, holding meetings with White Hawk as recently as 1987 and 1993. His accounts of the case have been reprinted or reworked in various forms: in articles for *Twin Citian* magazine, in a separate work, *Thomas James White Hawk*, in sections in *Tribal Scenes and Ceremonies*, *Wordarrows*, and *Crossbloods*, and in Vizenor's own autobiography, *Interior Landscapes*.

Vizenor introduces White Hawk as a "handsome tribesman and premedical student at the University of South Dakota" (*Wordarrows*, 126) who had been a good student, a noted high school athlete, an "exceptional Indian" (*Tribal Scenes*, 13). White Hawk was orphaned at age eleven and had become the pet project of various workers in the educational institutions he attended. After he had completed ninth grade, his self-appointed guardian, Philip Zoubek, transferred him from the "Indian Christian environment" of one school to the "military Christian environment" of a supposedly better school because, Vizenor writes, "he had great ambitions for this little Indian boy" (*Tribal Scenes*, 13). This move, controversial according to Vizenor's accounts, isolated White Hawk from a familiar Indian environment, affected his emotional well-being, and ultimately left him with "his uniform, bangles of acceptance and stomach trouble" (*Tribal Scenes*, 13). Vizenor suggests that the ambitions and expectations of those who saw themselves as philanthropists actually contributed to the development of White Hawk's mental instability.

In White Hawk's childhood years on Rosebud Reservation and at an Indian boarding school Vizenor sees the beginnings of a cultural conflict: "He lived with Indians and expressed his internal feelings with Indians. He was their rhythm, their psyche, but some people told him that he was different" (*Tribal Scenes*, 13). Authority figures who recognized White Hawk's "potential" worked to mold him into their image of success. The more he became immersed in the white educational system and was pressured to conform to white standards of success, the more his internal conflict escalated. Vizenor describes the forces operating on the boy this way:

> The ambitious guardians of the *indian problem* hovered over this exceptional Indian. They wanted him to go all the way. The dominant way. His guardians would teach him that he was entitled to many things. And he would acquire the ingravescent fear of failure in the dominant society. Thomas White Hawk would become a white man and fulfill their ambition. A cultural schizophrenic. He would become their beauty mark. (*Tribal Scenes*, 13)

White Hawk was bright and played his role well. According to one of White Hawk's teachers, "Tom was the way an Indian should be, he was the person you would like an Indian to be" (*Tribal Scenes*, 15). Ironically, of course, all the indoctrination worked to make the young Sioux as white as possible. Such an intent obviously operates out of a notion of racial superiority. Vizenor exposes the veiled cultural genocide that is so often glossed over with a multitude of euphemisms and justifications. Stripped bare of pretense and aliases, the underlying goal remains the same as it was when Captain Richard Pratt made it the motto for the Carlisle Indian boarding school: "Kill the Indian, save the man."[12] Vizenor summarizes the dominant culture's condescending characterization of White Hawk this way: "He was well accepted. Handsome. Pleasant. Verbal. A most unusual Indian. White Hawk was a beauty mark. White Indian" (*Tribal Scenes*, 27). White Hawk had become "the exceptional tribesman on the narrow white road to assimilated success" (*Wordarrows*, 128).

But his cultural brainwashing resulted in the loss of personal identity and freedom, and beneath the surface, a storm was brewing:

> Thomas White Hawk had given up his right to cry and he was giving up his freedom to dream. His unconscious was a burden of the past. When he walked alone he was bird or animal. He was one soul but he found himself in a prison of agreements with the burdens of opportunity and the false promises of success. He was becoming a white Indian. The youthful passion to know himself was displaced and consumed by his need to be successful in things that other people planned for him. He was dissociated from himself by his own greed for acceptance. He was among strangers. He watched himself respond. In a dream he saw the evangels of controlled words placed around him like empty boxes. He understood the exploitation of other men better than he understood himself. His unconscious was his *winter count*. He would have trouble in the spring. (*Tribal Scenes*, 16)

In this and other passages, Vizenor depicts the conflict between White Hawk's conscious actions and unconscious feelings that characterize the "cultural schizophrenia" he thinks led to the boy's violent actions.

Vizenor also alludes here, as he did in "Marlene American Horse," to the differences between tribal and nontribal world views. He recognizes White Hawk's link to his tribal past as residing in the unconscious, having been forced out or "schooled" out of his conscious mind. This tribal connection includes dreaming and transformation: "he was giving up his freedom to dream" and "when he walked alone he was bird and animal." Vizenor equates the record keeping of White Hawk's unconscious with the traditional Lakota system of recording significant events in the tribal life: "His unconscious was his *winter count*." At odds with the tribal freedom of dreams and transformations were White Hawk's conscious thoughts and actions, those being molded by his self-appointed saviors. These thoughts Vizenor characterizes as confining and hollow in phrases like "a prison of agreements," "burdens of opportunity," "false promises of success," and "evangels of controlled words placed around him like empty boxes." Vizenor sees a dangerous schism in White Hawk's personality: "White Hawk has an Indian unconscious and a white man's conscious mind" (*Tribal Scenes*, 44).

Eventually the young man paid the emotional price. The internal conflict bubbled over and violent behavior erupted. He murdered a white jeweler and raped his wife. In the ensuing legal, political, and social battles Vizenor sees the core of the problem overlooked amid the verbal jockeying for position. The psychiatric reports contain "no discussion of White Hawk's Indian identity," and there is "no information in any of the psychological reports about White Hawk's problem of unconscious and conscious links of identity, dissociation and cultural schizophrenia" (*Tribal Scenes*, 44).

Ultimately, White Hawk pleaded guilty and drew the death sentence. This is when Vizenor, as a board member of the Minnesota chapter of the American Civil Liberties Union, became involved in the case and tried to focus the attention on the causes of White Hawk's problem. He says of his involvement in the appeal for the commutation of the death sentence:

> I strongly oppose capital punishment for any reason. And he was an Indian and I felt there was a case that should be argued more publicly about his experience. So, if nothing else, there had to be a lesson here. I had to learn something. And then I felt it was the consequences of a bourgeois expectation, a neocolonial breakdown in a culture that led to his violence, not directly, but indirectly. (Interview)

The Indian wars, Vizenor shows, have not ended. The tactics have changed, the weapons have changed, but the battle rages on. Vizenor notes the tragic ironies of the White Hawk (and American Horse) situations in which "the very society which creates the sickness in which Indians have had to live . . . is the very society which now every day becomes the doctor," and in which a man is "condemned by an institution of that dominant culture which has actually led to the problems he has to live with" (*Wordarrows*, 154).

Self-Victimization

In the stories of American Horse and White Hawk, Vizenor centers largely on illuminating the role white society plays in creating a troubled Native American psyche. The battle lines in the "cultural word wars" are not drawn merely between tribal and nontribal, however, for Vizenor's vision is hardly that simplistic. He shows the true confusion of the new verbal combat when he depicts "terminal creeds," "invented Indians" and "tribal simulations." These concepts, which become a basis for much of Vizenor's social criticism and satire, surface in one form or another in nearly all of his works.

In early works like *Earthdivers*, *Bearheart*, and "I Know What You Mean," he employs the phrases "terminal creeds" and "terminal believers" to characterize a closed and limited view, static ideas. In "I Know What You Mean" he defines "terminal believers" as "those believing in only one vision of the world" (96). "Terminal creeds," claims a character in *Bearheart*, "are terminal diseases" (185). Whether sacred or secular, tribal or nontribal, terminal creeds destroy. In *Earthdivers* Vizenor writes of "anthropologists" who "approach diarrhetic levels of terminal theoretical creeds" (xv). In *Bearheart* he writes of "tribal religions becoming more ritualistic but without vision" and of "pantribal urban emptiness" with the "crazed and alienated" who are "desperate for terminal creeds to give their vacuous lives meaning" (12). Any zealot, of whatever static belief, threatens life, continuance: "There are no last words to the world" (*Bearheart*, 188).

Vizenor points out the folly of terminal creeds in a lighthearted narrative, "Fruit Juice and Tribal Trickeries," in *Wordarrows*. The "terminal believer" in the story, Girlie Blahswomann, is a "South Dakota born mixedblood prom queen turned Kundalini yogi" (75). Blahswomann, who runs a fruit wagon at the University of California in Berkeley, has followed one hollow dream after another, never finding the fulfillment or peace she seeks. When visited by "tribal trickster Erdupps MacChurbbs" and accused of "turning outer spheres into inner spheres" (79), she attempts to defend herself by listing all her past "spiritual" accomplishments:

> Inner spheres now. Listen here, I attended the Institute for Postural Integration, Fort Help, and Le Center du Silence. . . . Studied at the Holistic Life University, audited programs at Dare to Dream, the Center for Conscious Human Living, which was more like thinking about thinking about living than living, and then there was the Laughing Man Institute, the feminists fought me about that . . . Dancing Fool and Ishmael House, and then settled for Kundalini yoga at the end because at least the

brothers and sisters are clean and they had a comfortable place to live together. (79)

Vizenor undercuts the validity of Blahswomann's supposed spiritual experiences by creating bogus titles for the organizations she has sought out, by emphasizing the academic quality of her encounters through her use of verbs such as "attended," "studied," and "audited," and by revealing how her ultimate "inner sphere" choice depended on such externals as cleanliness and comfortable surroundings. MacChurbbs calls her various encounters "insideout spheres" and recognizes them as "terminal creeds":

> In all the places you have studied has no one taught you how to see and move through tribal time and space? Have all your worlds become word wars? . . . Words settle on dumb animals like terminal creeds. . . . Your vision is rerecorded in your head unsided and backward. . . . You have turned tribal secrets into white words. (80–81)

Terminal creeds and their consequences also figure heavily in Vizenor's first novel, *Darkness in Saint Louis Bearheart*. In fact, the main action of the novel, the cross-country pilgrimage of tribal clowns, results from America's too-loyal dedication to consumer culture. The country is out of oil, the cogs of civilization simply stop, anarchy rules. The tribal pilgrims, lead by Proude Cedarfair, travel from a Minnesota reservation to New Mexico in search of the vision window to the fourth world.

Maureen Keady sees Vizenor's novel as "a teaching tale about truth and choice, about those who are willing to sacrifice their 'Terminal Creeds' for real meaning, and those who will not."[13] "Survival of the fittest" is the rule in *Bearheart*, according to Keady, and the fit are those who adapt and change. The terminal creeds of the novel's pilgrims lead to their death, and only those who relinquish their word creeds survive and enter the new spiritual dimension of the fourth world. Vizenor does not isolate certain beliefs as faulty; instead, the novel's unlikely clutch of characters, each with his or her own idiosyncratic ideology, demonstrate that clinging blindly to any creed isolates and ultimately destroys an individual.

In the chapter "Terminal Creeds at Orion" Vizenor presents the key to maintaining proper mental balance: humor and continual questioning. One character claims, "We avoid terminal creeds with questions"; another, "People are the living dead with the unquestioned church in them" (*Bearheart*, 188). Still another describes "the mind" when it is "the perfect hunter": "The perfect hunter turns on himself. . . . He lives on the edge of his own meaning and humor. . . . The humor is in the contradictions of the hunter being close and distant at the same time, being the hunter and hunted at the same time, being the questioner and the questioned and the answer. The believer and the disbeliever at the same moment of mental awareness"(189). Here again Vizenor underscores vitality and ongoing dialogue as essential.

The individual fates of *Bearheart*'s pilgrims exemplify the self-destruction that awaits all who fail to continue the dialogue but opt instead for static or terminal beliefs. Perhaps the most interesting case among the terminal believers is that of Belladonna Darwin–Winter Catcher, because she espouses some of the tribal beliefs we expect that Vizenor himself might endorse.[14]

"We are tribal," says Belladonna, "and that means that we are children of dreams and vision. . . . Our bodies are connected to mother earth and our minds are part of the clouds. . . . Our voices are the living breath of the wilderness" (190). And, she says, "My blood moves in the circles of mother earth through dreams without time. My tribal blood is timeless and it gives me strength to live and deal with evil" (192). Her statements closely echo many of Vizenor's own descriptions of the tribal. Compare, for example, Belladonna's statement that tribal people "are children of dreams and visions" and Vizenor's claim in *The People Named the Chippewa* that "woodland identities turned on dreams and visions" (24). Belladonna claims her blood moves "through dreams without time"; in *Earthdivers* Vizenor says of the tribal trickster, "he dreams out of familiar time and space" (xi). Belladonna speaks of being "connected to mother earth" and having voices that are "the living breath of the wilderness." Vizenor talks about "tribal world views" in *Earthdivers* saying: "Sacred names, dreams, and visions are images that *connect the bearer to the earth*; shamans and other tribal healers and visionaries *speak the various languages of plants and animals* and feel the special dream power to travel backward from familiar times and places" (xvii; emphasis added).

Despite the character's and author's seemingly compatible views about tribal identity, Vizenor nevertheless indicts Belladonna because her beliefs have become static—terminal creeds. As Louis Owens comments in his afterword to the 1990 reprint of *Bearheart*, the attempts of terminal creeds to "impose static definitions upon the world" are "destructive, suicidal, even when the definitions appear to arise out of revered tradition."[15]

In her talk about "tribal values," Belladonna recites a list of clichés phrased mostly in comparative language that distinguishes Native people from the white race. Vizenor leaves no doubt that it is a recitation. Belladonna becomes defensive at questions or challenges of her view. She is unable to deviate from her trite catechism because, as one challenger declares, she "speaks from terminal creeds," not as "a person of real experience and critical substance" (*Bearheart*, 192). Belladonna's rigidity is revealed, for instance, in the story of her betrayal of her travel companion, a white dove. Because of a medicine man's dictum, that it was "an evil omen to be seen with a white bird," she first tries to drive the bird off, then ultimately murders it. She fails to examine her relationship with the bird or the judgment of the shaman. She fails to consider the contradiction between her professed connection with all creatures and her murder of the bird. As a terminal believer, Belladonna holds blindly to "the rules," relinquishes her responsibility for growth, and becomes, as one character says, "her own victim" (195).

Belladonna is poisoned and dies for the sake of her static beliefs, but Vizenor, in *Bearheart* and throughout his discussion of "terminal creeds," implies that terminal believers suffer a spiritual and intellectual death as well. This threat of "death by terminal beliefs" Vizenor finds particularly ominous for Native Americans, and he devotes much of his writing to delineating the "invented Indian." He makes distinctions between playing Indian by following the Indian "rules" and actually living out the tribal beliefs in the contemporary world, between the static words or "dead voices" of "mouth warriors," who like Belladonna merely recite the Indian "terminal creed," and the living words of tribal oral tradition. A failure by tribal people to recognize these distinctions means in effect that they have been outwitted in the "cultural word wars" and have allowed themselves to be captured as "Indians," imprisoned by words and stereotypes.

Victims of Invention: "This Portrait Is Not an Indian"

A complicated set of circumstances and issues are involved in the contemporary debate over tribal identity, integrity, and authenticity. First of all, although before contact the hundreds of tribal societies living on this continent maintained individual cultural identities, many early settlers, missionaries, ethnographers, or historians tended to generalize about the tribes using the label "Indians." As Momaday notes: "The Indian has been for a long time generalized in the imagination of the white man. Denied the acknowledgment of individuality and change, he has been made to become in theory what he could not become in fact, a synthesis of himself."[16]

The earliest accounts of tribal people were written almost entirely by non-Indians from an outsider's view, with tribal words and concepts translated into a foreign language—English. And as many scholars, including Richard Drinnon and Richard Slotkin, have suggested, these accounts themselves were slanted owing to the political or philosophical motives at work (whether or not the original authors intended or recognized the biases).[17] Ultimately, two contrasting stereotypic images of the Indian arose in the mind and culture of America. Both images— noble savage and murdering heathen—came into being to fulfill one aspect of the culture's romantic vision of itself.

In the meantime, the actual tribal cultures were being systematically destroyed through forced assimilation and cultural genocide. Tribal people could survive and win some degree of acceptance and therefore pride by becoming as much like the mainstream as possible. While some took this route, others learned to assume the white accouterments to avoid reprimand at boarding or mission schools. Throughout this time the old traditional ways suffered a deterioration; many of them were lost.

Eventually, when the tribal people no longer posed any kind of military threat and the mythical American Eden was rapidly becoming civilized, romantic images of Native Americans (the dime-novel versions of the Indian) began to capture the popular imagination. The fictional noble savage became a means for satisfying the ageless human longing for knowledge of the mythical lost past, for contact with man in his most pristine state. Scholars and tourists alike turned to the remnants of the decimated tribes expecting to find the Indian of their imagination and their fiction. Native people could win a kind of acceptance in the white world by filling that role or pretending to be that idealized Indian.

The situation becomes increasingly more complicated, however, when the popular invented image, the pose and posturing, gets mixed up with reality on both sides of the racial line. As Robert Berkhofer, Jr., notes in *The White Man's Indian*: "Whether as a conception or a stereotype, however, the idea of the Indian has created a reality in its own image as a result of the power of the Whites and the response of Native Americans."[18] Held up in comparison to the romantic stereotype, Native Americans once again have their authentic tribal identities invalidated: if they do not meet the mainstream's criteria regarding appearance, percentage of Indian blood, lifestyle, and so on, they are not considered authentic Indians. If Native peoples themselves mistake the invented standard for the real, they become a romantic "simulation," for the invented Indian does not exist, cannot exist, never existed outside the pages of a book except as a simulation in hyperreality.[19]

Because no living person, no culture, remains unchanging, the white culture, Vizenor holds, must relinquish their image of the invented Indian in order to accept the tribal people of today, and Native Americans must relinquish their romantic vision of the past in order to maintain the life of their culture in the present. This, according to Linda Ainsworth, is Vizenor's most significant message in *The People Named the Chippewa*: "Unless and until the people named the Chippewa can accept that they can not be the Chippewa and the Anishinaabeg at the same time, they will not be able to exercise the control over the past that will allow for a vision of the future. The Chippewa can not hold onto romantic dreams about the past without continuing to conspire in the victimization of traditional cultures." Elaine Jahner, too, identifies a similar core message in Vizenor's writing on survival: "People have to escape the conceptual inventions that trap them, have to stop being animated museums and use those features of their traditions that will help them find what is sacred."[20]

Vizenor variously explicates this whole complicated situation, fictionalizes the account, attacks the inventors of the idealized Indian, satirizes the Native Americans who assume that romantic pose and the whites who buy into it, exhorts tribal people to avoid the timebound identities, and outlines strategies for surviving the invention. These subjects, Native American consciousness, identity, and survival, have remained central subjects in all of Vizenor's works. From the humorous tale of the skin dip in "The Chair of Tears" from *Earthdivers* (3–29)— which provided tribal people with the chance to change their skin tone to better suit their political needs—to the commentary debunking the romantic poses of Dennis Banks and AIM in *The People Named the Chippewa* (124–38), Vizenor's essential points remain the same. As he wrote in one of his earliest works, *The Everlasting Sky*:

> The dominant society has created a homogenized history of tribal people for a television culture. Being an indian is a heavy burden to the *oshki anishinabe* because white people know more about the *indian* they invented than anyone. The experts and cultural hobbyists never miss a chance to authenticate the scraps of romantic history dropped by white travelers through the *indian country* centuries ago. White people are forever projecting their dreams of a perfect life through the invention of the indian—and then they expect an *oshki anishinabe* to not only fulfill an invention but to authenticate third-hand information about the tribal past (15–16).

The same work makes another point about Native American identity which remains key in all of Vizenor's later treatments of the subject: "The inventions of the dominant society have nothing to do with the heart of the people" (13).

Vizenor's recent discussion of these issues in *Manifest Manners: Postindian Warriors of Survivance* carries his analysis further, taking account of the most current developments in Native American politics and literature, employing recent critical theory, and creating many new words and phrases to express the unique and convoluted circumstances of identity politics in "Indian country today."[21] For example, with his creation of the phrase "manifest manners" he demands recognition of the "cultural legacy" and contemporary manifestations of the theory and policies of manifest destiny, which surface in such places as universities, the various branches of government, our legal system, and our popular media. He has used the term, for example, in describing a 1990 statement by University of Oklahoma president Richard Van Horn which encouraged students to "say hello to minority students on campus." Vizenor criticized the suggestion, calling it one of the "measures of manifest manners," and explained: "Racial salutations and other public relations snobberies serve those who dominate minority students rather than those who liberate the human spirit from institutional racism" ("Manifest Manners: The Long Gaze of Christopher Columbus," 232). Other examples of manifest manners indicted by Vizenor include "the Boy Scouts of America, the wild simulations of tribal misnomers used for football teams, automobiles, and other products, Western movies, and the heroic adventures in novels by James Fenimore Cooper, Frederick Manfred, Karl May, and others" (31).

He also claims that the "simulations" of manifest manners continue through "the surveillance and domination of the tribes in literature" in what he calls "the ruins of representation" (4). The "literature of dominance" that threatens tribal survivance includes critical as well as creative voices. In addition to Cooper, Vizenor includes Thomas Jefferson, Francis Parkman, and George Bancroft among the "masters of manifest manners in the nineteenth century" (8). Among those of the contemporary era he accuses of "surveillance and domination of the tribes in literature" are poet Robert Bly, fiction writer Lynn Andrews, and scholars Andrew Wiget and Charles Larson. Vizenor, for example, criticizes Larson's faulty conception of Indian identity, challenges the four categories he created for Indian novels and novelists in *American Indian Fiction* (assimilationists, reactionaries, revisionists, and qualified separatists), and characterizes Larson's work as "simulations" that have "more in common with political theories in the literature of dominance than with the wild memories and rich diversities of tribal and postindian literature" (80).[33]

The word *simulation* itself Vizenor borrows from Jean Baudrillard, and it becomes key in his theorizing about the postindian condition. We begin with his bold claim that the "Indian" never existed in reality: "the word has no referent in tribal languages or cultures" (11). It is an "absolute fake." All we can have, then, are "hyperreal" simulations of Indian, created from a model without actual "origin or reality." "Simulations are the absence of the tribal real" (4).[22] Although we cannot have "Indian," we can have "postindian," which replaces the Indian invention. The postindian "ousts the invention" through "humor, new stories, and the simulations of survivance" (5). As Robert Lee notes, "Vizenor . . . has positioned himself as postindian, an ongoing pursuer of all simulations that essentialize or ossify tribal people."[23] Although "postindian warriors" still operate through simulations, their "theatrical performances" can become a "recreation of the real," but only if they bear "simulations of survivance" to overcome the "simulations of dominance" (5). Vizenor offers examples of both kinds of performances by postindians, upholding, for example, the "postindian warriors" who "create a new tribal presence in stories" (12) and criticizing the "contrived performances" of the "specious shamans and tribal healers in urban areas," which "have no shadows of survivance" (46). He warns: "The warriors who turn simulations into prohibitions, rather than liberation and survivance, are themselves the treacherous taboos of dominance" (20–21).

Although difficult, the distinctions in Vizenor's theory reflect the complexity of the contemporary rhetoric surrounding Indianness and offer a rich groundwork from which to evaluate contemporary tribal politics and literature. We can see the application of the theory in Vizenor's own writings about tribal simulations, not only those pieces published in *Manifest Manners*, but works published earlier as well. His statement of theory is particularly helpful in reading his pieces on the photographs of Edward Curtis, on AIM, and on Ishi, the last Yahi.

In his essay "Socioacupuncture: Mythic Reversals and the Striptease in Four Scenes" from *The American Indian and the Problem of History* (another version of which appears as "Graduation with Ishi," in *The Trickster of Liberty*),[24] Vizenor uses the imaginary tale of one contemporary tribal leader's imprudent but short-lived pose as an invented Indian or tribal simulation to recall the subjugation of the tribal survivor Ishi to living-museum status and to shed light on what he sees as attempts at simulation by the AIM leaders. The fictional protagonist, Tune Browne, acquires the feathers, braids, beads, and leather of the "ideal museum specimen" of an Indian to assist him in his candidacy for alderman. He uses as prototype the photographs of Edward Curtis, which, both Browne and Vizenor claim, were posed and retouched to present a dramatic and romantic vision of Native Americans.

Vizenor employs the works of Roland Barthes, Susan Sontag, and John Berger to show how such photographs make possessions of tribal people, render them mere "consumable objects of the past" and deny them authentic existence in the present.[25] "All photographs," Berger writes, "are of the past, yet in them an instant of the past is arrested so that, unlike a lived past, it can never lead to the present" (quoted in "Socioacupuncture," 183). When tribal images have been manhandled by those Vizenor calls "jingoists, historians, anthropologists, mythologists, and various culture cultists," the result is "linguistic colonization of oral traditions and popular memories" (183). In other words, the literal and figurative picture of the tribal person in America has become the timebound Indian stereotype validated by the academic disciplines, a distorted, larger-than-life caricature representative of neither the historical nor the contemporary Native American, but which nevertheless serves as the model against which all tribal "specimens" are evaluated. Unhappily, Native Americans themselves have as often as not been schooled to accept that invented image as the measuring stick. As Vizenor's protagonist, Tune Browne, states: "We were caught dead in camera time, extinct in photographs, and now in search of our past and common memories we walk right back into these photographs, we become the invented images . . . to validate those who invented us on negatives" (186).

Browne recalls his past acquaintance with the historical figure, Ishi, the last Yahi Indian, who was captured in northern California in 1911, taken in by Karl Kroeber and the staff of the Museum of Anthropology at the University of California, and lived out his life there. Kroeber, an anthropologist, Saxton Pope, a medical doctor, and Thomas Waterman, a linguist, were among those who left interviews or book-length accounts of their study of and relationship with the Yahi Indian who came to be called Ishi. Ishi's story and its many implications have captured Vizenor's attention, and like the White Hawk story, it has appeared in various manifestations throughout his work.[26]

Ishi to America was a figure symbolizing "the obscure other," "the mortal evidence of savagism, and the vanishing race (*Manifest Manners*, 126). To Vizenor he becomes the supreme symbol of "tribal simulations." Ishi became a living museum specimen, with his language, his hunting skills, and his appearance all studied. He was repeatedly dressed and posed, then photographed, as a "savage" simulation, and "captured" again by the camera. But Vizenor also sees Ishi as a symbol of "tribal survivance," the real who endured in spite of or alongside of the simulation. He notes, for example, the way that Ishi never revealed his sacred tribal name, and claims of Ishi's storytelling: "his stories were his survivance" (*Manifest Manners*, 134).

Vizenor's interest in Ishi led him to repeatedly petition the University of California at Berkeley to name a building in honor of the man. When those efforts were not fruitful, he critiqued the actions of the university's regents in his essays on manifest manners. Ultimately, he succeeded in getting an interior court named in Ishi's honor.[27]

In Ishi's story and in Tune Browne's, Vizenor confronts the "dead voices of racial photographs and the vanishing pose" (*Manifest Manners*, 126). In his works on AIM, he confronts the mimicry of those simulations. Like the fictional Tune Browne, Vizenor sees Dennis Banks, Russell Means, and Clyde Bellecourt of AIM acquiring the accouterments of the museum Indian artifact so aptly rendered in Curtis's photographs. "The poses of tribal radicals," he writes in *The People Named the Chippewa*, "seem to mimic the romantic pictorial images in old photographs taken by Edward Curtis for a white audience" (130). Banks, for one, "wore beads, bones, leathers, ribbons, and a cultural frown, for his appearance in court" (124). With his cutting sarcasm, Vizenor makes certain we don't mistake the AIM member's dress for anything other than a cultural costume meant to fulfill "noble savage" expectations. For example, he contrasts Banks's dress during his AIM confrontation days with his appearance eight years earlier when he "dressed in dark suit, white shirt and narrow necktie" (*Tribal Scenes*, 51). And he labels Banks's newly acquired simulated "Indian" clothing his "secular vestments," perhaps alluding to Banks's vision of himself as a tribal religious leader (*The People Named the Chippewa*, 124). In his description of Delano Western's attire, he humorously notes that that AIM member wore, among other things, "two bandoliers of heavy ammunition, none of which matched the bore of his rifle" ("I Know What You Mean," 109).

But Vizenor depicts the group's attempted acquisition of the romanticized Indian qualities as going beyond mere physical appearance. They likewise attempt to fulfill the stereotypic vision of hunter and warrior and to espouse the tenets of traditional tribal religion. He describes a press conference held on a rifle range and Banks's bungled attempts to quick-draw with a sawed-off shotgun. He recalls the repeated failures of the tribal "hunters" to bag a deer to feed their group during one takeover episode and the game warden's donation of a deer killed by an automobile. He also reports on their testimony about tribal religious ideas in "Speaking for Mother Earth," from *Tribal Scenes*, quoting from the opening statements Banks and Means made to jurors in a federal court and describing their statements as "poetic metaphors" (78). Although words like Means's "It is our philosophy that because all living things come from one mother, our Mother Earth . . . we have to treat one another with the same respect and reverence that we would our own blood relatives" (78) seem hard to oppose, Vizenor's emphasis on the AIM leaders' recent change to such espousals succeeds in alerting the reader to their possible (maybe even probable) use as rhetorical artifice. According to Vizenor, the two leaders "are *now* emphasizing in prophetic monotones their traditional religious connections with Mother Earth," and Banks "*no longer* rails at white people in an angry voice, he *no longer* practices disruptive tactics at public meetings. He speaks in mellow tones *now*, and his gestures are gentle" (78–79; emphasis added). Vizenor goes beyond a hint that at least part of the motive behind their change might be that "the mellow vision of a religious revival is . . . a good defense posture in federal court" (80).

Vizenor offers harsher criticism of one fictionalized radical leader in a chapter of *The Trickster of Liberty*, "The Last Lecture at the Edge" (107–19). Here, the description of Coke de Fountain, an "urban pantribal radical and dealer in cocaine," often echoes in details and phrasing Vizenor's descriptions of actual AIM members. For example, like Banks, Coke is described as wearing a "cultural frown" (111); like Bellecourt, he is accused of drug dealings. Vizenor describes the AIM leaders as "urban radicals" with "stoical poses" (*Crossbloods*, xiii), Coke as bearing "radical and stoical postures" (*Trickster*, 111). Coke is introduced by a master of ceremonies in the fictional scene as "the man who took the most and gave the least back" (112). Audience members heckle him as he tries to speak, belittling his rhetoric and supposed accomplishments, and whirling accusations at him. One tribal woman claims: "He's a killer of our dreams" (113). An elder suggests Coke went to Wounded Knee for "money and women" (112). The fictionalized urban radical's pose is destroyed, much as Vizenor's accounts of the AIM members deconstructs their simulations.

In his discussion of Means in *Manifest Manners*, Vizenor's complex deconstructive moves include an analysis of an Andy Warhol portrait for which Means posed, *The American Indian*, which is used as the cover illustration for Vizenor's book. The double simulation of the portrait Vizenor undercuts by using a variant of René Magritte's "Ceci n'est pas une pipe." He repeatedly follows his descriptive comments on Means with "This portrait is not an Indian." The phrase becomes almost a chant, and is used throughout the "Postindian Warriors" essay to challenge tribal simulations and to allude to the larger discourse on identity politics.

Vizenor coins another phrase, "kitschyman," to highlight the hollow fakery of Indian simulations. He describes the AIM leaders as "kitschy-men of resistance" (150); Banks he specifically calls the "kitschyman of reservation capitalism," Bellecourt, the "kitschyman of liberal bounties" and "foundation monies" (43). Besides the definition of *kitsch* from Matei Calinescu, which Vizenor supplies in the text—"a world of aesthetic make-believe and self-deception" (*Manifest Manners*, 154)—the word has another possible connection in the Ojibway language. The sound of kitschyman is very like *gichi-mookomaan* or *chi-mookomaan*, words for "white man." If Vizenor intends this verbal echo, the implication is of a yet more radical disjunction between tribal identity and Indian simulations.

These kitschymen, Vizenor claims, are "the simulations of the media, with no real power of their own" (151). Their posturing for the media works to reinforce and perpetuate the romantic Indian stereotype, the tribal simulation. Vizenor clearly finds this unacceptable. But more deplorable still is the "inappropriate" use of words by the radicals, their active participation in the empty rhetoric of the "cultural word wars." For example, Vizenor calls Bellecourt "a word warrior on commission, a man who has abused the honor of tribal communities to enhance his own simulations" (154). Indeed, the major weakness of the AIM leaders, Vizenor points out, is their empty rhetoric, their failure to go beyond confrontation and back up their rhetoric by actually working with the people. Vizenor calls them a "symbolic confrontation group" and makes this distinction between confrontation and negotiation: "The confrontation idiom means punching out the symbolic adversary of racism and oppression at the front door, with the press present, and walking out the back door. The negotiation idiom means punching out the adversary at the front door with the press present, but waiting around for an invitation to return and grind out some changes" (*Tribal Scenes*, 52).

Vizenor further belittles the AIM rhetoric by means of an implied comparison. Before a battle with the whites after the Wounded Knee massacre, the Oglala holy man Black Elk spoke the heroic phrase "Today is a good day to die." At several of their takeover attempts, various members of AIM deliver their spinoff "We came here to die." Vizenor closes one of his commentaries on AIM with the mocking "Yesterday was a good day to negotiate because tomorrow may be a new confrontation" (*Tribal Scenes*, 55).

In other instances, Vizenor finds the radicals' rhetoric not only pompous but inconsistent, actually running counter to their actions. On the one hand, Vizenor reports, AIM criticized tribal officials at Cass Lake, Minnesota, for negotiating a monetary hunting and fishing rights agreement with the state. On the other hand, when the organization took over the Bureau of Indian Affairs building in Washington, he claims, they stopped negotiating on behalf of tribal people when they were offered "more than $60,000 to leave the building and the city" (*Tribal Scenes*, 54). What Ainsworth calls "conspiracy in the victimization of traditional cultures" succinctly summarizes the charge I see Vizenor leveling against these AIM leaders.

Perhaps Vizenor's view of the radical leaders' disjunction with authentic tribal tradition can best be illustrated by his applying to them the telling epithet of "peripatetic mouth warriors" (*The People Named the Chippewa*, 138) or by his describing Banks as less like the "raucous and wise" raven some have envisioned him to be and more like a "killdeer with an overdone wounded-wing act" ("Dennis Banks," 4). He variously labels the AIM bosses "simulated leaders," "media warriors," and "aesthetic inventions of dominance" (*The People Named the Chippewa*, 152, 150). But whatever the epithet, the pose of the AIM leaders has muddied the waters of identity politics in the "cultural word wars": they are "the absence of the tribal real," which has "become the real in the public media" (149).

The pull of radical politics, the romance of postindian simulations, the camaraderie of a popular movement—Vizenor denies none of these. Indeed, in *Interior Landscapes* he relates his own near surrender to the enticements of the American Indian Movement. He tells of his attendance at a meeting on February 27, 1973, two days before AIM began the occupation of Wounded Knee. He recalls being "obsessed with a sense of spiritual warmth," "transmuted by the power of the drums," and "close . . . to spiritual conversion" (235). He writes of this dramatic turning point in his life: "I might have raised my rifle to that airplane over the village in the morning; instead, my pen was raised to terminal creeds. . . . I listened to the voices, the racial politics, the ironies, and the lies, and tried to turn the sound of drums in my heart into a dream song, into literature. I would not become a mixedblood true believer" (235).

Contemporary Survivance

How can Native Americans survive manifest manners and the simulations of dominance, or in Jahner's words, "stop being animated museums"? Vizenor offers portraits not only of the victims of the word wars but of the survivors as well. Although the survivors surface in a multitude of different circumstances, they share significant common characteristics. Survivors actively engage themselves in the ongoing process of discovering and creating their own lives. Those who survive are those who continuously evolve. If stasis characterizes the victims, vitality and adaptability characterize the survivors. Vizenor's survivors adjust; they examine, question, shift, stretch, bend, change, grow, juggle, balance, and sometimes duck—for surviving doesn't necessarily mean winning. "The ritual of a spider building his web on the wind," writes Vizenor. "That is survival!" (*Bearheart*, 187). Survival in Vizenor's accounts is not an end but a constant delicate balancing, achieved primarily through the vehicles of story and humor. Like Angela Sidney, Yukon Native elder interviewed for Julie Cruikshank's *Life Lived Like a Story*, Vizenor believes that "stories are our wealth."[28] He claims, "We can tell stories to ourselves . . . and prevail" (Interview). The most powerful stories, according to Vizenor, are trickster stories of liberation and comic survivance, stories from which we learn "how to balance the forces of good and evil through humor" (*Wordarrows*, 30).

Taken together, Vizenor's various tales about those who manage to outwit evil and maintain tribal integrity in the contemporary world form a composite picture of his vision of survivor in the word wars. One of his earliest book-length works, *The Everlasting Sky: New Voices from the People Named the Chippewa*, offers portraits of contemporary Ojibway, people he calls the "oshki anishinabe" or the "new people of the woodland." Indeed, the book seems to have been a search for those qualities that sustain the tribal identity in the modern world. Although Vizenor does not specifically present or analyze the material as tactics for survival, we can still detect his early efforts to uncover those connecting threads. Note, for example, the emphasis on survival in these chapter headings: "Making It Off the Reservation," "Daydreaming in a White School," "Keeping the Family Together." The emphasis on a unit of survivors is also there when he writes, "The new people of the woodland are complex, and *they* have many different views and ideologies, but *we* share the secrets of the heart from the tribal past" (xv).

Among these early portraits of tribal survivors, one holds particular significance because it reverberates throughout Vizenor's later work. Vizenor's description of the poet and educator Ted Mahto in "Daydreaming in a White School" and "Dreams in the Fourth Dimension" (27–42, 65–79) attributes to Mahto the survivor many of the qualities Vizenor later attributes to his various fictional trickster personas. His summary of Mahto's ideas on the Anishinaabe language and tribal unconscious, like the various phrases he uses in his imaginative characterization of Mahto, recur in similar form throughout his later writing. And most significantly, many of the methods and goals Vizenor attributes to oshki anishinabe creative writer Mahto later serve oshki anishinabe creative writer Gerald Vizenor.

Mahto's background includes time in federal boarding schools, military service, and several colleges and universities. And Mahto, like White Hawk, experiences the internal tug-of-war resulting from two culturally different modes of measurement and sets of expectations. But while White Hawk fell victim to cultural schizophrenia, Mahto has managed to keep his balance. Although Mahto is by no means simply a foil to White Hawk, Vizenor's rendering of both men's characters and actions sheds light on his own ideas about the sources of strength and sanity, and how a connection to the vital tribal tradition would allow White Hawk, Mahto, or himself to preserve a sense of identity while adjusting to life in mainstream culture.

In the *Everlasting Sky* piece, Vizenor offers evidence of what he sees as Mahto's ongoing identification with tribal oral tradition and cultural values. For example, he includes Mahto's references to "reverence for nature," "sharing," "visual thinking," "communication through silence," and "tremendous awe for the independence of another individual" as recognizable core elements in tribal tradition. "These are things the people have never lost," Vizenor quotes, "they are part of the unconscious, they are part of the life meaning of the oshki anishinabe today" (41–42). The Ted Mahto of Vizenor's portrait clearly feels a sense of tribal rootedness at the same time that he lives and works in mainstream culture. With a degree in German and English and a teaching certificate, he had worked as a teacher, school administrator, and writer. At the time of Vizenor's interviews with Mahto for the book, he was working on a curriculum revision for the public schools, evidence of his adjustment to the requirements of white society.

But Mahto and Vizenor also recognize and discuss the oppositional forces acting on the Anishinaabe today and together identify one of the most significant areas of conflict as occurring in language. In describing the distinction between the white and Indian understandings of language, Vizenor calls the white way "structural social thinking" and the tribal "sensitivities of visual dreams" (75). He quotes Mahto as saying: "That symbolizing process that Western man has become so adept at is not true with tribal languages because tribal languages carry more feelings. Modern languages have abandoned the feeling for information and fact . . . the independent information about technology in the language of the dominant society is reflected in tribal linguistic thoughts as visual feelings" (74–75). Mahto places great emphasis on "visual thinking" as a key quality in oral tradition, noting how it generates a sense of connection with the past. "There is something spontaneous and religious about visual thinking," Mahto claims, and he sees the "ability to tell a visual story" as part of a tribal inheritance regardless of whether the ability is ultimately manifested in tribal languages or in English (40). Mahto's "visual thinking" has rich links to Vizenor's own "word cinemas" and his use of pictomyth.

Throughout Vizenor's characterization of Mahto, he emphasizes the notion of visual thinking and shows Mahto to have the survivor's understanding of the interconnectedness of past and present:

> Ted Mahto moves through time in the *anishinabe* spirit like a bishop on an evening walk, reluming his experiences of the present through the conscience of the *anishinabe* past. He is a metaphorical speaker and listener, showing that the past and the present have the same rhythm in stories about people.
>
> The *oshki anishinabe* writer is a visual thinker soaring on the rhythms of the woodland past through the gestures of the present—he is a poet, an autobiographer, a storyteller, an essayist, a public speaker and an epistler. The *oshki anishinabe* creative writer dreams in the fourth dimension of time and lives everywhere.
>
> . . . The *oshki anishinabe* writer tells stories now as in the past—stories about people, not facts. The ideas and visions can be seen more in human gestures than in words. Stories are a circle of believable dreams and oratorical gestures showing the meaning between the present and the past in the life of the people. The stories change as the people change because people, not facts, are the center of the *anishinabe* world. (69)

The characterization of survival Vizenor presents through his portrayal of Mahto also emphasizes adaptability. Although conscious of the schism between tribal methods and values and those of the American education system, Mahto attempts to work within the system to change it. Part of his interest in education, for example, centers on developing "innovative things in teaching *indian* children along the lines of visual expressions" (39). He wants to apply his understanding of the tribal heritage of "visual thinking" in the mainstream school system. He simultaneously maintains tradition and adapts to change, and thereby, he survives.

Vizenor published his portrait of Mahto in *The Everlasting Sky* in 1972. In the works that followed over the next ten years, the survival motif becomes a much more recognizable strain, and his effort to identify the characteristics of the survivor more pointed. In his preface to *Wordarrows* (1978), for example, he writes, "The arrowmakers and wordmakers survive in the word wars with sacred memories" (viii). And in his preface to *Earthdivers* (1981) he directly refers to the people of the stories as "survivors" and clearly underscores their characteristic adaptability: "The earthdivers in these twenty-one narratives are mixedbloods, or Métis, tribal tricksters and recast cultural heroes, the mournful and whimsical heirs and survivors from that premier union between the daughters of the woodland shamans and white fur traders. The Métis, or mixedblood, earthdivers in these stories dive into unknown urban places now, into the racial darkness in the cities, to create a new consciousness of coexistence" (ix).

In one survivor story originally published in 1979, "Land Fill Meditation,"[29] Vizenor creates a character whose emotional situation provides a clear contrast to the portrait of the tribal victim Marlene American Horse. Like American Horse, the fictional protagonist of "Land Fill Meditation," Martin Bear Charme, is a woodland Indian who finds himself displaced into the urban environment.[30] Vizenor describes him as "reservation-born, once poor and undereducated for urban survival" (137). But unlike American Horse, Bear Charme rejects the dictates of authority when they might mean sacrificing his own natural instincts. Rather than looking outside himself for validation of his self-worth, Bear Charme operates with an independence of spirit: he refuses to fulfill stereotypic notions about tribal people, and he refuses to follow blindly the ordained rules of good manners or good taste.

Bear Charme, for instance, rejects a boring but respectable future as a welder in favor of "hauling and filling wet lands with urban swill and solid waste," a job guaranteed to cause the persnickety of society to literally turn up their noses (138). But the imaginative entrepreneur of Vizenor's invention, unruffled by the distaste with which his occupation and his personal odors are received, not only makes his fortune in landfills but also audaciously preaches the need for "land fill meditation." He contends that humankind's attempts to isolate itself from its own waste are delusions that separate us from the earth and leave us easy victims to diseases such as cancer. The cure, according to Bear

Charme, is to "come to our reservation on the land fill to focus on waste and transcend the ideal word worlds, clean talk and terminal creeds, and the disunion between mind and the earth" (141).

Although Vizenor obviously presents this portrait in the spirit of play, it nevertheless emphasizes certain qualities of the survivor that save him from falling victim to the cultural word wars. While American Horse allowed herself to be defined by white society as a "drunken Indian" and thereby captured in the word wars, the survivor Bear Charme rejects the ordained roles of good Indian/bad Indian, which would brand him a "low-life," and instead imagines or invents his own identity and place in society unimpeded by false stereotypes. He is one of the many tribal entrepreneurs and "tricksters of liberty" who populate Vizenor's works and exemplify his sense of comic survivance.

As the theme of survival builds in Vizenor's writing, not only do the attributes of the survivors increase in clarity, but so does Vizenor's identification with the survivors of his stories and his aspiration to teach survival through his writing. Indeed, one of the most detailed pictures of a tribal person surviving the word wars is Vizenor's rendering of his alter ego, the trickster persona Clement Beaulieu, in *Earthdivers* and *Wordarrows*.[31] Vizenor's later characters, especially the tricksters of *Griever* and *The Trickster of Liberty*, often bear great similarity in spirit to Beaulieu/Vizenor, but in these two works the connection is more nearly autobiographical, since many of the stories arose from Vizenor's own encounters. In the tales, Beaulieu is a mixedblood surviving in the urban environments of Minneapolis or Berkeley. In some stories he appears as a tribal advocate, in others as a writer, and in still others as an academic. But most importantly, Vizenor consciously invests his persona with the attributes of a trickster survivor and therefore portrays him as categorically unlike the followers of terminal creeds or the postindian simulations of dominance. Beaulieu does not seek nor profess final answers or a static identity, as do terminal believers. Beaulieu does not speak empty words or use language merely as rhetorical strategy. He is a comic survivor, a postindian warrior of survivance.

In the *Wordarrows* piece "Laurel Hole In The Day," the trickster survivor, here a nameless "tribal advocate," makes living arrangements in Minneapolis for a family from the White Earth Reservation. Although the arrangements ultimately fail, the tale is significant because it illustrates the survival power that the advocate's connection to oral tradition affords him. Grounded in tribal tradition, he confronts the sometimes hopeless situations of contemporary life with realism, humor, and amazingly, optimism.

For example, when he finds assembly work and a small apartment on the urban reservation for the Hole In The Day couple, and the apartment owner makes unreasonable demands, the trickster advocate understands the character of the landlord as "a despicable overweight slumlord who smoked stout cigars, the reincarnation of the evil gambler from the tribal past" (51). Here, like the tribal survivor Mahto, he is "reluming his experiences of the present through the conscience of the *anishinabe* past. . . . showing that the past and the present have the same rhythm in stories about people" (*Everlasting Sky*, 69). By recalling the tribal story of the evil gambler, the advocate gains a new perspective. Knowing that the evil gambler of the story was outwitted, he refuses to waste his time fruitlessly lamenting the injustice of evil and instead enlists his wits to work around obstacles. He uses creative financing to meet the demands of the "despicable" landlord. He doesn't save his people from death at the hands of the evil gambler as Naanabozho did in the tribal tale, but he does achieve a small victory over the contemporary incarnation of the evil gambler. He faces life with the legacy of a survivor, the sense that he can handle whatever may come his way because he has seen it all before in a different disguise. He might say with Old Grandma, the character from Leslie Silko's *Ceremony*: "It seems like I already heard these stories before . . . only thing is, the names sound different."[32]

Vizenor comments directly on the benefits that result from participation in oral tradition in his introduction to *Wordarrows*. He first briefly summarizes the historical trials Native Americans have faced at the hands of white settlers and then claims the triumph of oral tradition through all of those circumstances: "The oral tradition has prevailed in fine humor over the grim realities of colonial suppression" (3). To prove his claim that the power of oral tradition endures and continues to foster survival in contemporary tribal culture, he relates an experience he had while executive director of the American Indian Employment and Guidance Center in Minneapolis, in which both he and a destitute tribal woman became immersed in the healing power of that tradition (3–5). The encounter haunts Vizenor, and he has retold the story in several works and interviews.

He describes an incident involving an unnamed tribal man and woman who come into his office one day at closing time. A ragged pair looking for a handout, they blame all their troubles on racism. When Vizenor challenges the man to abandon his excuses for failure and confront his real problems, the woman is shaken out of a drunken state and seems to experience a vision of the "traditional tribal staff of eagle feathers" being carried into the office. In response, she sings "in a powerful voice" a tribal honoring song, which Vizenor describes, saying, "The rhythm of her soul was like a bird soaring through the dreams of freedom (*anishinabe nagomon*, 133). He also writes of the dramatic effect of her singing: "Tears trailed down the deep dark creases on her cheeks. Through her singing she became sober, her dark eyes were clear, and when she extended her small hands to me, she said in a gentle voice: 'It feels so good to just talk again.' Singing she was talking in the oral tradition. We touch hands. Her smiles pulled the creases on her face into peaceful curves" (*Wordarrows*, 4).

"Talking in the oral tradition" has produced a transformation in the woman. Vizenor quotes Momaday's essay "Man Made of Words" to explain what has taken place and to underscore the function of oral tradition and its indispensable role in tribal survival. According to Momaday, storytelling is "imaginative and creative in nature. It is an act by which man strives to realize his capacity for wonder, meaning and delight. It is also a process in which man invests and preserves himself in the context of ideas. Man tells stories in order to understand his experience, whatever it may be. The possibilities of storytelling are precisely those of understanding the human experience" (*Wordarrows*, 4).

With her singing, the woman has begun to break out of her isolation: "The old tribal woman in the vomit-stained shirt must have thought about talking again, telling stories in good time, expressing her visual wonder and meaning, even from shame and drunkness [*sic*], about her experiences in the new urban world and her collective memories from the tribal past" (*Wordarrows*, 5).

Vizenor calls the incident "profound . . . one thing I have never gotten over." He describes his own reaction to the encounter and the power he felt in what he calls the woman's "spiritual . . . hallucination": "I was just tingling everywhere. I was so transformed by the power of this—instinct" (Interview).

The story, given as an introduction to a collection of Vizenor's own tales, becomes a comment on his storytelling method and his belief in the healing power of story. In *Manifest Manners* he writes of the "literature of survivance" (63), and in *The Heirs of Columbus* of "story energy," "stories and humor" that become "the energy that heals" (164). He characterizes the liberation and survival power in contemporary tribal literature more clearly when he claims: "The purpose of poetry among some Indians is the same as ceremonials in the traditional culture. There's a balance, a reassertion of the creation, a celebration of place on the earth, origin myths, imaginative resolutions, balance." That balance, Vizenor explains, belongs to the mythic or spiritual realm; it is "balance in a symbolic healing sense, that life can go on."[33] By seeking balance in and through story, we can continue. In *Dead Voices* Vizenor repeatedly exhorts us to do exactly that, when an adaptation of a Samuel Beckett line becomes a chant heard throughout the novel: "We must go on."

Indeed, throughout the Vizenor canon, the same basic exhortations on behalf of survival sound again and again, gaining variation from their context and the new Vizenorese in which they are phrased. In *Wordarrows* he writes, "Tricksters must learn better how to balance the forces of good and evil through humor in the urban world" (30). In *Manifest Manners* he calls for the "trickster hermeneutics of liberation" to deny the "obscure maneuvers of manifest manners" (66). Again and again, Vizenor upholds the same basic keys to survival: balance, humor, imaginative liberation, connection, continuance—and story. He invests his own stories with each of the other elements, attempting not only to teach but also to write survival. As a wordmaker in the cultural word wars, his "pen is raised to terminal creeds" (*Interior Landscapes*, 235).

3

The Wordmaker

Subverting "Strategies of Containment"

Artists are the Indians of the white world. They are called dreamers who live in the clouds, improvident people . . . people who don't want to face "reality." . . . The world in which you paint a picture in your mind, a picture which shows things different from what your eyes see, that is the world from which I get my visions. I tell you this is the real world.
    —John (Fire) Lame Deer, *Lame Deer Seeker of Visions*

The teller of stories is an artist, a person of wit and imagination, who relumes the diverse memories of the visual past into the experiences and metaphors of the present.
    —Gerald Vizenor, *The People Named the Chippewa*

Shadow Writing

Amid the philosophical and legal finagling Vizenor dubs the "word wars," he rages against what he sees as static, monologic words, against "dead voices." He criticizes simulations, claims of representation, and neocolonial historicism. Vizenor's struggle with the written involves dissatisfaction with both the underlying philosophies and structures of language use in contemporary society, and the particular appropriations and misrepresentations of the Native American which have resulted. He recognizes, for example, how the representation of a static Indian image in literature denies and replaces the reality of contemporary Native Americans. When he addresses this issue in *Manifest Manners* and in the essay "The Ruins of Representation: Shadow Survivance and the Literature of Dominance," he quotes Larzer Ziff's claims that the Native American "could continue living only in the white man's representation of him" and that "the process of literary annihilation would be checked only when Indian writers began representing their own culture."[1] The impetus in Vizenor's work is exactly that of checking the process of literary annihilation and freeing Native American identity from the grasp of literary colonialism. He does this both by struggling against established literary and linguistic structures, practices, and images, and by working to create new ones: by undermining the colonial "strategies of containment"[2] and replacing them with strategies of liberation.

The quandary in which Vizenor finds himself and the battle in which he is engaged are by no means peculiar only to him. His is the same dilemma faced by most contemporary Native American authors. His responses, however, reflect a particular genius, one willing to engage the intellectual elite on their own turf, as he not only enacts a literature of rebellion but theorizes it as well in the language of the academy. In this chapter I examine Vizenor's theoretical deconstruction of three literary genres and the resulting metamorphoses. Vizenor deconstructs the classic styles of journalism, history, and autobiography, bringing to each new materials, new approaches, and a new understanding of the genre.

The tensions apparent in Vizenor's involvement with literary and academic pursuits arise from several cultural and historical intersections common to many Native Americans, common as well to many other postcolonial cultures. "The Indian author," Louis Owens claims in *Other Destinies*, "is writing within the consciousness of the contextual background of a nonliterate culture" wherein "every word written in English represents a collaboration of sorts as well as a reorientation (conscious or unconscious) from the paradigmatic world of oral tradition to the syntagmatic reality of written language."[3] These tensions between oral and written, English and Native languages, still have currency even though Vizenor, as many Native American writers, grew up with

The Wordmaker / 73

English and with the written mode, for a deep and affecting cultural investment in orality and Native languages remains. Indeed, the work of Vizenor and other Indian writers contains many tangible manifestations of a commitment to as well as the descent from orality and Native speech patterns. But for Vizenor or anyone who professes the power of the oral and pursues the vocation of a writer, the inherent contradiction remains. "The printed word," Vizenor writes, "has no natural evolution in tribal literatures" ("Ruins of Representation," 142). So, as Robert Silberman has said, "There is something paradoxical about the attempt to keep alive mythical, oral values through literary . . . means."[4] Elaine Jahner comments on the negotiation involved in Vizenor's struggle to "find a place on the written page":[5] "At the beginning of his career, Vizenor saw all writing as an act that destroys the life of the oral exchange. Over time he has come to a more accepting view of what writing is and can be if it avoids the constraints of single interpretations which are then easily turned into instruments of domination."[6]

The philosophical and practical dilemmas of writing are complicated yet further when the problems and practices of translation—cultural and literary—are brought to bear. Kenneth Lincoln asks: "How can the translator carry Native American oral traditions—hundreds of indigenous literatures permeated with religion, mythology, ritual, morality and heuristics, national history, social entertainment, economic skills and magic formulas, healing rites, codes of warfare and hunting and planting and food-gathering, visions and dreams, love incantations, death chants, lullabies, and prayers—into printed words in books for modern audiences?"[7] In fact, translation itself, particularly as it has been practiced in conjunction with Native American literatures, comes to represent a process of domination. It is always in principle the privileging of one language and culture over another, and offers validation for the indigenous literature only as an object of study by the dominant culture, or, as Arnold Krupat has noted, as an object of comparison with the dominant culture's models functioning as the master template.[8] The task facing Native writers, trespassing as it does on the grounds of so many political and cultural issues, becomes more difficult.

Vizenor, as already noted, does not believe that Native traditions and literatures can be translated. He believes they can be "reimagined" and "reexpressed," however, and claims, "That's my interest."[9] This process of reexpression, and the process of Native writing in general, has in most instances meant writing, in the language of English, and often in the literary and aesthetic forms of the dominant culture. As such, it requires certain adjustments, and the use of certain tactics to overcome the inherent constraints. But with competence in the dominant language and familiarity with the expectations of the publishing industry, the voices of Native peoples have been allowed to be heard without (or with limited) interpretation or translation. Native writers have learned to use the literary forum to their own ends. They have, in Owens's words, learned to "appropriate, . . . tear free of its restricting authority, another language—English—and . . . make that language accessible to an Indian discourse."[10] The following passage reveals both Vizenor's ambivalence about his relationship to writing in English and the subversive stance that allows him to ameliorate that ambivalence.

> The English language has been the linear tongue of colonial discoveries, racial cruelties, invented names, simulated tribal cultures, and the unheard literature of dominance in tribal communities; at the same time, this mother tongue of paracolonialism has been a language of liberation for many tribal people. English, a language of paradoxes, learned under duress by tribal people at mission and federal schools, was one of the languages that carried the vision and shadows of the Ghost Dance, the religion of renewal, from tribe to tribe on the vast plains at the end of the nineteenth century.
> . . . English, that coercive language of federal boarding schools, has carried some of the best stories of endurance, the shadows of tribal survivance, and now that same language of dominance bears the creative literature of distinguished crossblood authors in the cities. . . . The shadows and language of tribal poets and novelists could be the new ghost dance literature, the shadow literature of liberation that enlivens tribal survivance. ("Ruins of Representations," 162–63)

Vizenor envisions a powerful tribal literature capable of restoring the future to the "vanishing race" of American history and literature. This "new ghost dance literature" appropriates the written tradition and then re-creates that tradition on its own terms.

As a part of this process, many Native American writers have assumed a subversive stance in regard to issues of literacy and literary aesthetics. In their work, they often find themselves negotiating against the authority of the very written tradition in which they are engaged: challenging the rules of writing, challenging the truth of historical accounts, challenging the privileging of text. Their own work often rewrites, writes over, writes through, writes differently, writes itself against the Western literary tradition. Native writers often tell a different story, tell it from a different perspective, from a different worldview. They challenge the reigning literary conventions and the enshrined styles of writing both in principle and in practice. Emma LaRocque, for example, comments on the connections between enforced literacy and the First People's literary aesthetic and practice in *Writing the Circle: Native Women of Western Canada*:

> Native Writers have a dialectical relationship to the English (or French) language. Not only do we have to learn English, we must then deal with its ideology. . . . We may . . . disagree with what is aesthetically pleasing. We may prefer Basil Johnston or Louise Erdrich over Stephen Leacock. We may bring our oratorical backgrounds to our writing and not see it as a weakness. What is at work is the power struggle between the oral and the written, between the Native in us and the English. And even though we may know the English language well, we may sometimes pay little attention to its logic—perhaps we will always feel a little bit rebellious about it all.[11]

LaRocque's comment suggests the kind of self-conscious subversion that becomes its own art form in Vizenor. He, too, has challenged the "logic" of English in its basic structures. He also challenges and subverts the acceptable literary forms.

He begins first with a refusal to abandon the intentions of the oral event, even in written text. Writing for Vizenor becomes "word cinemas." He "finds his place on the written page" not by abandoning the oral, but by his attempts to bring the oral tradition into his written works: "What I go after that's like the oral tradition is I leave it open, I don't resolve it. Now that leaves open the possibility for discourse. . . . And that is liberating and healing" (Interview). Other Native writers have undertaken similar attempts to imbue texts with orality. Simon Ortiz identifies his goals in *A Good Journey*: "I wanted to show that the [oral] narrative style and technique could be expressed as written narrative and that it would have the same participatory force and validity as words spoken and listened to." Momaday, too, has spoken of an attempt to "bring those traditions [the spoken and the written] closer together" and says he believes they "can be informed by the same principle."[12]

That principle Vizenor has variously described as involving "sacred memories," "spiritual energies," "imagination," "liberation," and "rituals." He has also characterized it as a shadow presence, using the metaphor of shadow to explain the multiple referents of imaginative language performance:[13]

> The shadows are the silence in heard stories, the silence that bears a referent of tribal memories and experience. The shadows are active memories, and the memories of heard stories. The shadows are intransitives, an animate action in the silence of stories. The word *agawaatese* is heard in the oral stories of the *anishinaabe*, the tribal people of the northern woodland lakes. The word hears silence and shadows, and could mean a shadow, or casts a shadow. The sense of *agawaatese* is that the shadows are animate entities. The shadow is the unsaid sense in names, the memories in silence, and the imagination of tribal experience. ("Ruins of Representations," 143–44)

This notion of shadow becomes crucial in understanding Vizenor's objection to and subversion of traditional forms and genres. It is this shadow presence or referent that "dead voices" lack; it is this shadow presence that Vizenor tries to bring into being with his writing. He compares its force to that of the vision: "Some personal visions and stories have the power to liberate and heal, and there are similar encounters that liberate readers in the novels and poems of contemporary tribal authors" ("Ruins of Representation," 162). The shadow force of Vizenor's literature works in direct opposition to what Tejaswini Niranjana calls the "strategies of containment."

Objectivity versus Reality

Perhaps the most revealing example of Vizenor's struggle with the "strategies of containment," the sense of confinement he perceives in the conventional written style, and a perfect demonstration of his attempts to break out of those strategies, is "Sand Creek Survivors," a short piece from *Earthdivers* (33–46). In the narrative, Vizenor appears as Clement Beaulieu, a "mixedblood writer and college teacher" on assignment for the *Minneapolis Tribune*, covering the suicide jail death of a thirteen-year-old tribal child in Sisseton, South Dakota. But while "Sand Creek Survivors" includes excerpts from the news stories printed by the *Minneapolis Tribune*, the impetus behind the piece is to tell the real story, a story that had to be left out of the conventional journalistic report, a story that can be discovered only in the shadow regions of oral tradition.

The central tension explored in the work is that between the hard facts, the supposedly objective story of Dane Michael White's death, and the more inclusive story that incorporates images of the social milieu, a sense of historical context, and a subjective analysis of blame. Though Vizenor does relate the kind of information found in conventional journalism, throughout the piece he repeatedly and self-consciously transgresses the limits of objective reporting, using various methods to extend the scope of his story and to underscore what he sees as the truth of the situation. "We know that there's no such thing really as an objective fact," says Vizenor. "Newspapers don't argue that way though. They pretend as if there is an objective truth and they've just discovered it. But . . . you know how simplistic[ally] experiences are presented [in news stories]" (Interview).

In "Sand Creek Survivors," Vizenor clearly exposes the discrepancy between objective and subjective accounts when he juxtaposes the acceptable story, the story that fits the news format, with the story his persona would like to tell. When Beaulieu calls his editor at the *Tribune*, the editor rejects the story Beaulieu begins to dictate, demanding instead the standard "objective" news:

> "Traditional white colonial racists banished tribal cultures and isolated the survivors. . . ."
> "Save it for the archives," said Premack.
> "What is the news?"
> "Start dictating," said Premack, grinding his teeth.
> "November 21, 1968, dateline Sisseton.
> "Catholic funeral services for Dane Michael White were held here Wednesday. . . ." (39)

Then, after recording a segment of the dictated news story given by Beaulieu, Vizenor follows with a different story, a different explanation of Dane White's death: "Dane White lost his balance with the more complicated burdens than the separation between tribal words and white institutions, dreams and social manners; he stumbled through the memories, expectations, and contradictions of two families. . . . Dane White was stranded between cultures and between families" (40).

Although Vizenor's vision of the truth behind the surface story of Dane Michael White's death becomes more clear as he develops the piece, this explanation is significant because it abruptly cuts off and abuts the news story, becoming the shadow reality of the news account. Later in the story, we get another indication of where Vizenor thinks the real story, the real truth, lies. He again delivers the shadow story by recording what the fictional editor rejects. Beaulieu proposes to write about "politicians and their apologies for violence and suicide," but Premack ignores the suggestion and continues interrogating him about the hard facts.

But Vizenor devalues the standard factual fare in journalism through the voice of his persona Beaulieu, who rates his own writing for the *Tribune* as nothing more than "newspaper side shows in the word wars" (44). Beaulieu embodies the ambivalent position of Native writers and Vizenor dramatizes his fractured loyalties, contrasting his actions as newspaper reporter with his role as tribal "wordmaker," one who "shapes his words in the oral tradition" (*Wordarrows*, vii). Beaulieu first records the words of the priest at the funeral services, then identifies his notetaking as merely the work of "a dutiful scribe" (35) and goes on to record his own violent reactions to the funeral service: "How can his words be so soft, so restrained, Beaulieu wrote in his notes. Dane knows no pleasure in the words of the white world; he was trapped and executed in a white institution" (36). Although in the news account he submits to the *Tribune* Beaulieu must say White "took his own life," in this passage he challenges that interpretation and identifies White's death as execution, a word which more accurately reflects the shadow reality of the story.

This idea of discrepancy between an objective news story and the true story does not originate with Vizenor. It became, for example, the premise for Norman Mailer's *The Armies of the Night* when Mailer set his own personal version of the 1967 march on the Pentagon against a news story from *Time* magazine: "Now we may leave *Time* in order to find out what happened."[14] But with Vizenor, the true story must include not only the personal and social aspects of the events as it did with Mailer and many others among the "new journalists"; it must also include the "intransitive shadows," "the unsaid sense," "the memories in silence," "the imagination of tribal experiences": it must include a sense of cultural continuity and ongoing tribal history.

For Vizenor, the Dane Michael White story can be understood only as part of a larger tribal story, understood in that context. Although, as Owens has pointed out, "in the oral tradition, context and text are one thing," Vizenor here must invest his written text with the trace of shadows to advertise their presence, thus allowing the readers to find their place in the context of tribal story.

Matthias Schubnell has identified a method of writing that "emulates the tribal mentality by focusing on mythical and ancestral precedents" as well as "considering . . . individual existence."[15] In "Sand Creek Survivors" Vizenor emphasizes the mythic, historic, and communal significance of Dane Michael White's story. Specifically, he invests it with a sense of timelessness and interconnection by identifying in White's story the shadow of the Sand Creek Massacre, which took place in Colorado on November 29, 1864, identifying the context as that place where "tribal worlds converged in imagination and individual memories" (35): "Dane White and the Sand Creek Massacre in Colorado are three generations apart in calendar time, but in dreams and visual tribal memories, these grievous events, and thousands more from the White Earth Reservation to the damp concrete bunkers beneath the interstates in San Francisco, are not separated in linear time" (33–34).

Vizenor goes on to extend both the political and the tribal significance of Dane White's story by linking the present, the execution of the thirteen-year-old boy, with the tribal past, the slaughter and mutilation of innocent children at Sand Creek: "Now the apologists mutilate this child with funeral words, in the same place in the tribal heart where tribal children were tossed on bayonets and women were dismembered by savage white soldiers" (36). This passage draws parallels between the emotional and spiritual mutilation of a young boy held forty-one days in jail in virtual isolation, the mutilation of White's memory by those who want to write it off, gloss it over with pretty words and vague promises—with manifest manners—and the horrifying physical mutilation of Indian women and children at Sand Creek. The coupling of these incidents challenges, or perhaps indicts, those who would dismiss with trite phrases and mumbled apologies the Dane White case as an isolated, tragic instance. Both, Vizenor implies, cast the same shadows of racism and cultural genocide.

He reinforces his message by bringing in material on the Marias River and Wounded Knee massacres, by quoting from the Lakota holy man Black Elk, by bringing up evidence from the senatorial subcommittee on Indian education of similar Indian youth jail deaths, and by reporting on the lack of remorse and near-hero status of the leader and participants of the Sand Creek Massacre. Ironically, by his apparent digressions, Vizenor succeeds not in obscuring but in bringing into sharper focus the truth of the present events. As he sets the story in the all-too-clear historical and social context, the death of Dane Michael White becomes only the latest episode involving the killing of tribal people.

The multilayered montage of Vizenor's story takes the events out of linear time and creates a vivid shadow reality of "political violence and white horrors in the memories of the tribe" (37), a superimposition of experiences visual, audible, animate: "Hear these primal screams, the tribes scream with the trees and rivers, from diseases, the massacres and mutilations of the heart . . . racist isolation and the repression of the heart in white schools and institutions" (37). Vizenor has created what Silko describes in *Ceremony* as "the pattern, the way all the stories fit together to become the story that was still being told," and as "the world as it always was: no boundaries, only transitions through all distances and time"; what Frank Waters describes in *The Man Who Killed the Deer* as "the web which binds us to the invisible shapes that have gone and those to come, in the solidarity of one flowing whole."[16] Vizenor brings to journalism both the timeless shadow reality that permeates Native American fiction and the literary methods that recreate it. In so doing he deconstructs and subverts the journalistic form, breaching its "strategies of containment" in order to allow it access to the multiple levels of reality including the spiritual, the visionary, and the mythic, and finally replacing it with a new form, one equally valid artistically and with access to the fuller truths of experience.

In the flux of Vizenor's narrative, he refers to White as both a "victim of dominant white colonial institutions" and a "survivor from Sand Creek" (33). White survives tragic suicide or execution by benefit of the same vehicles through which Vizenor's words survive textualization: the shadows of story and the transformative powers of myth. White's story is not separated from its context, nor are his shadows "contained" in the literary form; rather, both are liberated in mythic memory. Allusions in the story to the ghost dance religion, references to the "new world," and suggestions of White's transformation or reembodiment in other physical elements imply a new spiritual and imaginative existence. Vizenor underscores the reader/listener's shared responsibility for the transformative power of story by identifying its communal origins: "Dane Michael White was buried in an isolated grave, but he must not be forgotten. He must soar in memories with millions of tribal people from the past, their faces in the sun, their smiles in the aspen, their death and our memories a revolution in the heart. We are dancing in the sun . . . we are the pallbearers and the ghost dancers" (39).

The liberation of the narrative is achieved only through participation. Ortiz explains that the listener-reader has "as much responsibility to the poetic effect as the poet," and when together they achieve this effect, "the compelling poetic power of language is set in motion towards vision and knowledge."[17] Insisting upon engagement in the event of story, Vizenor resists containment in the "dead voices" of journalistic form, and language is "set in motion."

Righting the Story in History

In accounts of history, too, Vizenor insists on the presence of shadow and the engagement of the reader in setting the historical story in motion. "The postmodern shadows," he writes, "counter paracolonial histories, dickered testimonies, simulations, and the banal essence of consumerism" ("The Ruins of Representation," 139). In historical accounts, as in journalism, Vizenor struggles against the sterility of conventional method; he rejects the static, the formal, and the mono-logic. In uncovering the story in history, he invokes the voices of all its actors and "archshadows" and traces its many connections. In works throughout the Vizenor canon we find theoretical arguments lamenting the traditional historical methodologies, most notably in the book devoted to "righting" history, *The People Named the Chippewa: Narrative Histories*. The title itself succeeds in challenging the colonial imposition of historical identities as it advertises Vizenor's own narrative historical method.

Vizenor's objections to conventional accounts of history center on three major issues: the deliberate or inadvertent slanting of the accounts as a result of political, religious, or cultural agendas; the limited vision of conventional history reflected both in its failure to admit certain kinds of evidence or ways of knowing and in its linear, monologic form of presentation; and the various ways in which history becomes a tool of containment and domination. Each of these conditions of historiography arises out of the long-standing colonial struggle for possession in America—not only possession of the land and its resources, but also ideological possession, because to a large degree the two have gone hand in hand: those who control the land have controlled the story (the his-story) of the land and its people.

This possession of history has compelled not merely the "facts" but the perspective of the accounts and the methods of representation as well. Lester Standiford, for example, summarizes the message in David F. Beer's "Anti-Indian Sentiment in Early Colonial Literature" with this comment: "From the beginning, European Americans wrote of the Native Americans only for the allied purposes of religious conversion and political exploitation." While Standiford points to deliberate slanting of material, Calvin Martin identifies less intentional but equally damaging distortions of history. In his introduction to the collection *The American Indian and the Problem of History*, for example, Martin discusses the standard imposition of an anthropological perspective onto the history of Native American people who themselves proceed from a biological metaphysic, and he characterizes such a move as "ideological colonization." Richard Drinnon has also attempted to expose the cultural bias of historical accounts. Writing about cultural conceptions of time, for example, he claims, "With our objectified Time, we historians have hidden the cyclical world of myth under our linear writings and have thereby robbed tribal people of their reality." Finally, Larzer Ziff characterizes those who present the popular vanishing-race perspective as writing "Indian history as obituary" and claims that such accounts actually cooperate in efforts of cultural genocide.[18] The whole situation is further complicated because, of course, the creation and interpretations of histories have also functioned directly as the justifications for possession or dispossession, and the forums for supposed historical accounts have always included the various literary genres.

Vizenor has traced the formation of the history of the Anishinaabeg through the auspices of political, academic, religious, literary, and popular culture media, noting the irony of a culture's history being recorded by the group most committed to changing, if not completely destroying, that culture: "The cultural and political histories of the Anishinaabeg were written in a colonial language by those who invented the Indian, renamed the tribes, allotted the land, divided ancestries by geometric degrees of blood, and categorized identities on federal reservations" (*The People Named the Chippewa*, 19).

Among the other contemporary scholars who have recognized the connections between history, literature, and colonization are Richard Drinnon (*Facing West: The Metaphysics of Indian-Hating and Empire Building*), Richard Slotkin (*Regeneration through Violence: The Mythology of the American Frontier, 1600–1860*), and Ward Churchill, whose recent study *Fantasies of the Master Race: Literature, Cinema, and the Colonization of American Indians* includes subsections entitled "History as Propaganda of the Victors" and "Literature as a Weapon in the Colonization of the American Indian."

Among Native writers, the responses to the representations and misrepresentations of history have appeared in many forms, ranging from John G. Neihardt's rendering of Black Elk's account of Little Big Horn and Wounded Knee in the "autobiography" *Black Elk Speaks*, to Linda Hogan's dramatization of the Oklahoma oil boom in her novel *Mean Spirit*, to Simon Ortiz's exploration of the history and implications of mining in the Grants uranium belt in the poetry and narrative of *Fight Back: For the Sake of the People, For the Sake of the Land*, to Vine Deloria Jr.'s challenge of the bases and tenets of Western history in essays like those from *God Is Red*. Within these various literary forms, the tacks Native authors have taken also run the gamut of possibility and have included revisionist accounts, preemptive interpretations of contemporary historical events, "eye-for-an-eye" propagandistic distortions, attempts at completely autonomous representations, and multiple combinations of all of the above.

Vine Deloria, Jr., has characterized the work of Native American writers in general as presenting a "reflective statement of what it means and has meant to live in a present which is continually overwhelmed by the fantasies of others of the meanings of past events."[19] The most compelling and ultimately most rewarding literary representations of history by Native American writers are those which, by their humor, work to unmask and disarm history, to expose the hidden agendas of historiography and thereby remove it from the grasp of the political panderers and return it to the realm of story. It is among this group that Vizenor falls, among those who have approached the deadly serious business of history with trickster humor. Through play and intellectual bantering he forces a reconsideration of the processes and powers of historical reckoning and thus essentially liberates the reader from preconceived notions, inciting an imaginative reevaluation of history and a fuller engagement with its shadow texts.

Key to the ability of Vizenor and other Native writers to undertake such a liberation is their keen awareness of the contested visions of history and their imaginative rendering of the places (both physical and intellectual) of cultural and historical contact. In discussing American literature, Louis Owens makes an important distinction between notions of territory (unoccupied space) and frontier (place of contact).[20] Vizenor writes works about the frontier; that is, they do not proceed from the illusion of any pristine historical territory, untouched by previous, and perhaps contrasting, accounts; instead, they draw their humor and power from an awareness of the reality of the place where the diverse accounts of history come into contact with one another. His works take for granted, and force recognition of, the already embattled visions all readers bring to the text. Is America virgin land or widowed land? Did Native peoples migrate to this continent or emerge here? Are the stories of Native peoples to be classified as myth or history? Was America discovered or invaded? Vizenor expends little of his wit and energy to advance either of the opposing sides of these arguments; instead, he writes to flesh out the frontier in all its immense complexity. He shifts and reshifts his stories' perspectives, turns the tables of historical events, unmasks stereotypes and racial poses, challenges the status of history's heroes, and emerges somewhere in a new frontier of Indian literature, somewhere between fact and fiction, somewhere between the probable and the possible, in some border area of narrative that seems more true than previous accounts of history.

Vizenor's method combines a narrative structure with a kind of writing Manina Jones has called "documentary collage."[21] Into the telling of history he brings imagination. He does more than record or catalogue facts; he tells an imaginative story in order to "relume" the past, to bring it to life. "Stories are the truth," writes Vizenor, "facts are the end" ("Reversals of Fortune," 27). The storytelling, the narrative method, allows him to imbue the facts with suggestion, implication, and possibility—with the shadows of history—thus invoking a fuller truth.

Momaday has likewise noted the importance of imagination or what he calls "speculation" in the work of nonfiction: "It is speculation which is not fact in the ordinary sense, but neither is it fiction. I believe that this speculation, which is an act of the imagination, is indispensable to the writing of non-fiction prose." Here Momaday's and Vizenor's thinking seems similar to E. M. Forster's in *Aspects of the Novel*: "Fiction is truer than history, because it goes beyond the evidence, and each of us knows from his own experience that there is something beyond the evidence." The contemporary author Barry Lopez also claims story as the most truthful mode of telling: "The best we can have of those substantial truths that guide our lives is metaphorical—a story. . . . The truth reveals itself most fully not in dogma but in paradox, irony and contradiction that distinguishes compelling narratives—beyond this there are only failures of imagination: reductionism in science; funda-mentalism in religion; fascism in politics."[22]

Paradox, irony, contradiction: these are the lifeblood of Vizenor's method. To Lopez's list of the failures of the imagination, Vizenor might add "colonization of history," for such, he believes, has been the result of linear historical writing. When, in *The People Named the Chippewa*, he criticizes the work of many historians, anthropologists, and others who give accounts of the tribal past such as Edmund Danziger, Barbara Jackson, Henry Rowe Schoolcraft, and George Copway, he repeatedly refs to their works as "invention," clearly challenging the supposed truth of these linear accounts.[23] He contrasts academic invention with tribal imagination; the social scientific accounts he views as lifeless and false, while the imaginative tribal accounts he portrays as vital and true:

> Traditional people imagine their social patterns and places on the earth, whereas anthropologists and historians invent tribal cultures and end mythic time. The differences between tribal imagination and social scientific invention are determined in world views: imagination is a state of being, a measure of personal courage; the invention of cultures is a material achievement through objective methodologies. To imagine the world is to be in the world; to invent the world with academic predicaments is to separate human experiences from the world, a secular transcendence and denial of chance and mortalities. (*The People Named the Chippewa*, 27)

Obviously, his choice of the storytelling mode, with its inclusion of material systematically excluded from most conventional history, implies a challenge of both the method and the truth of the historical canon. So too does his use of documentary collage. Vizenor draws on some of the same kinds of documents most historical researchers tap for their information: letters, memoirs, court records, old newspapers, photos, and other historical manuscripts. He even makes use of the accounts of other historians. But he creates this multilayered manuscript in order to bring the texts into dialogue with one another and ultimately to challenge the authority of certain "official" accounts or documents. Read in the contemporary context, some of the materials advertise their own bias. The subjectivity of other materials Vizenor unmasks by juxtaposing them with additional "official" or "accepted," but contradictory, accounts. Vizenor's work also explores the processes of history: how, from these variously tainted sources, history is constructed.

To the "official" documents of history he adds other sources, frequently unrecognized or undervalued. He allows for the historical significance of oral tradition, dreams, and visions. For Vizenor, material does not have to be written or endorsed to be true or to be historical. He contrasts the two ways of viewing historical material: "The Anishinaabeg did not have written histories; their world views were not linear narratives that started and stopped in manifest binaries. The tribal past lived as an event in visual memories and oratorical gestures;

woodland identities turned on dreams and visions" (24). So, like other literary and historical scholars who have begun to tap the resources of oral history, he readily accepts as evidence the informal spoken memories of tribal elders, giving as much, perhaps more, credence to these accounts than he does to the formal written memoirs or the so-called official accounts of the various eras or events.[24] And just as he allots the oral its place in history, he also includes accounts of tribal tales, dreams, and visions, recognizing the effects of each on historical events and their position in the relationships that create history.

The sources for Vizenor's "narrative histories" are thus more numerous and, I will argue, much richer than those of more conventional, linear, or academic accounts. Vizenor includes these various sources to expose the shadow silences of history (what is lacking in the evidence), the sometimes unacknowledged transitions between evidence and historical accounting (how and why evidence is read in certain ways), and the way that historical accounts often blissfully build on older "established" accounts, blindly taking for granted their accuracy. Vizenor's narratives include not only the story of historical events but also the story of the creation of history and a depiction of the "frontier" of American history where divergent accounts come into contact. His narratives both enact and offer a critique of the movements involved in historical accounting.

"Shadows at La Pointe" from *The People Named the Chippewa* displays the multiple dimensions that characterize Vizenor's narrative histories and the theoretical beliefs that lie behind his methods (37–55). Vizenor tells a story through the eyes of two young mixedblood women from Madeline Island. He allows us to experience vicariously the exhilaration of these two schoolgirls as they play hooky from school, romp in the spring weather, recall the fine stories they have heard at the trading post, dream of their place in history, and hatch a plot to stow away on a steamer.

In this narrative Vizenor clearly intends to expose the invisible seams that lie behind the apparent gloss of history, to reveal the inevitable effects of personality on historiography and the effects of historical accounts on culture. To illustrate these interconnections, Vizenor employs a metahistorical strategy that mimics the realistic complexity of any accurate account. He creates a kind of house-that-jack-built affect. "Shadows at La Pointe" at once encompasses the events of an era, the historical story about the events of an era, the tales that were told about the inventors who wrote the historical story of an era, the life stories of those who told the tales about the inventors who wrote the historical story of an era, and finally, the thoughts and dreams of those who ultimately have their identities formed by all the previous stories.

We can extend the range of the piece yet further if, as Linda Ainsworth says, the probable target audience for the book is made up of contemporary "people named the Chippewa" whose survival, Vizenor hopes, will be the next story.[25] That survival, though, depends on a recognition of the lie of history and the truth of imagination. For only if the Anishinaabeg refuse to accept the invented history that has written off "the people named the Chippewa" as a dead or dying race can they survive as a free people to continue to imagine their lives, the ongoing story that is narrative history.

In "Shadows at La Pointe" Vizenor thus sets out both to expose the questionable nature of what we call history and to enliven the reader's imagination on page after page. He uses overheard conversations, secret hiding places, stories, gossip, letters, description, questions, implication, suggestion, ambiguity, contradiction, pantomime, and dreams to create a sense of adventure and imminent discovery, to incite the active reading with which he believes we should approach historical story. From the outset, Vizenor's imaginative style runs counter to what we might consider normal for historical accounts when he opens with the descriptive scene-setting more common in the fictional mode:

This morning the lake is clear and calm.
    Last night a cold wind washed slivers of ice clear over the beach, the end of a winter to remember. Now, the pale green becomes blue on the horizon. Spring opens in the birch, a meadow moves in the wind. The trees thicken down to the water, an invitation to follow the sun over the old fur trade post to a new world of adventures. (37)

But this descriptive opening does more than establish a literary quality; it sets the story and the storyteller in a tribal context, in a physical and mythic space. Julie Cruikshank notes the important connection between place and story in Native traditions and explains one function of place in narrative: "By imbuing place with meaning through story, narrators seemed to be using locations in physical space to talk about events in chronological time."[26] Vizenor explains the kind of innate connections activated by metaphors of place: "The past is familiar enough in the circles of the seasons, woodland places, lakes and rivers, to focus a listener on an environmental metaphor and an intersection where the earth started in mythic time, where a trickster or a little woodland person stopped to imagine the earth" (*The People Named the Chippewa*, 7).

Later in the piece, through the voices of his protagonists, the two mixedblood girls, Vizenor offers a more specific account of the historical and mythical significance of Madeline Island, the setting for the narrative:

> Madeline Island is our tribal home, the place where the earth began, the place that first came back from the flood. Naanabozho, the trickster was born here, on this island; the old men told us he was the first little person in the world. He stole fire from across the lake. We are little people. This is our place on the earth, this place is in our bodies, in our words, and in our dreams. Our new names, there in the sand, hold back the next flood, but nothing holds back the tall people who come from the East. Naanabozho must have stolen fire from them; now the tall white people are here and they want the whole earth back as punishment. (47)

The island clearly has ancient significance for the protagonists, and this mythical and historical reality affects, and in some instances actually effects, their understanding of the current events of their lives. In the above quotation, for example, the protagonists use myth to explain tribal history and their present condition. Momaday has commented on the necessity of storytelling, saying, "Man tells stories in order to understand his experience," and "Only by means of that act [storytelling] could they bear what happened to them thereafter." Cruikshank, too, has recognized "the contribution of expressive forms like storytelling to strategies for adapting to social, cultural, and economic change."[27] Here in Vizenor's story, the protagonists use a Naanabozho story to try to make sense out of what is happening to their people and their island at the hands of the white settlers. If they felt that the sufferings of their people were senseless, they would find themselves in the kind of existential void that humankind through the ages has found unbearable. They save themselves the same way Beckett's characters Vladimir and Estragon do in *Waiting for Godot*, by creating meaning, creating hope—creating story.

Thus Vizenor sets up history and myth not as existing on separate nonintersecting planes, not as fact versus fiction, not as reality versus nonreality, but as interrelated, interacting elements that together affect or create present reality. By such a conception and such a depiction of the two in narrative, he again clearly aligns himself with the Native American tradition wherein, as Momaday has claimed, "The imaginative experience and the historical express equally the traditions of man's reality."[28] Vizenor enacts these beliefs in his narrative histories, as Momaday does in *The Way to Rainy Mountain*. He depicts Native American characters for whom tribal myth and history are equally real and equally affect their actions. He also anticipates and blocks the arguments of naysayers who might dismiss such a belief in the equal "reality" of myth and history as nothing more than the uneducated belief of primitives. In the narrative, he also writes of biblical stories, biblical "history," significant to white settlers, and shows how those Christian beliefs, which some call myths, affected the historical actions of their believers to as great a degree as did the tribal myths the actions of Native Americans. Set in such a context, the designates "myth" and "history" no longer seem to be clearly distinguishable categories but divisions created on the basis of personal beliefs. Vizenor thus succeeds in blurring the established perimeters of history and prepares the reader to more readily accept his unorthodox vision and methods.

Vizenor continues this challenge of the orthodox when dealing with recorded events of history, the written accounts that we have previously been programmed to accept as indisputable. He does so, not by substituting an alternative "gospel" of history, but by imaginatively depicting the circumstances and individuals involved in the events and implying that the human factor necessarily leads to subjective accounts of history. He presents scenes and information through the voices of numerous firsthand observers or participants. Thus, whether these multiple points of view collaborate or contradict one another, he has moved the black-and-white accounts of history into the gray areas of reality. Following the logic of his method, we arrive at the ironic conclusion that conventional history conveys a fictional account, while Vizenor's narrative or fictionalized histories convey a more realistic account of historical occurrences.

In "Shadows at La Pointe" Vizenor multiplies points of view both through storytelling and through documentary collage. The two mixed-blood women, Margaret Cadotte and Angelick Fronswa, relate the stories they remember being told growing up and the stories they hear the old men of their tribe telling at the trading post. Into the dialogue of his characters Vizenor often incorporates quotations from various historical documents. For example, material from an autobiographical letter by a real-life resident of Madeline Island, Eliza Morrison, becomes one of the stories remembered by the two protagonists in "Shadows at La Pointe." Other real-life figures whose words or deeds play a part in Vizenor's narrative include the missionaries Reverend Sherman Hall and Father Francis Pierz, the ethnologist Henry Rowe Schoolcraft, the treaty commissioners Lewis Cass and Colonel Thomas McKenney, and the tribal writer William Whipple Warren.

Vizenor patches together a story from the real-life figures and their words or deeds, or he overlays the imaginative story with these elements of documentary collage. The seams of history become apparent, and through the interaction of the imaginative and the historical, he succeeds in rounding out the accounts of history to include that "something beyond the evidence" that Forster speaks of as bringing us closer to the truth. When he writes of Schoolcraft, for example, he humorously contrasts two viewpoints of the man: one tribal and one held by white society "back east."

History texts credit Schoolcraft with numerous discoveries during his expeditions into Ojibway territory in the early to middle 1800s, including the discovery of the source of the Mississippi River.[29] But through the voice of an "old mixedblood" storyteller, through Vizenor's imaginative interjections into history, Schoolcraft's supposed achievements are belittled or devalued:

"Schoolcraft believes he found the sacred copper back on the Ontonogan River but he was mistaken. The shamans planted a chunk of mined copper there; the explorer thought that he had discovered more than the next white man. . . . He tried to change the name of this place to Virginia Island. Madeline, the mixedblood wife of Michel Cadotte, remained the favorite name, the place name on the maps.

"He also asked tribal people, even a few mixedbloods, where to find the source of the Mississippi River. He asked his way and then revealed his discoveries back East.

". . . He became an expert on the 'red race' and . . . he invented the 'Algic tribes,' as he called us out here. This copper hunter learned all he knew about tribal people from his mixedblood relatives, but he gives them no credit for his discoveries." (41–42)

This imaginary recounting of the other side of Schoolcraft's recorded activities expands our grasp of histories by making us dwell on the possible omissions or bias of conventional accounts. Vizenor reinforces his point about subjective history and the two opposite reputations Schoolcraft earned through a humorous depiction of physical size mirroring status. In the fictional mixedblood's story, Schoolcraft alternately grew or shrank as did his status. The same actions that made him sprout inches back east decreased his size with the tribe. At his death, according to the speaker in the narrative, Schoolcraft was buried in a ten-foot coffin in the east while the tribe only built a four-foot grave house. And, the story concludes, "Some tell that his coffin is two feet longer since his death, and still growing. . . . The grave house out here has become a bird nest, and even smaller" (42). Vizenor's playful treatment of Schoolcraft exemplifies his unwillingness to pay homage to any of the supposed "giants" of American history.

Vizenor delivers an additional blow to conventional ideas of history through the ambiguity that surrounds the major fictional action of the narrative: the protagonists' departure from the island as stowaways. He leaves the way open for various interpretations of the text's description of the protagonists' actions. In an early segment of the narrative, for example, he relates these thoughts of the protagonists: "We will be remembered in the future because we boarded the first steamer that followed the sun in our dreams" (38). But the passage leaves us wondering: was boarding the steamer a fulfillment of the girls' bright dreams, did the steamer figuratively "follow the sun" in their dreams; or did the two girls only dream of boarding the steamer, which, like the sun, moved off over the horizon? How we interpret the line, or whether we choose to pin the passage down to one interpretation, will affect how we understand the rest of the tale.

Later in the piece, the schoolgirls' story continues:

> We waited on the dock near the steamboat until no one was watching and then we climbed into two huge brown trunks with bright brass corners. The sun leaped through thin cracks and seams on the curved trunk cover, enough light inside to read our secret maps, the ones we charted with places from all the stories we had heard in the store. . . .
> We traveled to Fond du Lac.
> We listened. (50)

What the two girls hear is the account of a treaty conference including the formation of an article that would provide for the halfbreeds as well as the full bloods. And, they tell us:

> We imagined our names on these treaties, we marked these places on our personal dream maps, places the old mixedbloods told about in their stories, around the stove at the store. . . . Our places on the dream maps, our shadows in the stories. (54)

Multiple possibilities exist for interpreting these passages: We can see the protagonists' journey as one they envision together, plotting their course based on the stories they heard the old men tell in the store, or as an actual journey being undertaken, or even as an imaginative journey they dream of as they are in the act of listening to a story. The treaty conference is likewise either one they imagine based on stories they have heard, one they actually overhear as stowaways, or one they invent or imagine while they actually are stowaways. Vizenor limits what he reveals to his audience about the girls, just as the information in any history is limited. Then, by drawing attention to the multiple possibilities in the story, he, by extension, likewise exposes the multiple possibilities of history. And just as what we believe about one passage in the story colors our interpretation of the remaining story, in history our beliefs about certain events as clearly color our interpretation of later events.

In this last passage, Vizenor also suggests much about the shadow realities absent from conventional historical accounts. The girls, we are told, imagine themselves into history (they imagine their names on the treaty) because they are a part, however unrecognized, of that history, and they both affected it and are affected by it. They are "shadows in the stories," just as the unrecorded treaty stipulation about halfbreeds, and any other omissions, are shadows in the written histories.

In both his narrative histories and his literary journalistic pieces, Vizenor concerns himself with putting into his writing all that is left out of the conventional accounts. Alfonso Ortiz offers this observation about the weaknesses of conventional history: "There is a difference between writing about a period and getting lost in it. Too many historians of Indian/white relations fall into this trap and are overcome by a moral myopia, a failure to see the modern applications and implications of their findings from the past."[30] Through Vizenor's subversive accounts, he attempts to incorporate the multiple visions of reality. Into the present of the Dane Michael White case he incorporates the past of the Sand Creek Massacre; into the past of Madeline Island's history he incorporates the present of Margaret Cadotte and Angelick Fronswa; into the factual content of both he introduces the power of imagination. He incorporates the shadows of history and thus forces the reader's recognition of the way all historical accounts depict only possibility and probability, not actuality.

Vizenor's challenges of history surface throughout his work, in his novels and short fiction as well as in his essays or "narrative histories." Perhaps the work that best demonstrates the wild irreverence with which he treats our nation's "gospels" of history is his novel *The Heirs of Columbus*. Published just before the 1992 quincentenary observance of Columbus's coming to the Americas, *Heirs* distinguishes itself from the mass of Columbus materials that appeared at that time by the unusual twists it gives to the legacy of the Columbus myth, boldly imagining the genes of the explorer as a source of contemporary healing. For Vizenor, merely rejecting the errors of historical accounts and relegating Columbus to the past would be both too simple and too unsatisfying, an absolution without the benefit of new revelation and without the pleasure of humor. As Will Roscoe noted in his review of the novel, "Columbus is loathed by Indians on general principle. But

Vizenor isn't satisfied with resentment. He wants revenge. And so he claims Columbus as one of his own."[31]

In *Heirs* Vizenor writes Columbus into the history of the Anishinaabe, carves his name in the family tree. He recounts the sexual union of Columbus and Samana, a tribal woman, from which issues the mixed-blood "heirs" whose story is told in the novel. But Vizenor's trickster humor goes further: Stone Columbus, heir and namesake of the great explorer, claims that the "Admiral of the Ocean Sea" was himself American Indian, having descended from Mayan ancestry. By Stone's account, "The Maya brought civilization to the savages of the Old World," and Columbus's misguided adventure to the Americas was a return to "his homeland" (9).

Columbus a Mayan, Mayans the carriers of civilization to the savage European nations, American Indians as "heirs" of the great explorer: these are the kinds of trickster reversals which make up the story in *The Heirs of Columbus*. Vizenor embellishes history's staid accounts of Columbus with a wild, irreverent tale of sex, gambling, murder, and general mayhem. His goal obviously is not to replace one historical account of Columbus with another, not to "re-possess" history, but to place the realm of history beyond the reach of what he calls "the striven western gaze," "the colonial gaze" (184, 153). History, he believes, should be not possessed but imagined. History should be, not an emblem or a tool of social and political power, but a vehicle of personal and communal empowerment. History should not enslave but liberate. With the political satire of *The Heirs of Columbus*, Vizenor essentially disarms history.

We see his satirical wit at work in scenes involving the repatriation of remains, both those of Pocahontas and those of Columbus. As Roscoe has noted, "Whoever controls the artifacts of history, controls history."[32] Having claimed possession of both the bones and the persona of Pocahontas, colonial culture has made her into the perfect stereotype of the primitive "other," an Indian princess, emblem of the romantic past and of the primitive's adoring devotion and humble gratitude for the salvation of civilization. The "act of recovery" undertaken in Vizenor's novel is not only of her bones but also of her identity, an identity representative of the larger tribal culture.[33]

Vizenor's account of the battle over the bones also serves as a comment on the consumer culture he so frequently attacks. The heirs want to reclaim the remains of Pocahontas to bury them. Such a plan arouses great uproar among the collectors of cultures who recognize the monetary value of such artifacts. At issue, of course, are opposing ideas about the proper disposition of remains: reburial or display in private or museum collections. And these opposing ideas stem from deeper philosophical differences about what constitutes value. Are tribal artifacts and remains sacred, imbued with inviolable rights, as Vizenor argues in "Bone Courts," or with what he calls "pious intentions" (*Heirs*, 76)? Or are they valuable only as commodities subject to barter and ownership? Must they be made "useful" in some economic terms to be deemed valuable, or do they have inherent value?

Vizenor raises the ante in this debate when he adds intrigue over the remains of Columbus, since it is one thing to discuss the remains of "primitive" cultures as museum objects, quite another to afford the same honor to one of the supposed giants of Western history. Ultimately, Columbus's remains are "discovered" to bear the genetic "signature of survivance," a DNA encoding. Columbus's "seventeen gene signature" contains "healing genes," and the heirs found a new nation dedicated to healing through "genetic implants" and "story energy." Ironically, the explorer whose appearance in the Americas signaled the beginning of an era of destruction of Native American cultures becomes the source of their survival.

Vizenor's *Heirs* also works to reduce the status of the historical persona of Columbus by showing the Admiral of the Ocean Sea relying on the assistance of Native peoples in the "discovery" of valuable minerals, depicting Columbus as a closet Jew in an anti-Semitic civilization, and showing Columbus afraid at sea, suffering from a physical deformity, and as a man unnerved and haunted. Finally, Vizenor challenges the notion of Columbus as a representative of a superior race, whose right and duty it was to civilize the inferior, by representing Columbus himself as a mixedblood.

Vizenor also challenges the professed motives of the conquerors. Although he quotes Ronald Reagan as calling Columbus "the inventor of the American dream" (189), Vizenor identifies that dream as one of possession: "Columbus arrived in the New World with a striven western gaze. . . . Tribal people he saw as naked servants with no religion. . . . The record of that first stare inscribed the end of peace on the islands and the source of loneliness in the New World" (184). For proof, Vizenor offers excerpts from Columbus's diary. His method for undercutting Columbus's declarations of ownership is to mock them, to overturn them and reveal their ludicrous nature by recounting a similar declaration by the heirs. The account of Columbus's claiming of the West Indies, taken verbatim from the diaries, reads this way:

> The Admiral called to the two captains and to the others who jumped ashore and to Rodrigo de Escobedo, secretary of the whole fleet, and to Rodrigo Sanches of Segovia, and said that they should bear faith and witness how he before them all was taking, as in fact he took, possession of the said island for the King and Queen, their Lord and Lady, making the declarations that are required, as is set forth in the testimonies which were taken down in writing.[34]

Vizenor's account of the heirs' claiming of Point Assinika offers a wonderful revision and an implied commentary on Columbus's declaration: "The Heirs of Columbus bear faith and witness that we have taken possession of this point in the name of our genes and the wild tricksters of liberties, and we made all the necessary declarations and had these testimonies recorded by a blond anthropologist" (119).

This trickster mockery continues throughout the novel. The pages of the book are filled with historical and contemporary references and with playful misreadings of both. Although every reader may be equipped to distinguish between fact and fiction in some cases, few will know the "truth" in all instances. We are thus left wondering which is which. This, of course, is Vizenor's point. We should read history with vigilance and active engagement as we try to ferret out the truth or falseness of the accounts.

Truth, Vizenor repeatedly illustrates, may lie outside the realm of simplistic distinction between fact and fiction. For example, in talking of an encounter between Columbus and Samana, Stone Columbus first gives the date as October 28, 1492, then as October 29, 1492. When the discrepancy is challenged, Stone responds, "Columbus is ever on the move in our stories" (11). In another instance, the stories we are told by Louis Riel, who also appears as a character in the novel, are recognized as "sacred stories, true or not" (166). And according to Riel, "Whether the heirs believe their stories is not the point, because no culture would last long under the believer test; the point is humor has political significance" (166).

Of course, this too is the premise behind and the raison d'être for Vizenor's fiction. Clearly his humor has political significance and a political purpose—to overturn the "striven western gaze" that corrupts and prevents liberation. His humor takes on Columbus, not by relegating him to a closed history, but by bringing him into the present. Custer may have died for the sins of the colonizers, but clearly Vizenor's Columbus lives. And those who think death is the final revenge haven't read *The Heirs of Columbus*.

Transforming the Self in the Autobiographical Moment

In his autobiographical writings, as in the historical, Vizenor's attention is again given to undercutting the conventional claims of the genre and to exposing the unacknowledged processes involved in the creation of autobiographical story. The title of his book-length autobiography, *Interior Landscapes: Autobiographical Myths and Metaphors*, suggests that his will indeed be a nonstandard way of telling a personal story. "My memories and interior landscapes are untamed," he declares (*Interior Landscapes*, 263). Defined as a form in which an individual recounts the "true" story of his or her life, autobiography, Vizenor recognizes, is an implausible concept. In one of his short autobiographical essays, "Crows Written on the Poplars," for example, he quotes Paul John Eakin's *Fictions in Autobiography*: "What we are ready to believe—and what most autobiographers encourage us to expect—is that the play we witness is a historical one, a largely faithful and unmediated reconstruction of events that took place long ago, whereas in reality the play is that of the autobiographical act itself, in which the materials of the past are shaped by memory and imagination to serve the needs of present consciousness" (102).

Of course, Eakin's (and Vizenor's) stance is not new. The accuracy or validity of one's personal accounting of his or her experience has been frequently challenged. Note, for example, how a collection of memoirs edited by William Zinsser carries the same implication in its title: *Inventing the Truth*.[35] But Vizenor's challenge of the genre involves more than just the impossibility of objectivity: it involves the equally implausible concept of individual story. Many scholars of Native American autobiography have commented on the incompatibility of this notion with a tribal worldview. Arnold Krupat, for example, writes: "'The autonomy of the . . . individual' was always subordinated to communal and collective requirements. That egocentric individualism associated with the names of Byron or Rousseau, the cultivation of originality and differentness, was never legitimated by native cultures, to which celebration of the hero-as-solitary would have been incomprehensible."[36]

If the idea of autobiography is, as Krupat and Brian Swann claim in *I Tell You Now*, "foreign . . . if not also repugnant" to tribal cultures, then naturally, as they say, "The form of writing generally known to the West as autobiography had no equivalent among the oral cultures of indigenous inhabitants of the Americas." Although, as Hertha Wong notes, Native Americans did have their own methods of recording events and images in art or oral tradition, theirs was not autobiography in the Western sense.[37] The autobiographical form, when employed by ethnographers, anthropologists, and other collectors and translators of Indian culture, thus becomes (however unintentionally) one of the "strategies of containment," a genre aesthetic that redesigns a Native accounting of life, forcing it to conform, for example, to strategies of lineality and cause-and-effect, to rhetorical patterns of paganism and conversion, savagism and civilization.[38]

Although also upheld as the format for Native Americans when they become literate and capable of telling their own lives in English, the autobiographical method has been appropriated by Native writers and has undergone significant alterations. Often, for example, the story becomes that of a people, a history, and a place, and only secondarily that of an individual. The autobiographical method has been steeped in myth and in elements of the oral storytelling aesthetic. Krupat, for example, contrasts the individual or distinctive voice thought to characterize autobiography in the Western model with the dialogic or collective voice characteristic of Native American life stories, and

Cruikshank's work with three Yukon women illustrates the way that storytelling often provides a frame for past and present life experiences, offering a kind of parallel text to the subject's own life story.

Vizenor, too, recognizes the imposition of the Western concept and form of autobiography on Native American lives, and his own autobiographical accounts display many of the subversions characteristic of Native-authored autobiographies. But he challenges the form on broader grounds. He claims that the idea of an individual life is fallacious in itself, not merely incompatible with a Native concept of identity. In several discussions on autobiography he quotes George Gusdorf's statement on this point:

> Throughout most of human history, the individual does not oppose himself to all others; he does not feel himself to exist outside of others, and still less against others, but very much *with* others in an interdependent existence that asserts its rhythms everywhere in the community. No one is rightful possessor of his life or his death; lives are so thoroughly entangled that each of them has its center everywhere and its circumference nowhere.[39]

Vizenor's challenges of these bases of autobiography, his challenge of the validity and method of the genre, manifest themselves not only in theory but also in the form of his own autobiographical works, which include "I Know What You Mean, Erdupps MacChurbbs" (1976), "Gerald Vizenor: Ojibway/Chippewa Writer" (1980), "Crows Written on the Poplars: Autocritical Autobiographies" (1987), and *Interior Landscapes: Autobiographical Myths and Metaphors* (1990), as well as segments from *Wordarrows: Indians and Whites in the New Fur Trade* (1978), and *Earthdivers: Tribal Narratives on Mixed Descent* (1981). Portions of many of his fictional works are also highly autobiographical. Vizenor's challenges of the enshrined autobiographical method also surface in the theoretical relationships he enacts in and between his own various works. A chronological look at his various autobiographical works reflect his own evolving views about the genre and demonstrate through their changing forms the development of his autobiographical method. The movement, in what Arnold Krupat has called Vizenor's "serial autobiography," is from early accounts (such as "I Know What You Mean" and "Gerald Vizenor: Ojibway/Chippewa Writer") that seem to accept the idea of autobiography, if they do not neatly follow the entrenched method, to later works (such as "Crows Written on the Poplars" and *Interior Landscapes*) that reject both the tenets of the genre and the formal models.[40]

Notable elements of Vizenor's subversion of classic autobiographical form include his use of a fictional persona, his sparse accounting of even the most basic details of his personal relationships, his use of the third person in writing autobiography, his use of names as a form of autobiography, his self-conscious invention of his own personal words and phrases, his casual juxtaposition of fantasy and realism in personal story, his self-conscious critique and deconstruction of his own earlier works of autobiography in those which follow, and his use of myth and metaphor as a vehicle of personal story. All of these characteristics of Vizenor's self-writing illustrate his consciousness of the process of autobiography, his understanding of it as the creation and not the recounting of story, and his understanding of the reader's role in activating the dialogues of the autobiographical texts.

In fact, Vizenor's "true" autobiographical work becomes the larger story, the *Bildungsroman*, or perhaps more accurately, the *Künstlerroman*, embedded in the texts and among the spaces between the works of the Vizenor canon. Like many tribal stories, it is an ongoing story, a continual source of puzzlement; and in that way it accurately reflects the puzzle that is his life: "I am still discovering who I am, the myth in me. Once I was a lady bird devouring aphids in the tomato plants. Once I made my home among the marigolds at the edge of the garden. I am part crow, part dragonfly, part squirrel, part bear. I kick the sides of boxes out. I will not be pinned down. I am flying home in words and myths" ("Gerald Vizenor," 168).

Indeed, in Vizenor's autobiographies more than anywhere else in his literary creations, we see his mythic storytelling at work. As the subtitle to *Interior Landscapes* suggests, Vizenor employs myth and metaphor to tell a personal story; but more than that, he recognizes the inherent, the inextricable presence and influence of both in the story of all human life. Autobiography for Vizenor must not only cross the lines of genre but also challenge their very existence. In his own accounts he recognizes and delights in the inevitable transformations of myth into life and life into story. Again and again the autobiographical Vizenor discovers amid the harsh circumstances of his life small moments of beauty or connection, and the author Vizenor tells the tale of how his younger self fashioned from those moments a meaning (his own story, his connection to myth, a metaphor for his life) that allowed him to survive. Robert Lee recognizes in these accounts a double "self-authoring": the "literal" creation of self and the literary.[41] Indeed, the levels of creation inherent in Vizenor's autobiography may be yet more numerous and more complex.

In one incredible scene from *Interior Landscapes*, for example, after finally having experienced a secure home with his stepfather for a short five months, Vizenor again finds himself alone when his stepfather dies, his mother abandons him to foster care, and his foster family forces him to move out and holds his belongings ransom when his care is not paid for. Just finishing his junior year in high school, Vizenor finds a room to rent and a summer job to pay expenses. This is his literal self-authorship, his basic life choices, his simple survival. Later, when the autobiographical Vizenor writes of that time, "So much depended on a time card then: identity, money, and the need to be distracted by labor," we see his literary self-authorship as he creates a story, and thereby a meaning, from his earlier experiences (99). The author's understated comment conveys not only the terrible isolation and pitiful heroism of his adolescence, the conditions he took so much for granted, but the tiny seed of exhilaration he managed to keep alive, his indomitable spirit.

Vizenor closes the account of that era in his life noting his "insecurities" and "past miseries" as well as his "humors" and "a new sense of adventure and liberation" (100). The use of understatement becomes the silent self-authorship, the unsaid creation, evidence of the shadow realities of any autobiographical moment, the reader's entrance into the story. Finally, when Vizenor writes of the stark urban poverty, abandonment, and foster homes, he claims, "The tricksters raised me in imagination," and "The tricksters were with me in stories, and we remembered how to turn pain and horror into humor" (74). In this mythic self-authoring, his own experience is first informed and then transformed by trickster story; his placing of his life in a mythic context invests it with a new meaning.

When the levels of Vizenor's autobiography, particularly as informed by their crossblood nature, are explored by Betty Louise Bell in "Almost the Whole Truth: Gerald Vizenor's Shadow-Working and Native American Autobiography," Bell notes the degree to which the reader is compelled to "inhabit and textualize the shadows" of *Interior Landscapes* and the "overwhelming sense of absence in Vizenor's autobiography, the sense of things not said and not found."[42] Of course, Native-authored autobiography has seldom aspired to a confessional mode wherein the many personal details of an individual life are traced chronologically and causally. In fact, many tribal autobiographies, like Vizenor's, have proceeded episodically, by selective rendering of telling scenes or commentaries or oral stories. Julie Cruikshank, for example, who collected the life accounts of three Yukon elders, reports a notable shift in her expectations during her interview sessions with the women:

> In the beginning, I asked about their childhood experiences, about seclusion, about marriage and childbirth, and about how events like the gold rush and Alaska Highway construction had affected their lives. The women would give brief answers to my direct inquiries and then suggest that I write down a particular story they wanted to tell me. Usually such stories involved a bewildering series of characters and events, but with practice I learned to follow the complex plots and to understand that when women told me stories they were actually using them to explain some aspect of their lives to me.[43]

In the case of Vizenor's account, because he does offers such intimate details of his encounters with prostitutes or his humiliation at the hands of childhood bullies and later army officers, the reader may at first not notice the absence of details about his two marriages, his relationship with his son, or his day-to-day experiences within the literary and academic worlds. But in fact, Bell's comments illuminate an important aspect of Vizenor's self-authoring: the degree to which the autobiographical in Vizenor is engaged not with the personal but with the mythic, the metaphorical, and the theoretical, particularly the degree to which it is engaged with the mythic Anishinaabe trickster.

Indeed, the primary myths and metaphors of Vizenor's autobiographies arise out of the trickster tradition. In *Earthdivers*, for example, Vizenor recalls the Anishinaabeg creation story and identifies his mixedblood trickster persona as one of the new earthdivers who "dive into unknown urban places now . . . to create a new consciousness" (ix). He even sees "the experiences of the autobiographer" as "similar to those of the earthdiver" (xix). Both, after all, are in the process of creating or recreating their own place in the world. In *Interior Landscapes* Vizenor opens his story by associating himself with the crane clan, identifying the crane as among the original six tricksters who "posed as humans when the earth was new" (3), and noting the crane clan's reputation as tribal "orators" (4). He thus establishes his mythic connections to trickster and to story. In several places in his autobiography Vizenor also uses the myth of Naanabozho and the evil gambler as a metaphor for his own life and as a metaphor for his father's life. He writes, for example, of his father, who was murdered in an unsolved urban crime: "Clement William Vizenor lost the game with the evil gambler and did not return from the cities" (*Interior Landscapes*, 27). This same trickster myth becomes an important source for multiple fictional, historical, and personal accounts throughout the Vizenor canon. He employs a version of the myth as the prologue for the "Narrative Histories" of *The People Named the Chippewa*; he renders one version in the short story "The Moccasin Game"; his fictional "heirs of Columbus" retell the story in his Columbus novel; and his persona Clement Beaulieu often finds himself playing a role in a modern-day version of this mythic trickster/evil gambler contest of wits.

This ready trespassing of mythic, personal, historical, and fictional boundaries clearly characterizes Vizenor's autobiography as well. Friends, family, acquaintances, enemies, and public figures who appear in his autobiography often find themselves or their caricature cast in a work of his fiction as well. His accounts of familial, historical, and personal myths often become the sources for some of his fictional settings and events. A somewhat macabre personal encounter involving the butcher of chickens and told by Vizenor in *Interior Landscapes* seems to reappear transformed by Vizenor's imagination in a marketplace scene in the novel *Griever: An American Monkey King in China* (53–54) and in an early story, "Paraday at the Berkeley Chicken Center" (8–9). Vizenor recognizes these transformations of story and the transgressions of the genres as the common human experience. The mythic, the metaphorical, the personal, the historical, the fictional always inform one another; the shadows of each are always present in the telling of any of the others.

Because of these inevitable attachments of the personal to other levels of being and knowing, and because of the natural shifts in perspective brought about by the passage of time, Vizenor rejects as inaccurate autobiographical accounts in the first person. "First person pronouns," he claims, "have no referents" ("Ruins of Representation," 158), and "We are reduced in remembrance to scenes on color television in the back seat of a white limousine" (*Interior Landscapes*, 262). So Vizenor's autobiographies attempt in various ways to reference the multiple shadows of experience and to reflect the complicated nature of autobiographical writing. In "Crows Written on the Poplars," for instance, he analyzes his own earlier autobiographical work "I Know What You Mean" and retells the same squirrel story he told in that work, but tells it from a new perspective, one informed by an analysis of autobiographical process. Writing about his own autobiographical presence in the third person, in one passage Vizenor claims, "Ten years ago he wrote about what he chose to remember from an experience twenty years before that" (103). Clearly here he exposes autobiography as "invention."

In many places Vizenor also moves to unmask the multilayered reality of autobiography by advertising his changing perspectives from actor to viewer to commentator to interpreter. We see not only the younger Vizenor but also the adult Vizenor viewing the young man. We see both the account of the younger man's creation of his existence through myth and metaphor and the older Vizenor's comments on those efforts, his own contemporary re-creation and reevaluation of the meaning of the younger man's life. The continual re-creation inherent in Vizenor's autobiographical process subverts the "strategies of containment" of the traditional form and essentially redefines autobiography.

Just as Cruikshank admits having to alter her expectations in her gathering and understanding of the Yukon women's stories, Vizenor's readers too must learn to expect and value not detailed biographical information but metaphorical story, silence, and intellectual dialogue. When they do, they find that his accounting offers a satisfaction different from that of chronological, confessional autobiography. Vizenor's autobiography becomes "a remembrance past the barriers" of genre distinctions and formal characteristics ("Crows Written on the Poplars," 101).

But like all of Vizenor's shadow writing, his autobiographical method becomes more than a literary exercise in subversion; it becomes a mode of tribal survivance, a way in which Native peoples can assert and create a new identity, one not contained by tragic or romantic visions of a vanishing race nor threatened by "literary annihilation." It becomes the voice of a new social consciousness, one destined to liberate and heal. It becomes part of the "new ghost dance literature, the shadow literature of liberation that enlivens tribal survivance" ("Ruins of Representation," 163).

4

Multiple Traditions in Haiku

Native American poets attempt in their insistent utterances to lessen the distance created by print, to transform the "passive word of the written page" into an "active immediacy." . . . The poems do not withdraw into style, but project into life.
—Brian Swann, Introduction to
Harper's Anthology of Native American Poetry

By understanding more about our immediate locale, the native soil we stand on and the other living things that share our world, we expand our imaginations and expand our culture.
—Rick Simonson and Scott Walker,
Introduction to *The Greywolf Annual Five: Multi-cultural Literacy*

Throughout his career, Vizenor has enriched his writing with the interweaving of multiple traditions. As the previous chapter has shown, he has often worked against the accepted definitions of truth and the constraints of genre, to establish links, combine forms, and play one idea or genre off of another. Vizenor's cross-cultural, mixed-genre tendency is perhaps most clearly manifested in his haiku poetry (published in six collections between 1962 and 1984 and frequently anthologized), which seeks to combine the traditions of the Ojibway dream song and the Japanese haiku.

The range of relationships, however, ultimately reaches beyond these two traditions. The Native American imprint on Vizenor's haiku involves more than the narrowly defined dream song and expands beyond the bounds of Ojibway culture. Many of Vizenor's haiku, for example, readily exhibit a connection to the trickster tradition in Native American literature and to pan-Indian concepts of spirituality. The haiku tradition itself has frequently recognized links to Zen philosophy and practice. In addition, haiku, by its minimalistic nature, tends to lend itself to reading in another tradition, that of reader-response aesthetics. An understanding of haiku in Vizenor's style, then, has clear links to multiple cultural, philosophical, literary, and theoretical traditions.

Haiku Form, Ojibway Dream Songs, and Whether the Twain Meet
Having served in Japan in the military in 1954 and 1955, Vizenor developed an interest in Japanese culture and especially in haiku. Later, in both his undergraduate and graduate work at the University of Minnesota, he was involved with the Asian studies program. His publications from the 1960s include collections of haiku and reexpressions of traditional Ojibway songs, two kinds of expression he saw as similar in form and intention. About the haiku form he said, "There is a visual dreamscape in haiku which is similar to the sense of natural human connections to the earth found in tribal music, dream songs" (*Matsushima*, 3). And about Ojibway dream songs he said, "They are sort of the Ojibway haiku—in song" (Interview).

Reviewer Robert Glauber, writing in 1966 after the release of Vizenor's collection of Ojibway songs *Summer in the Spring*, was one of the earliest commentators to make a connection between the two forms in Vizenor's work. In the *Beloit Poetry Journal*, he noted: "Here is a fascinating collection of Ojibway pieces that strongly remind one of haiku. All are brief and extremely evocative. One cannot say, however, if the Japanese quality is actually in the original or has only crept into Vizenor's 'interpretations.'"[1] The line of inquiry suggested in Glauber's brief comments might be satisfied by the knowledge that Vizenor's "interpretations" were really "reexpressions" of Frances Densmore's translations of Ojibway song poems and that a haiku-like quality was earlier noted in these original translations. However, that information leads to a more central question about whether the Japanese quality was inherent in the original Ojibway dream songs or merely "crept into" Densmore's translations. Lively scholarly debate continues on this issue.

Although scholars date the origin of the Japanese haiku differently, all agree it has a long literary and cultural history, and many fine studies analyze this history as well as haiku form, philosophy, and function.[2] Briefly, the haiku is a short poem (generally classified as a lyric) usually made up of seventeen syllables in three lines, which follow a 5-7-5 syllable pattern. Although English and Japanese haiku may differ in regard to the use of poetic techniques such as rhyme and alliteration, both rely mainly on cadence, not meter, for their rhythm. The poem most frequently has as its subject some aspect or observation of nature and usually includes a seasonal element. Tightly constructed, it offers vivid images with little or no commentary or interpretation. The Japanese haiku has frequently been associated with the Zen philosophy and, like Zen, the haiku celebrates the "suchness" of things themselves and frequently has its origin in an experience of personal enlightenment.

Like haiku, the Ojibway dream songs also stem from a moment of intense personal awareness, which, as the name indicates, may have come during a dream or visionary experience. The subjects of the songs might be an image in nature, an action, the experience of a moment, a state of mind, or an emotional response. Frances Densmore, in the two volumes of *Chippewa Music,* transcribed close to four hundred Ojibway songs of various types in the early years of the twentieth century. Her transcriptions of the dream songs include descriptions of their musical or oral performance or enactment, as well as explanatory notes concerning pertinent social or cultural background and providing some understanding of the songs' allusions. Densmore's literal translations of the songs themselves, later "interpreted and reexpressed" by Vizenor in *anishinabe nagoman* and *Summer in the Spring: Ojibwe Lyric Poems and Tribal Stories* (1970, 1965), tend to be very brief, averaging about four lines in length.[3] The lines themselves consist of one to generally no more than six words or vocables and are presented with little or no punctuation or capitalization and usually without obvious grammatical connections to the other lines of the song.

Similarities in the forms and subjects of haiku and dream songs have been recognized and commented on since shortly after the original publication of *Chippewa Music* in 1910 and 1913. The comparisons were frequently made with reference to a third (and at that time both new and radical) poetic movement, imagism. The imagists, who were fascinated with the haiku as well as with other "primitive" forms such as the Chinese written character and Native American song poems, championed a new form of poetry: compact in form, based not on meter but on natural rhythm, using common speech, presenting precise images, and refraining from comment. A review of Densmore's *Chippewa Music* by Carl Sandburg in 1917 playfully noted the similarities between the Ojibway songs and the imagist movement: "Suspicion arises that the red man and his children committed direct plagiarism on our modern imagists and vorticists."[4]

Later observations continued to point to similarities between haiku, imagism, Chinese poetry, and Native American song poems. In 1918 Mary Austin wrote about the "extraordinary likeness between much of this native product [Native American songs and chants translated in *The Path on the Rainbow*] and the recent work of the Imagists, vers librists, and other literary fashionables." Margot Astrov, writing in 1946, was more specific about what constituted the similarities between haiku and Native American songs. The tribal songs, she says, are "remindful of the best of Japanese Haiku that turn the listener into a poet himself, for it is his part to fill the sketch into completeness." In his 1951 study *The Sky Clears: Poetry of the American Indian*, A. Grove Day analyzes the attraction Native American poetry held for the imagists, who "found in the short verses like the Chippewa songs collected by Miss Densmore the sort of compressed word-pictures they also sought in other foreign forms like the Chinese poems collected by Ernest Fenellosa [*sic*] and the rigid seventeen-syllable Japanese form called the haiku."[5]

Many contemporary scholars, including James Ruppert, Michael Castro, Kenneth Rexroth, Larry Evers, Felipe Molina, Karl Kroeber, and Lester Standiford, have discussed this historical apprehension of similarity between these three forms and have debated the accurateness of such a claim. In addition, some scholars have questioned the accuracy of the work of Densmore and other early collectors. Although it is not within the scope of this chapter to take up each of these debates and all associated issues, I raise these topics in order to give some indication of the place of Vizenor's work in this larger scheme.[6]

Vizenor has himself commented on the twentieth-century poets' exploration of the trend of relationships between haiku, tribal songs, and the imagist movement, and claims: "The first American imagist poets were the American Indians. . . . Many modern imagist poets have sought models of concise poetic expressions in Oriental literature. They may have found these qualities in the lyrical poetry and songs of the American Indians" ("The Ojibway," 18–19). Michael Castro, however, argues that "these similarities are, in fact, superficial at best and more apparent than real," and that "when the translators used imagist concepts and techniques to produce their English translations, the results were bound to bear a striking resemblance to imagist forms."[7] However, this objection of Castro's can be answered at least in part by Kenneth Rexroth's observation about the differences in poetic type that result from Densmore's translations of songs from various tribes:

> The resemblance to Japanese poetry is indeed startling, particularly in the Chippewa songs. This is not due to the influence of Amy Lowell and other free-verse translators on Miss Densmore. On the contrary, she worked with the Chippewa many years before such Japanese translations and their imitations in modern American verse came into existence. As the years have gone by she has moved on to tribes which do not show the same kind of resemblance either in music or in lyric.[8]

Yet even if we accept that Densmore's poetic style may have arisen organically from the various tribal songs themselves, Castro, Kroeber, Molina, and Evers raise other important points about the methods and problems of translation that cannot be ignored. For example, Castro notes:

> The originals on which these poems are based are not written. They are sounded, not silent. Their dimensions of music, movement, and relation are more complex, more physical, for they are literally embodied in their singers. The translation, because it shifts the ground of the poem from the media of the singer's body and voice to the medium of the page, can only provide, at best, the roughest equivalent of the original.[9]

Here and elsewhere he challenges the very application of the term "poetry" to oral tradition; noting the diminished dimensions of the translations and the changed contexts of the finished products, he seems to question the wisdom of attempting to make of vital life activities mere written words.

Actually, Castro's uneasiness with what translation attempts and his keen awareness of the transmutations (or mutations) that result parallel Vizenor's concerns. As I noted at the beginning of Chapter 1, Vizenor has spoken of his own original wariness of the written word and has himself bemoaned the inadequacies of translation. As that previously quoted statement indicates, however, his response is not to forgo the attempt: "I don't think the oral tradition can be translated well, but I think it can be reimagined and reexpressed and that's my interest."[10]

One exploration of the difficulties of translation particularly pertinent to Vizenor's work is Arnold Krupat's "Post-Structuralism and Oral Literature." Krupat discusses the opposing tendencies of translators, who seek *either* "unmistakable" *or* "undecidable" meanings, and suggests not only that both methods are lacking, but that "what each method in itself is and can offer is always a function of what it is not and what it can never produce. What the very best mythographers make present to us can only fully be understood in relation to what they have left out, to the absences whose traces we must somehow take into account if we are to understand anything at all." While translators will continue to "fix" texts after whatever fashion they deem most worthy, readers, Krupat holds, must read the texts "as in need of unfixing" in order to gain understanding of the works as part of the oral as well as the written tradition.[11]

Vizenor's style seems to encourage a similar method of viewing and of reading literature. To meet not only the challenge of translation or reexpression of oral tradition but also the broader challenge of all writing—the translation or reexpression of life deeply experienced into static words—Vizenor frequently creates an "open" text, a text that advertises its absences and requires the response of the reader to bring it to fruition, a text that works to activate the reader's imagination and thus to engage the reader in the process of "unfixing" the text. By making what is present attempt to include what is absent by allusion,

Vizenor works to break through the boundaries of print. Among his earliest experiments in this vein are his haiku collections.

Vizenor, unlike Castro, finds the similarities between tribal song poems and haiku to be more than superficial. One important similarity between the two which Vizenor identifies involves their ultimate purpose, their supraliterary (perhaps even antiliterary) intentions. Both, Vizenor feels, intend to surpass or forgo the goals of any philosophy of literary aesthetics for the sake of actual experience, for a moment of enlightenment.

It is exactly this supraliterary quality that many, including Castro, have pointed to as distinguishing tribal song poems from the mainstream literary movements, including imagism. For example, Rexroth writes that American Indian "poetry or song does not only play a vatic role in society, but is itself a numinous thing." A. LaVonne Ruoff writes of the Native American's "attempt to order its spiritual and physical world through the power of the word, whether chanted, spoken, or sung." And Kroeber speaks specifically of the Ojibway dream song as "a transactional event, a process by which dream power is realized as cultural potency." Castro, too, points out that in their origin most tribal songs were not "aesthetic objects," but sources or channels of power: "Indian poetry seeks to be effective, not merely affective."[12] The following statement from Densmore illustrates this effective intention of the Ojibway dream songs specifically:

> The songs in this group are not composed in the usual sense of the term, but are songs which are said to have come to the mind of the Indian when he was in a dream or trance. Many Indian songs are intended to exert a strong mental influence, and dream songs are supposed to have this power in greater degree than any others. The supernatural is very real to the Indian. He puts himself in communication with it by fasting or by physical suffering. While his body is thus subordinated to the mind a song occurs to him. In after years he believes that by singing this song he can recall the condition under which it came to him—a condition of direct communication with the supernatural.[13]

Although Vizenor does see a distinction in purpose between much mainstream poetry and the tribal songs, he sees the haiku poetry as like the tribal songs in this respect, as likewise pursuing (although admittedly perhaps not to the same degree) an experiential, and not merely a literary, reality. This supraliterary quality of haiku was likewise identified by the imagist poet John Gould Fletcher: "The merit of these haiku poems is not only that they suggest much by saying little; they also, if understood in connection with the Zen doctrine they illuminate, make of poetry an act of life."[14]

Vizenor, then, sees in the haiku method a way of writing that most nearly approximates the essence of an oral tradition and, therefore, can most nearly embody a tribal worldview. In his own characterizations of the haiku form—as he identifies what kind of experience gives origin to haiku, how the haiku engages the reader, what demands it makes on the reader, what powers it awakens, and what quality of experience it leads to—he weaves the Japanese tradition of Zen and haiku with Native American spirituality and oral tradition (or perhaps he merely expresses the similar vision held by the two traditions).

Haiku Poets and Tribal Dreamers: Singing Nature's Songs

One striking similarity between the two literary expressions is the quality of the experience that gives rise to the creation of the poetry. The "haiku moment," the kind of encounter from which haiku issues, has been described by the haiku poet and theorist Otsuji (pen name for Seki Osuga) as "the instant when our mental activity almost merges into an unconscious state—i.e., when the relationship between the subject and object is forgotten. . . . when it is said that one goes into the heart of created things and becomes one with nature."[15] Note the obvious similarity between the state described here and that described in Densmore's comments on dream songs. Dream songs, she writes, are "songs said to have come to the mind of the Indian when he was in a dream or trance" when "the dreamer contemplates nature in a certain aspect so long and so steadily that he gradually loses his own personality and identifies himself with it." Frequently the dreamer claims to have learned the song from some other being or spirit (deer, thunderbird, trees, etc.). This state Densmore describes as "a condition of direct communication with the supernatural" wherein the dreamer often "learns from manidó."[16]

In their study of Yaqui deer songs (the Yaqui near equivalent of Ojibway dream songs), Larry Evers and Felipe Molina describe a similar state that gives rise to the deer songs: "The hunters learned the secrets of the deer and their language and that deer language came to be translated into the deer songs of the hunter." When the songs are performed, they explain, "the deer dancer takes on the spirit of the deer, giving him physical form even as the deer singers . . . bring his voice." The Yaqui poet Refugio Savala has also explained that deer songs "come from the wild—just like when you dream, you go to a place in nature."[17]

When Vizenor himself enumerates the similarities between haiku and dream songs, he, too, identifies this common state of mind or spirit. Both haiku and dream songs he sees as reflecting "the kind of touch with nature, the twist on natural experience that's almost a transformation, human consciousness derived from other living things" (Interview). Ideally, then, both forms of poetry emanate from a moment of vision, what Zen calls enlightenment or *satori*, what Rexroth has called "transfiguration and transcendence," and what Vizenor calls "dreamscape."

Both haiku and dream songs also seek not merely to give voice to this visionary experience but, acting as stimuli, to assist the reader or listener in the attainment of a similar moment of spiritual awareness or illumination. For example, Mary Austin, an early student of Native American poetry, emphasized the "state of mind evoked by tribal song" and writes of the "inherent power of [tribal] poetry to raise the psychic plane above the accidents of being." Evers and Molina describe the deer songs as "speaking the sacred" and comment on "the inspiration manifested in the deer song," and Savala compares singing the deer songs to praying: "It is like a prayer because the songs are inspired."[18] Similarly, when Suzuki talks of the purpose of haiku and Japanese art, he notes both their spiritual quality and their transcendent effect:

> The mysteries of life enter deeply into the composition of art. When an art, therefore, presents those mysteries in a most profound and creative manner, it moves us to the depths of our being; art then becomes a divine work.
>
> . . . Great works of art embody in them *yūgen* [also called *myō*, meaning mystery and spiritual rhythm], whereby we attain a glimpse of things eternal in a world of constant changes: that is, we look into the secrets of Reality.[19]

So it is in Vizenor's haiku theory and practice. The power of his haiku lies in its engagement of the reader's imagination and its ability to move the reader beyond the words to an individual moment of illumination, its ability to incite the reader to find what Vizenor calls "a dreamscape in natural harmonies beneath the words" (*Matsushima*, 11). "The reader," he notes, "creates a dreamscape from haiku; nothing remains in print, words become dream voices, traces on the wind, twists in the snow, a perch high in the bare poplar" (*Matsushima*, 1).

The Nothingness That Is Not Absence:
Reader Response and Haiku Dreamscape

Note that Vizenor credits the reader, not the poem, with the creation or attainment of dreamscape. The haiku serves only as a spark to the reader's own powers. The dreamscape of haiku lies not in words but in experience. Similarly, in the Native American tradition, both the role of the singer and the role of the community is to hear more than is sounded or spoken. Molina and Evers make use of a Yaqui story of a talking stick to make this point, explaining, "The focus of the story is not so much on what the talking stick sounded like as it is on what the young woman is able to hear."[20]

Scholars of haiku such as Dorothy Britton, Kenneth Yasuda, and Donald Keene (all of whom are familiar to Vizenor and mentioned or quoted in his own discussions of the art of haiku) frequently emphasize the reader's role in haiku. For example, Britton says:

> These short verses are thought-provokers. The haiku poet rarely describes his own feelings, but lets the juxtaposition of his images make us feel his emotions instead. Seemingly objective, a good haiku should rouse in the reader's mind a deeply subjective response and set in motion a world of thoughts. A haiku makes demands. So much is left unsaid that its three brief lines need more than a casual reading. One should try to immerse oneself in the poem and let the images propel one's thoughts to deeper meanings[21]

When Vizenor discusses the participation of the reader in his introduction to *Matsushima*, he quotes both Donald Keene—"a really good poem, and this is especially true of haiku, must be completed by the reader"—and Daisetz Suzuki—"the meaning of such objects . . . is left to the reader to construct and interpret it according to his poetic experience or his spiritual intuitions" (3).

This participation of the reader is not only a recognized result of haiku but also an important goal of the form, one clearly linked to the philosophy, method, and purpose of the poetic process. Haiku's conscious attempt to engage the reader has its source in what I have called the form's supraliterary intentions. The goal of haiku is its own annihilation. Haiku exists solely to be obliterated and replaced by experience. Kenneth Yasuda makes the distinction between poetry that is *about* experience and poetry that *becomes* experience itself.[22] The best haiku become experience. "The visual description [of haiku]," claims Vizenor, "is enough to enter a visual experience. You don't need the poem anymore" (Interview). Therefore, as literature, haiku must work for its own effacement. Vizenor's discussion in *Matsushima* of these supraliterary aspirations of haiku quotes from R. H. Blyth: "A haiku is not a poem, it is not literature; it is a hand beckoning, a door half-opened, a mirror wiped clean. It is a way of returning to nature" (2). Vizenor also makes use of Roland Barthes's assertion that haiku is the "literary branch" of Zen and that it is "destined to halt language" (9).

Both of these statements, which speak of the haiku form's desire to escape the capture of language and literature, become more understandable when we consider the attitude of Zen toward conceptualization. Daisetz Suzuki explains: "Zen is not necessarily against words, but it is well aware of the fact that they are always liable to detach themselves from realities and turn into conceptions. And this conceptualization is what Zen is against. . . . Zen insists on handling the thing itself and not an empty abstraction." Suzuki claims that Zen distinguishes between "living words" and "dead words," the dead ones being "those that no longer pass directly and concretely and intimately on to the experience. They are conceptualized, they are cut off from the living roots." The haiku master, then, aspires to create not a work of art but a work of life. Japanese art, including haiku, avoids merely "copying or imitating nature," and instead attempts to "give the [artistic] object something living in its own right," to "go beyond logic" and point to "the presence in us of a mystery that is beyond intellectual analysis."[23] A haiku that fulfills these intentions is the enlightenment or *satori* of Zen artistically expressed.

In these referential artistic aspirations of haiku, although there is not a direct correspondence, we can see some similarity to the goals and artistry of dream songs and a connection to the broader practices of tribal oral tradition. Traditional tribal songs, like haiku, resist conceptualization; language remains connected to being. The songs did not so much report as participate in or embody life. "The words and rhythms themselves," Vizenor claims, "had intuitive power" ("The Ojibway," 19). In tribal cultures, coup stories were the medium by which one told of one's deeds; dream songs were the means to renew a visionary connection or to access or share a power channel. H. David Brumble comments on a scene from the autobiography *Two Leggings: The Making of a Crow Warrior* that illustrates this reaccess of power through a dream or vision song: "The people assumed that the vision had a store of power, and that this power could be shared by the people if the vision could be enacted. . . . Two Leggings, for example, after building the miniature sweat lodges, sang for his raiding party the song he had heard in his vision."[24]

Molina and Evers, in describing the role and power of deer songs, also explain how the songs do not merely report but foster continuing communication with the "wilderness world" of the Sonoran desert: "Deer songs continue in Yaqui communities as a very real vehicle for communication with the larger natural community in which the Yaquis live." This communication with "plants, animals, birds, fishes, even rocks and springs" certainly stands outside intellectual and logical realms and participates in the realm of experience and mystery of which Suzuki speaks.[25] Having their source in a visionary experience of a natural dimension outside the limits of time and space, these songs embody that mystery and invite its rediscovery.

How are the lofty goals of these two poetic forms achieved in practice? Both haiku and dream songs proceed by means of an "open text," a text that works by suggestion, implication, absence, allusion, and juxtaposition, that works through intentional gaps, indeterminacy in various forms, and the practice of many kinds of restraint in language. For example, Yasuda describes the haiku method as "the representation of the object alone, without comment, never presented to be other than what it is, but not represented completely as it is." Similarly, in describing Native American song poems, Margot Astrov claims that "few of these short songs are complete in themselves": "The singer sketches only a thought or an impression and it is left to the poetical imagination of the listener and his resources of mythic knowledge to supply the gradations of color and mythical context."[26]

The restraint on the part of the author or singer allows for and encourages the participation of the reader or community. In Native American song poems, the associations may be not so much "poetic" as cultural and mythical, but the implications of absence still hold sway. The explanation of Marie Chona, Ruth Underhill's Papago informant quoted in Chapter 1, that a certain tribal song "is very short because we understand so much,"[27] clearly illustrates the allusive quality of tribal oral literature.

Suzuki identifies part of what this common guardedness in language preserves when he talks about the appropriateness and purpose of restraint in haiku: "When a feeling reaches its highest pitch, we remain silent, because no words are adequate. . . . When feelings are too fully expressed, no room is left for the unknown, and from this unknown start the Japanese arts." Activated by the suggestion of the haiku are the reader's imagination, intuition, and primal memory, all of which work to fill in the essence that language cannot capture, to discover things that have not been written. The goal, according to Suzuki, is "to grasp life from within and not from without."[28] What Vizenor calls the "internal transformation" comes about when "the listener-participant makes that [the haiku] a personal experience-event from his or her own experience" (Interview).

With the actualization of haiku, the words of the poem in essence dissolve or deconstruct, having been transformed or rendered into experience. The deconstruction of the words or the "art" thus accomplishes the ultimate unveiling. According to Vizenor:

> The images in haiku remain connected to our bodies; the words are rendered visual, transformed in primal memories, simple experiences, natural harmonies, and a dreamscape on the earth. Deconstruct the printed words in a haiku and there is nothing; nothing is a haiku, not even a poem. The nothing in a haiku is not an aesthetic void; rather, it is a moment of enlightenment, a dreamscape where words dissolve; no critical marks, no grammatical stains remain (*Matsushima*, 5).

For Vizenor then, haiku, like dream songs, succeed to the degree that they deconstruct as literature and undergo a transformation into experience and enlightenment—into dreamscape.

Vizenor's Haiku Method Employed

The open text of Vizenor's haiku generally works through images of the natural world, through unusual juxtapositions and through unfulfilled expectations. In his poetry, he employs natural images but refrains from dictating connections or meaning. Instead, he holds faith with the visual imagination of the reader. He describes his haiku method: "There is tension in haiku thought; little in human experience is without tension, but the tension in haiku is subtle, unresolved in narrative schemes. Tension is suggested, the reader touches the places in his memories" (*Matsushima*, 4).

The tension in Vizenor's haiku often stems from the juxtaposition of the sentimental with the mundane or from the juxtaposition of two apparently incongruous images. In this way, Vizenor's haiku seem to meet the qualifications set out by Donald Keene for effective haiku: "The nature of the elements varies, but there should be . . . two electric poles between which the spark will leap."[29] In Vizenor's poetry, the first line or first two lines in his haiku frequently set up edenic expectations, and the final line or lines diffuse these inflated romantic notions of reality, thus propelling his reader beyond the conventional, fictionalized or romanticized images of life toward an experience of authentic underlying harmony. This subtle undercutting of expectations, or in other poems, the unusual depictions of the ordinary or the revelation of surprising connections, have the effect of eliciting an internal gasp of recognition or an inadvertent glottal stop, either of which then provides the momentum for bridging the gap between mere words and experiential reality.

Although not all the haiku engage the reader in exactly the same way, a look at several from Vizenor's various collections illustrates his common methods and intentions and the probable effects on the reader. In the following poem from *Seventeen Chirps*, for example, Vizenor depicts a scene of natural, almost reverent solitude with its first two lines:

Morning mist
Rowing over the leaf pond (11)

The lines invite the reader to enter the scene through imagination: Damp morning mist seeming to hover or float silently over a pond, the invigorating moist chill of dawn still in the air, the slight musty smell of dampened leaves, and a hushed atmosphere that engenders stillness in any watcher. And then, the last line cuts across the scene with the shrill call: "Chick a dee dee dee!" Just as one standing at the scene might start at the tranquillity so suddenly broken, so does the engaged reader react. The ignited spark of excitement awakens a memory or a knowledge that, for an instant, transports the reader to the reality of just such an adrenergic experience, to an experience more alive than words on a page.

What the reader ultimately experiences, however, is not so much a physical moment as it is an unbidden perception of an intersection with the eternal, with the unbounded oneness. On one level the poem is the depiction of physical tranquillity followed by the momentary disruption of that tranquillity, which only serves to awaken an awareness of the underlying all-consuming tranquillity. The sound of the bird startles the reader over the hurdle of time and place into the realm of what Zen calls Emptiness. Thus she discovers the point of intersection of the momentary and the eternal and thereby is enlightened regarding the intersection of all dualities.[30]

Vizenor attempts to describe this kind of primal transcendence that is the "moment of enlightenment" in haiku when he writes, "Words are turned back to nature, set free in the mythic dreamscapes of a haiku" (*Matsushima*, 5). He continues the explanation by quoting from Susan Griffin's *Woman and Nature: The Roaring Inside Her*: "Behind naming, beneath words, is something else. An existence named unnamed and unnameable. . . . But in a moment that which is behind naming makes itself known. . . . This knowledge is in the souls of everything, behind naming, before speaking, beneath words." Molina and Evers report of the Yaqui understanding of a similar realm and refer to this "source of all things" in various ways in their study. For example, they describe one of the supernatural worlds, the "sea ania" or flower world, as "located in the east, in a place 'beneath the dawn'" and as being "a perfected mirror image of all the beauty of the natural world of the Sonoran desert."[31]

Suzuki, like Vizenor and Griffin, also speaks of the buried knowledge that can be uncovered within each person, and he delineates the several layers of consciousness that, he believes, make up the human mind. These include "dualistic consciousness," the limited level at which we generally move; a "semi-conscious" plane consisting of our ordinary memory; the "Unconscious," made up of buried memories; the "collective unconscious," credited with being the "basis of our mental life;" and finally, the "Cosmic Unconscious," which is "the storehouse of all possibility," "the principle of creativity . . . where is deposited the moving forces of the universe."[32] Although successful haiku should reflect and have the inherent capability to propel us to the level of the Cosmic Unconscious, the reader in activating a haiku may or may not tap all these levels of understanding.

Indeed, not all readers' experiences will necessarily be uniform or even similar, nor is this the author's intent. The goal is not to understand the author, to "get" the author's meaning, but to move beyond the words on the page and experience natural, underlying harmonies that are part of our primal memory—to create life from static words.

In a haiku like the following from *Matsushima*, for example, the awareness it recalls, the certain perspective on natural experience, stimulates in the reader endless connective memories of other instances of similar awareness:

> cedar cones
> tumble in a mountain stream
> letters from home (23)

In the first two lines, Vizenor simply visually describes a natural scene, allowing us to imagine it photographically. The final line, however, suggests a perspective that nudges the reader out of our observer status and gives us the role of discoverer. The phrase "letters from home" offers an image of the chain of natural relationships observable in nature and the potential for discovery: a cultural interpretation of a natural phenomenon. The cedar cones may have tumbled into the mountain stream from one natural setting (perhaps even from a cedar grove familiar to the writer) and arrived by water at another place, only to be discovered by him there. Thus they become "letters from home," remindful as they are of another place or environment, a different order. The responses of the reader might then entail memories of the multiple other instances when scents, sounds, or sights have in the past caused that same thrill of recognition.

A second kind of recognition awakened by the same closing line is that of the movement or life in nature. Although we may see something in nature hundreds of times, if we only view it in tableau, our view is limited. The poem's last line recounts that moment when something startles us into an awareness of the interconnections within the moving cycle of nature. The discovery about the cedar cones might be not only where they come from but the realization of how they travel from place to place or how the trees might spread to new locales. With the final line, the haiku incites us to recall the moments when the surprise of such discoveries in nature have caused us inadvertently to look around for a presence or have accelerated the beating of our hearts. The heightened intensity of the moments these haiku create or recall comes from awareness of life unseen, which always affects us more readily than the seen because it involves greater potential for discovery and ultimately leaves our expectations aroused.

Vizenor depicts another such moment in *Raising the Moon Vines* with the following haiku:

> Under the crossing log
> Fresh openings in the ice
> Haloed with footprints (89)

The poem obviously describes markings left by an animal who had come to the water to drink. But by describing the markings as "under the crossing log" (therefore not as readily observable) and the openings as "fresh," Vizenor heightens the sense of discovery and the awareness of vital processes occurring literally under our noses. By employing the connotations of "halo" and using the word as verb not noun, he implies a sacred quality or aura and links that with the activities, not the tableau, of natural life.

The invitation inherent in Vizenor's haiku is to be a participant in such sacred activities. The distinction between observing and being-engaged-in is key in Zen and in a Native American perspective of life and literature, for the idea of beholding nature automatically creates a division and sets up a subject/object relationship that makes of nature thing, not being. We understand our true position in nature when the separation brought about by ego vanishes to the degree that we not only experience the "merging of the self with the other" but also remain unaware of that oneness. When we become conscious of our altered state, we have already reverted to the isolation of self-absorption.

Vizenor's poetry, then, clearly reflects and requires not mere observation of but participation in nature. Recognizing the cycles that the fresh tracks or the tumbling cedar cones represent is not like passively observing physical creatures or elements in nature as abstracted "scenery" or conceptualized objects. We experience the reality of the cones, the tracks—a reality more spiritual than physical, more internal than external—because through what Suzuki called our Cosmic Unconscious we see in them the ultimate movement of all nature.

Although the sight of natural creatures—the flash of white tail as a doe leaps out of our sight, the porcupine that waddles off the path—inevitably excites the observer, the pleasure depicted in Vizenor's lines is more intense because it involves a moment of new awareness. Vizenor's haiku moment more clearly parallels our experience when we discover, not the creatures themselves, but the traces of them—the still-steaming scat in the snow, the trampled impression where deer had lain among the pines or the fresh animal tracks of the *Moon Vines* haiku. His is a moment of intuiting the hidden life beyond the evidence or the unraveling of one of the mysteries of nature. The verbalization of such an experience is not the "ahh" of delivered pleasure but the "aha!" of active discovery. The moment is not closed out, as it is when the physical animal leaps out of sight, but continues to haunt our every step because its connective possibilities are endless. Any discovery tends to increase our attentiveness to our surroundings and our susceptibility to additional discoveries. In various ways, then, the perspective on nature depicted in the foregoing haiku causes the realm of the poems to expand with the responses of the reader.

Indeed, haiku experiences are always subjective; readers will respond to the suggestiveness of haiku in their own way, to the degree that they are able. As Vizenor notes, "There isn't any predestination [in haiku]" (Interview). For example, in the following haiku from *Matsushima* the three images allow for multiple levels of interpretation:

> sunday morning
> children waddle in the park
> geese to water (70)

A reader might envision a scenario involving an after-church outing with little girls in frilly dresses and their first shiny patent leather shoes buckled across white, lacy anklets, and little boys in navy-and-white sailor suits. The baby plumpness of the children and their still-uneasy balance cause them to waddle like the geese they have come to feed. When the children run, inquisitive little hands outstretched to touch feathers and beaks, the geese retreat to the safety of their pond. Such an imaginative fleshing out of the poem's images, replete with squeals of delight and squawks of displeasure, would certainly create a vibrant reader experience and fulfill the intentions of the form.

The open text, however, implies and allows for a bolder reading from a tribal worldview. The last two lines seem to advertise an omission and compel the reader to make a connection—children waddle in the park / *like* geese to water—or to complete the symmetry: children waddle in the park / geese *waddle* to the water. This participation in the creation of the meaning results, not in closure, but in the further opening of the text. By supplying the link or the echo in the lines, we are drawn to acknowledge the implied correspondences between the children and the geese. The children may be "playing" geese or "becoming" geese by imitating the motion of the gaggle. The lines might also imply similarities other than movement between the geese and the children: the ecstatic feeling of play, the lack of schooled restraint, and an intangible natural bond or earth connection. If we take these ideas further, through the tribal idea of the shared reality of different elements of creation, we can arrive at the idea of transformation or the possibility of a dream experience of being another creature. As these hypothetical readings illustrate, the possibilities of the interpretation or co-creation vary depending on the participation and identity of the reader.

Vizenor talks about these variations and acknowledges that, while any person of any experience can find an entrance point in his haiku that can lead the reader to illumination, the implications for tribal readers may be more expansive. Vizenor employs the term "primal memory" (as opposed to the "racial memory" N. Scott Momaday has spoken of), but he does feel that, because of embedded cultural tradition and beliefs, most Native Americans have more ease of access to the realm of dreamscape by means of haiku.[33] The issue for Vizenor is not race but established patterns of thinking, what John Dewey called "funded experience": "those memories, not necessarily conscious, but retentions that have been organically incorporated in the very structure of the self."[34] What makes the situation of tribal people unique, Vizenor explains, "is it is only a few generations to our experiences of the past. And it's an immediate recognition of the kind of topography, and vegetation, and climate. I mean, that is in the genes, if it can be. And it's in the language and the vocabulary. It [primal memory] is a little more focused and direct. That's awfully mystical, but there is . . . a source of energy there" (Interview). In many cases, then, a person's earth connections and intuitions may have been further honed by the location, activities, and belief systems of tribal cultures, while they may have been dulled by disuse or weakened by the skepticism of science in mainstream cultures. And because haiku thought is frequently grounded in seasonal associations, the more familiar the associations to the reader, the more readily the reader can create with them.[35]

Vizenor's "Street Dancer": The Trickster Voice in Haiku

Although sensuous nature imagery does characterize much of Vizenor's haiku, his poems do not deal exclusively with humankind's experience of or interaction with the natural world. Vizenor talks about the range and voices of his poetry in his introduction to *Matsushima*, and he identifies what he calls "the soul dancer in me," who "celebrates transformations and intuitive connections between our bodies and the earth, animals, birds, ocean, creation"; but he also identifies other "interior dancers" involved in his haiku (6). Among these other voices, the one most prominent in his work is the "street dancer," who "is the trickster, the picaresque survivor in the wordwars, at common human intersections, in a classroom, at a supermarket, on a bus" (6–7). However, since both Zen and a tribal worldview see humankind as not only involved with but as a part of nature, as Otsuji notes, "Human affairs as they appear in haiku are not presented as human affairs alone."[36] We find this "street dancer," for example, in poems that have as their subject the human relationship to the larger world, unusual intersections between human nature and the natural world, and unusual intersections between civilization or technology and nature. (Although Vizenor's broad use of the trickster figure receives more elaborate attention in Chapter 5, here I look briefly at the "trickster signature" in his haiku.) His trickster street dancer frequently appears in the haiku that offer illuminating twists on the way we perceive ourselves, or in those which challenge our overserious or isolationist view of our actions.

Take, for example, this poem from *Empty Swings*:

> Newspapers are piled
> Day by day under the window
> Raising the cat (50)

Vizenor takes a mundane, seemingly inconsequential, daily action and suddenly shows it to have impact on another living creature. I doubt that the poem intends to provoke any sustained thought on the cat whose perch is inadvertently raised day by day by the action of his or her human companion. Instead, I imagine its value to lie in the wry comment it makes on our failure to concern ourselves with the larger relationships and the larger consequences of our actions. I see no note of indictment in the haiku; rather I see a playful and harmless little jab at our self-centeredness meant to jar us, if only momentarily, from our habitual monocular viewpoint.

Vizenor's haiku in the voice of the trickster or the "picaresque survivor" definitely calls us to reconsider our narrow views. Consider this poem, which gives title to the *Seventeen Chirps* collection:

> It took seventeen chirps
> For a sparrow to hop across
> My city garden (47)

This haiku seems intended to nudge us toward a new perspective on how we evaluate by enumerating—even when the event ill suits enumeration. Of course, the larger implication probably involves how much we miss by insisting on applying our standards of judgment to all we encounter. Or consider how the following haiku challenges our feeling of superiority over other creatures by grouping the egotistical human, as represented by the poet, with the lowly beast, as represented by the cow. It shows both creatures as equally subject to the rough track of the pasture and the pestilence of the flies. Operating as "a great equalizer," this haiku depicts both human and beast at the same action:

> Through knobby pasture
> Both the poet and the cow
> Swishing flies away (*Raising Moonvines*, 52)

In his haiku, Vizenor employs many of the same methods to shake up the self-satisfied reader that the traditional tribal trickster tales used to reproach the wayward tribal members. For example, the tribal tales frequently worked to enlighten the audience to their own flaws by exposing the ludicrousness of the trickster's actions; so, too, does the trickster voice of Vizenor's haiku employ this same tactic. Note that the following haiku, from *Empty Swings*, has as its nominal subject the imagined complaints of mice:

> Sliding in the loft
> The mice complained all Winter
> About the coarse hay (26)

By projecting onto the mice a typical (and unflattering) human reaction, however, Vizenor really highlights the silliness of our own petty complaints and dissatisfactions. In another haiku from the same collection, he offers a similar perspective of mundane human complaints and a comment not only on humanity's pettiness but perhaps on the practice of making petty complaints pass as poetry:

> Poet at the fence
> Would horses write about their burden
> Apple cores and blinders (63)

Multiple Traditions in Haiku / 129

In each haiku, Vizenor administers his mild reprimand with humor, much as a favorite uncle might tease or tickle a pouting child into better spirits.

But whether achieved through humorous or solemn means, the instant of revelation remains key in Vizenor's poems. Barbara Babcock has characterized trickster literature as having an "evaluative" function: "contributing to a reexamination of existing conditions and possibly leading to change."[37] Note how each of the following Vizenor haiku reveals something startling about the society humankind has created and, by so doing, questions the justice or wisdom of such a social arrangement:

> The old man
> Admired the scarecrow's clothes
> Autumn morning (*Seventeen Chirps*, 4)

> Against the zoo fence
> Zebras and Sunday school children
> Hearing about Africa (*Empty Swings*, 36)

The first, of course, depicts both the tragic social and economic imbalance of society and indicts a throwaway culture that shows so little compassion for the poor in our midst. The second registers the irony of a zoo system devised by our consumer culture that results in creatures unfamiliar with their own "natural habitats," and it depicts both human and animal as equal exiles.

Both haiku work to actualize the experience of the poem through the creation of a moment of unbalance. Their unusual perspectives startle the words into life and thus lead the reader to contemplate more than the scene depicts and to invite a reevaluation of conditions. The moments of illumination in Vizenor's haiku may vary in type and intensity from the new twist offered by a trickster perspective to the spiritual reverberations activated by a natural encounter, but they all stem from the open quality of the text, involve the engagement of the reader, and inevitably outstrip the written words.

"Ojibway Haiku—in Song"

The same method surfaces in Vizenor's transcription and reexpressions of Ojibway dream songs. Both in the rhetoric he uses to explain the working of the song poems and in the form of their actual translation, many similarities to his views and techniques of haiku surface.

In his introduction to his translations or reexpressions of the poems, Vizenor describes "the song poems of the *anishinaabeg*" as "imaginative events, magical and spiritual flights, and intuitive lyrical images of woodland life" (*Summer in Spring*, 11). Note that he sees dream songs, like haiku, as relying on imagination and intuition and involving images of woodland life. His reference to them as "events" and "magical and spiritual flights" is similar to his descriptions of haiku as "word cinemas" and "traces on the wind" (*Matsushima*, 1, 7). Vizenor also describes the Anishinaabeg song poetry as "a sympathy of cosmic rhythms and tribal instincts, memories and dream songs, expressing the contrasts of life and death, day and night, man and woman, courage and fear" (*Summer in Spring*, 13). Again the descriptive phrases here bear a striking resemblance to those he uses in discussing haiku. He speaks of "cosmic rhythms," "tribal instincts," and "memory" in this introduction to the dream songs; he speaks of "natural harmonies" and "primal memories" in his introduction to haiku (*Matsushima*, 5). In describing dream songs, he speaks of "contrasts"; in describing haiku, he speaks of "tension" (4). Finally, in his introduction to the lyric poems, Vizenor credits dreams with achieving a connection "between the conscious and unconscious worlds of the people" (*Summer in Spring*, 11), just as he credits haiku with bringing about "transformation" and "a moment of enlightenment." The correlation between Vizenor's descriptions of each only confirms his evaluation of their similar forms, philosophies, and intentions.

His methods of expressing them in words is likewise similar, as illustrated by the following pair of dream songs:

> with a large bird
> above me
> i am walking
> in the sky
>
> i entrust
> myself
> to one wind (*Summer in Spring*, 35)

Multiple Traditions in Haiku / 131

Note how each employs the same economy of words and makes the same kind of demands on the reader's imaginative powers as do Vizenor's haiku. Note also how our expectations are undercut in the same manner as in the haiku. For example, in the first song the opening three lines might cause us to envision a man walking and looking up to watch a bird as it flies. But the last line surprises us by locating the man "in the sky." We are thus called to displace our conventional thinking, just as we were in Vizenor's haiku. The possibilities for interpretation are left open much as they were in the haiku about the children and the geese. We may understand the dream song in terms of imaginative experience, dream experience, or transformation. In any case, our engagement in the song has undoubtedly transported us beyond the simple phrases of the text to the "visual dreamscape" experience likewise achieved by the haiku. The correlation is complete.

Another example from among Vizenor's reexpressions of tribal dream songs serves to emphasize both the "funded experience," or the knowledge presupposed on the part of the hearer or reader, and the imaginative demands made by the song:

> two foxes
> facing each other
> sitting
> between them (*Summer in Spring*, 34)

The breathtaking quality of this song poem becomes apparent only if the reader/listener has some experience or understanding of foxes on which to draw. Visually, the image multiplies in intensity with knowledge of the penetrating quality of a fox's gaze. Add to this visualization a familiarity with the creatures' fleet movements, the sometimes playful wrestling of the young, and the animals' instinctive avoidance of human contact, and the first two lines set up an expectation of impending motion, while the last two lines imply an unlikely and therefore extraordinary experience on the part of the singer. Whether we take that experience to be physical, spiritual, imaginative, or some combination of these, an appreciation of its uniqueness can only come about as the reader imaginatively fleshes out the words of the song poem with the help of an understanding both of foxes and of the realm of magical possibilities available to a tribal person who is in the appropriate state of mind. Like the haiku, the song poem only suggests; the reader creates: she first imagines and then experiences.

Haiku in Prose: Basho's *Haibun*

Just as Vizenor's early involvement with haiku form, philosophy, and methods undoubtedly affected his reexpressions of tribal dream songs, it has left its mark on most of his subsequent writing as well. Vivid nature imagery, building by suggestion, tension created by unusual juxtapositions, trickster consciousness, reader engagement—all of these traits surface again and again in Vizenor's work as methods to move beyond the written text itself.

Certain prose passages in Vizenor's writing greatly resemble his haiku and function in much the same way. Compare a statement from Vizenor's first novel, *Darkness in Saint Louis Bearheart*—"The ritual of a spider building his web on the wind . . . That is survival!" (187)— with a haiku from *Seventeen Chirps*:

> Patient spider
> Day after day in the wind bottle
> Building his web (30)

The extremely similar images used in each of the passages set up reverberations that extend well beyond an understanding of the spider's life: although the haiku does not name but instead embodies the quality of continuance, the revelation of each is about the spirit and deepest meanings of survival.

Here and elsewhere certain lines of Vizenor's prose embody what Makoto Ueda, in talking about the prose of the haiku master Basho, called *haibun*: a kind of prose "written in the spirit of haiku" (quoted in *Matsushima*, 10). For example, these passages also come from *Darkness in Saint Louis Bearheart*:

> We speak the secret language of bears in the darkness here, stumbling downhill into the fourth world on twos and fours, turning underwords ha ha ha haaaa in visions. *The bear is in our hearts. Shoulders tingle downhill on dreams.* The darkness moves through us in ursine shivers. (vii, italics mine)

Cedarfair circus in the morning. Clown crows. Incense from moist cedar. Time turns under the warm figures of breathing. *Moths and the sound of dew coming down the fern and pale waxen faces on poplar leaves near the river.* (1, italics mine)

The two italicized sections report images in the same succinct fashion as Vizenor's haiku; both suggest, by juxtaposition, connections between the phrases; and both rely for their meaning on the engagement and participation of the reader. As they imply a connection with certain tribal ideas or experiences in nature, the reader's own knowledge of these things must be plumbed in order to arrive at the full significance of the passages. The first involves the tribal ideas of dream vision, guardian spirit, and transformation. The second assumes an understanding of the position and role of animals in tribal culture and also contains references to the role of the clown, to the cleansing power of cedar smoke, and to the ceremony of sunrise prayer.

The second passage, though nominally prose, is cast in haiku's standard seventeen-syllable, three-line form (although Vizenor does not confine himself to this form even in his haiku poetry). The movement of the passage is similar to that of many of Vizenor's haiku, with the first two lines setting a scene and the last changing the quality of that scene. Here the first line evokes a sense of time and place: morning at Cedarfair circus (which, in the larger context of the book, we know to be a large circle of cedar trees near a river). The second line adds the presence of animal life and implies a tribal consciousness by imparting to the crows the significant role of "clown." Many ideas are taken for granted in the application of such a title—the possibility of human-animal transformation, the illusory nature of physical forms, the possibility of reciprocal human-animal relationships, and the importance of the role of clown or trickster—all of which establish a tribal milieu. The last line could conceivably be taken merely as sensory description, adding the smell of cedar to the scene. But I think the line turns on the universal connotations of the word "incense" combined with the tribal connotations of the word "cedar." Incense carries with it the suggestion of religious ceremony, and cedar smoke or incense is used for purification in tribal rites. Thus, taken together, the lines conjure something more than just an experience of early morning in a cedar grove. When the smell of damp cedar in the morning awakens in the writer/reader the memory of incense or becomes incense, the experience takes on religious dimensions. The passage may work to expose an innate connection between the natural and the religious. Or perhaps the last line may intend to transform the scene and recall the solemn morning rite of sunrise prayer.

In any case, the similarities between prose of this sort, Vizenor's reexpressions of dream songs, and his haiku are apparent. All work to invite the reader to break through the boundaries of print and find the essential experience beyond the words. As Suzuki has noted: "With all the apparatus of science we have not yet fathomed the mysteries of life. But, once in its current, we seem to be able to understand it."[38] The task of haiku in Vizenor's style is to thrust us into "the current of life" where we can find for ourselves a moment of understanding—of enlightenment.

Vizenor has bound multiple traditions in the form and philosophy of his haiku's "open text": traditions of both writing and speaking, traditions of postmodern and tribal aesthetics, and traditions of Native American and Japanese cultures. Such a linkage seems a fit illustration of the ultimate "nexus of infinite interrelationships" haiku profess to uncover.[39]

5

Trickster Signatures

The trickster upsets the balance, if for no other reason than to keep people alert to their own survival and powers to heal. The crossbloods are tricksters; they settle the new worlds in their own blood.
——Gerald Vizenor, "Bad Breath"

A trickster, contrary, muckraking political journalist and activist, poet, essayist, novelist, and teacher, Vizenor confronts readers with shape-shifting definitions, inhabiting the wild realm of play within language and seeking, trickster-fashion, to trick and shock us into self-recognition and knowledge.
——Louis Owens, Afterword to *Bearheart*

Trickster Engagement

The trickster of Vizenor's literature and imagination is a figure simultaneously old and new, a peripatetic figure who in his wanderings has made the transition from traditional oral tales to contemporary written literature. Cedarbird, the protagonist in Vizenor's short story "Four Skin Documents," proclaims, "I am a novelist, a tribal trickster in the written tradition" (*Landfill Meditation*, 164). He could well be voicing the author's own claim, for the use of Naanabozho, the Ojibway tribal trickster figure, does form one of the central links between

Vizenor's written work and the Anishinaabe oral culture. In his use of "trickster consciousness," Vizenor says, he is "drawing a configuration of an old idea in a different way, through a tribal literary practice" (Interview).

The culture hero appears in Vizenor's work in origin stories and long-told tales such as "Naanabozho and the Gambler," as well as in recast and contemporary versions of those older stories. Naanabozho and his pan-Indian counterparts also appear as ethos, as persona, and as fictional characters in Vizenor's own imaginative tales, transformed into modern-day denizens of every sort from college teacher to landfill director, transformed as well into animal forms from bear to flea. But the trickster signature of Vizenor's literature involves more than the inclusion of these physical manifestations of trickster and more than his use of a trickster persona; it arises from a certain state of mind, an anarchical energy, a liberating humor. In *Interior Landscapes* Vizenor describes trickster as "a spiritual balance in a comic drama" (26); in *The Trickster of Liberty*, as one who "liberates the mind in comic discourse" (xi). Ideas of balance and imbalance, spiritual and comedic, discourse and liberation, all inform Vizenor's use of trickster consciousness. Its employment becomes one of his most effective innovations in evolving a dialogue with his audience and in inciting the reader's dialogic relation with his or her larger experience. How the imaginative portrayal of trickster stimulates reader participation becomes more clear with an understanding of the traditional role of the trickster-transformer.[1]

Trickster Theories

The trickster figure of Native American culture appears in the oral literatures of numerous tribes, including the Klamath, the Navajo, the Crow, the Modoc, the Salish, the Winnebago, the Lakota, and the Ojibway. Often the stories form a cycle of tales, with both formal or causal relations between episodes as well as informal connections stemming from themes and motifs. Disagreements have arisen involving the overall structure, lack of structure, or antistructure of trickster cycles and the formal relationship, lack of relationship, or antiformal relationship between episodes.[2] These debates become significant in a reading of Vizenor because, grounded as his work is in the trickster tradition, it, too, draws similar criticism for its lack of a coherent structure and for its episodic nature. For example, among the several criticisms Kenneth Lincoln levels against Vizenor are comments on the "disjointed dream narrative" of *Griever* and a "point of view" that "rules out character development, dramatic structure, and thematic plotting."[3] But just as Barbara Babcock argues for recognition of a "deep structure" in the Winnebago trickster cycle (a view in contrast to those of Alan Dundes and Paul Radin), I claim the same deep structure for Vizenor's work, as well as a mythic structure stemming from its relationship to trickster tales, and an antistructure that deliberately subverts the formal Western ideals of literary aesthetics.

Trickster's identity is itself a subversion of the Western mode of classification, resisting singularity (and therefore becoming in Vizenor's work a perfect metaphor for the mixedblood). Known variously among the tribes as Coyote, Raven, Spider, Blue Jay, Dragonfly, Raccoon, Hare, Wolverine, or Old Man Coyote, as Toe'osh, Iktome, Pehrru, Wakdjunkaga, and Naanabozho, trickster is really multiform. Although among some tribes he or she is associated with a specific animal form such as the coyote or the raven (usually the hare among the Anishinaabe), even when these associations are made, the physical identification is not concrete. According to Kenneth Lincoln, trickster "resists the boundaries of any given species and is likely to appear at any time in any image." Babcock notes that tricksters "exhibit human/animal dualism" and "have an ability to disperse and to disguise themselves and a tendency to be multiform and ambiguous, single or multiple."[4] Vizenor especially resists the formal classification of trickster energy and emphasizes that trickster is "not representational" (Interview).[5]

Also subverted in any attempt to understand the nature of trickster are standard categories, divisions between realms or types of beings. Not wholly human, animal, or god, but simultaneously none and all of these beings, the polydemic trickster blurs these classic distinctions. In speaking of the Navajo trickster, Barre Toelken makes an important differentiation, saying "he is not a composite" that is made up of distinct and recognizable parts, but a "complex" whose makeup is intricate and interwoven.[6] Trickster is understood to have been one of what are called the First People in Native American tradition, one of those who were in the world in mythic time before humans as we now know them came to be here, one who has attributes of the various beings, including certain magical powers such as the ability to change shape at will. Like the trickster of oral tradition, Vizenor's characters (and his literary creations) frequently resist classification, subvert notions of concrete form, and inhabit more than one region of being.

In character and action, as in being, tricksters embody contradiction and ambiguity. The known cycles of stories reveal a wide range in trickster's personality and actions. Neither wholly good nor solely bad; neither completely wise nor only foolish; sometimes the wily perpetrator of tricks, sometimes the vice-ridden buffoon who falls victim to his own pride; sometimes the compassionate tribal benefactor, sometimes the bungler who spoils some aspect of the world for human beings; trickster seems aptly described by Toelken as "the exponent of all possibilities." Or, as Jarold Ramsey has noted, trickster may not be either/or but simultaneously both. Ramsey speaks of trickster and trickster stories as "a dynamic interposing of the mind between polar opposites, allowing it to hold onto both opposites, as if affirming either/and."[7] Trickster mediates between supposed contradictory forces or elements by retaining aspects of both, or by revealing them to be co-existing parts of one whole, interconnected, often indistinguishable elements of the one. This mediation becomes the raison d'être of the mixedbloods in Vizenor's prose and the central impetus behind much of his writing.

The actions of the culture hero, like his character traits, frequently appear self-contradictory. When Ramsey asks, "Of what is a . . . Trickster capable?" he answers:

Anything, it appears from the evidence, anything, that is, that does not express consistent restraint or altruistic, responsibly domestic, or executive motives. Coyote . . . wanders around, masquerades, lies, steals, attempts to defraud, hoards, gorges himself, commits rape, masturbates, schemes to commit incest, seeks unwarranted revenge, wastes natural resources, plays malicious tricks, is dismembered, is swallowed whole, expelled, publicly humiliated—all the while inventing important rituals, naming and placing the tribes, chartering fishing rights, laying down laws of marriage, warfare, and so on, and establishing the permanence of death.[8]

Yet within this infinite range of possibilities, certain of trickster's features can be pinned down. Trickster is most often characterized as a wanderer, a peripatetic figure likened by some to the picaro, and trickster tales frequently depict this motion. Trickster proves himself in the tales to be inquisitive, often reckless, with a gluttonous appetite for food, sex, and of course, tricks, and he proves himself to be adaptable, irrepressible, a survivor. Ramsey speaks of his "predilection, one might say his genius, for always being in the middle, in all kinds of middles, in muddles."[9] These general qualities describe both the traditional and the contemporary versions of this mythic figure and characterize quite accurately as well his manifestations in Vizenor's work.

Various contradictory explanations exist about why the traditional trickster tales came about and how they function in tribal society. These debates inform Vizenor's work as he immerses himself in the controversy, attempts to educate his audience about trickster dynamics, creates within the context of the mythic tradition, and enacts trickster methods in his own writing. Paul Radin treats the psychological necessity behind the trickster tales in his frequently quoted work *The Trickster: A Study in American Indian Mythology,* describing trickster tales as primarily "an attempt by man to solve his problems inward and outward." He sees the cycle of tales as the recounting of a process wherein the symbolic trickster acquires a certain knowledge and "at the end of his activities a new figure is revealed to us and a new psychical reorientation and environment have come into being."[10] In an essay reprinted in Radin's book, "On the Psychology of the Trickster Figure," Carl Jung explains what he sees as the "therapeutic effect" of the trickster myth:

> It holds the earlier low intellectual and moral level before the eyes of the more highly developed individual, so that he shall not forget how things looked yesterday. . . . Because of its numinosity the myth has a direct effect on the unconscious, no matter whether it is understood or not. . . . Two contrary tendencies are at work: the desire on the one hand to get out of the earlier condition and on the other hand not to forget it.[11]

Vizenor is aware of the theories of both Radin and Jung—indeed, he extracts phrases from the works of both—but only as background against which to advance his own theories. He objects to their theories for a variety of reasons.[12] The linear, progressive formulation underlying the interpretations and the privileging of cause-and-effect logic in the readings of the mythic cycles, for example, deny much of the humor, play, and chance of the tales. Furthermore, by defining the "worthwhile" uses of trickster cycles the theories limit them and confine the sense of possibility Vizenor sees as a crucial element in "trickster consciousness." And finally, by identifying a supposedly "pure" cycle, Radin's theory further limits possibility, effectively shelving the trickster tales of tribal oral culture and relegating them to a static state, making them a part of the "terminal creeds" Vizenor so abhors, tearing them from the contemporary literatures of tribal people to make them a part of the exclusive turf of academics and social scientists.[13] Jung, too, succinctly museumizes the trickster stories of the Winnebago and denies both their satiric sophistication and any claim to contemporary applicability by characterizing the myths as "a remnant" and distinguishing between the contemporary tribal people for whom the mythic cycle "still 'functions' provided they have not been spoiled by civilization" and the "thoughtful observer" who can presumably theorize more knowledgeably and disinterestedly about this "remnant" of culture.[14]

Such static views run counter to the tribal notion of ongoing story and to Vizenor's emphasis on dynamic and evolving culture. While his understanding of trickster involves engagement and dialogue, these kinds of theories, Vizenor writes in the prologue to *The Trickster of Liberty*, "separate readers and trickster" (xiv). In the preface to *Earthdivers*, while leveling criticism against Alan Dundes's "Earth-Diver: Creation of the Mythopoeic Male," he again faults the anthropological analyses of tribal tales for bringing about separation. "This secular seriousness," he writes, "separates the tribes from humor, from untimed metaphors" (xv). To one who identifies the goal of trickster consciousness as the creation of liberating discourse and who envisions the ultimate transformation of readers into tricksters, as Vizenor does when he writes, "The active readers become obverse tricksters," such separation is untenable (*Trickster of Liberty*, ix).

In response to what he sees as faulty, misleading, or incomplete academic theories about trickster, Vizenor frequently presents his own explanations about the "comic holotrope" alongside or intermingled with his creative attempts to invoke the presence of the "immortal" trickster. In *Earthdivers*, for example, he makes a specific distinction between Radin's view of trickster and the trickster of his own writings: "*Wenebojo* or *naanabozho* is the compassionate tribal trickster, not the trickster in the word constructions of the anthropologist Paul Radin, the one who 'possesses no values, moral or social . . . knows neither good nor evil yet is responsible for both,' but the imaginative trickster, the one who cares to balance the world between terminal creeds and humor with unusual manners and ecstatic strategies" (xii). When he gives one of his most lengthy and straightforward statements about trickster in the prologue to *The People Named the Chippewa*, we again sense that part of his effort is to respond to or fend off what he sees as false notions about trickster, especially in his emphasis on what Naanabozho is not:

> Naanabozho, the compassionate woodland trickster, wanders in mythic time and transformational space between tribal experiences and dreams. The trickster is related to plants and animals and trees; he is a teacher and healer in various personalities who, as numerous stories reveal, explains the values of healing plants, wild rice, maple sugar, basswood, and birch bark to woodland tribal people. More than a magnanimous teacher and transformer, the trickster is capable of violence, deceptions, and cruelties: the realities of human imperfections. The woodland trickster is an existential shaman in the comic mode, not an isolated and sentimental tragic hero in conflict with nature.
>
> The Trickster is comic in the sense that he does not reclaim idealistic ethics, but survives as a part of the natural world; he represents a spiritual balance in a comic drama rather than the romantic eliminations of human contradictions and evil. (3–4)

The contemporary scholar Andrew Wiget has criticized Vizenor's concept of trickster, claiming that despite Vizenor's negation of what he considers faulty theories, he is himself unable to successfully theorize trickster. Vizenor would most likely take this observation not as an indication of his failure but as a measure of his success, since in his conception trickster energy cannot be captured in academic theory. But Wiget's critique goes further, suggesting that Vizenor portrays trickster as an "absence" or "the palpable void beyond signification," and that his employment of the poststructuralist notion of the "perpetual deferral of signification" results in the "perpetual deferral of significance."[15]

Louis Owens, on the other hand, has seen in Vizenor's "trickster pose" the antidote to the postmodern threat of meaninglessness. He describes the two extreme views of language: "Within the straitjacket of a fixed, authoritative discourse the self is made lifeless . . . by stasis; within the unordered infinitude of pure possibility, the self deconstructs schizophrenically." Vizenor, he suggests, finds the balance between stasis and chaos in the process of trickster fiction, "allowing signifier and signified to participate in a process of 'continually breaking apart and re-attaching in new combinations.'" In Vizenor's trickster dialectic, "language" or "stories", Owens claims, "assert orders rather than order upon the chaos of experience."[16] The key, then, is vitality, adaptability, continuance. The "continual questioning" of the "perfect hunter" in Vizenor's *Bearheart* is not without answer; it is without a single ultimate answer. Similarly, the trickster of Vizenor's work is not merely absence or the lack of signification, it is the lack of a single presence or single signification. The commitment in Vizenor's work is to a new kind of interactive significance.

We can see the characteristic movement in Vizenor's analyses of trickster in his prologue to *The Trickster of Liberty*, one Jonathan Boyarin characterizes as "critico-fictional."[17] Here Vizenor mingles his ideas with comments by other theorists, placing them both in a narrative frame and presenting them in a playful, contradictory fashion that is trickster consciousness: he attempts to simultaneously explain and enact trickster fiction. His description of trickster can also be read as a description of the prologue itself: "The Woodland trickster is a comic trope; a universal language game. The trickster narrative arises in agonistic imagination; a wild venture in communal discourse, an uncertain humor that denies aestheticism, translation, and imposed representations. The most active readers become obverse tricksters" (ix–x).

These quoted passages from *The People Named the Chippewa* and *The Trickster of Liberty* clarify the character of the trickster as imagined in Vizenor's writing and describe Vizenor's metaphorical use of trickster consciousness. Within them lie the watchwords in his creation of a trickster signature: *contradiction, balance, between, humor, imagination, game, comic, communal, transformation, dream, mythic, imagination, agonistic, discourse, active,* and *survival.* Throughout the creative and theoretical works of the Vizenor canon, these terms surface again and again to elucidate or enact trickster engagement, trickster discourse and trickster liberation.[18]

One comprehensive theoretical analysis helpful in illuminating the characteristics and dynamics of Vizenor's use of this mythic figure is Barbara Babcock's "'A Tolerated Margin of Mess': The Trickster and His Tales Reconsidered." Babcock explores the place of the trickster among the various manifestations of marginality in literature and society, offers a sixteen-point summary of the characteristics of tricksters, summarizes and analyzes the Winnebago trickster cycle, and examines both the literary and the social roles or functions of trickster tales.

From her summary of trickster characteristics (nearly all of which surface at various times in Vizenor's numerous imaginative depictions of Naanabozho), perhaps those most relevant to this discussion are her claims that tricksters "exhibit an independence from and an ignoring of temporal and spatial boundaries . . . tend to inhabit crossroads . . . are usually situated between the social cosmos and the other world or chaos . . . are generally amoral and asocial . . . [have] creative/destructive dualism . . . tend to be ambiguously situated between life and death, and good and evil . . . in all their behavior, tend to express a concomitant breakdown of the distinction between reality and reflection.[19] These qualities clearly inform the revolutionary border existence most noteworthy among Vizenor's imaginative and metaphorical characters.

Babcock's discussion of the trickster dynamic is similarly helpful, contributing to an understanding of the ability of trickster consciousness to engender reader involvement. She notes six functions or roles of trickster tales, the first four of which have been fairly commonly acknowledged: (1) "narrative as entertainment"; (2) "myth as social charter," reinforcing the laws and customs of society; (3) tale as "projection and sublimation," with trickster tales working much as the saturnalian rituals have been thought to function, providing an outlet for negative feelings about society's rules; and (4) storytelling as "evaluative, as contributing to a reexamination of existing conditions and possibly leading to change" through the use of satire or social criticism. However, most helpful in arriving at a better understanding of Vizenor's claim that trickster tales liberate and serve as a catalyst for reader response and co-creation are the last two functions in Babcock's list. The fifth role Babcock notes is what she calls the "reflective-creative" function brought about by upsetting humankind's illusion of order:

> Caricature, parody, and other dialogic literary forms operate similarly by juxtaposing two or more incompatible frames of reference. By calling attention to the artificiality of literary expression and by being itself a play upon form, parody of other myths and serious narratives stimulates the perception of the as if nature of social forms and structures and the necessity but not the supremacy of control. Like the joke, the picaresque narrative or the trickster tale affords an opportunity for realizing that an accepted pattern has no necessity. Its excitement lies in the suggestion that any particular ordering of experience may be arbitrary and subjective. It is frivolous in that it produces no real alternative, only an exhilarated sense of freedom from form in general, though it may well provoke thought of real alternatives and prompt action toward their realization.[20]

Here Babcock underscores an important movement, showing how literary form can become social performance, can prompt action. The deconstructive act becomes a means to liberation and, ultimately, to continual reconstruction. Trickster, as Helen Jaskoski has noted, "is ever provisional, contingent, and metamorphic," and the process of trickster mediation is always ongoing. "Mediation," Ramsey has noted, "does not mean 'compromise and reconciliation.' . . . It is a continuing process of the mind, not a transitional step toward some conclusion." Therefore, as Owens points out, the "trickster pose" of Vizenor's literature avoids one of the pitfalls of postmodernism: "mere capitulation to chance or random event." It subverts "imaginative constructions that limit human possibility and freedom" as a way of clearing a space for asserting a new "coherent, adaptive, and syncretic human identity."[21] The responsibility for this "breakthrough into performance" ultimately rests with the reader. Alan Velie has noted how "Vizenor writes like a trickster, creating a narrator who is a professed trickster, telling a story of tricksters, all with the purpose of turning the audience into tricksters."[22] The deconstructive act and the reconstructive are equally central to trickster discourse. Vizenor imaginatively embodies the continual recurrence of both with this previously quoted image: "The ritual of a spider building its web on the wind . . . That is survival!" (*Bearheart*, 187).

In her analysis of the sixth and final function of trickster literature, Babcock identifies other arenas in which the trickster dialectic is played out, that of the primal and spiritual realms. This function Babcock calls the "creation of communitas . . . where hierarchies are leveled, distinctions dissolved, and roles reversed" and, she claims, it results in an awakening of the power of the imagination: "Recent research has shown a high positive correlation between creativity and fantasy and marginality and deviance—imagination freed from the constraints of social structural roles." Trickster tales, then, ultimately introduce the reader to what Victor Turner calls "a realm of pure possibility whence novel configurations of ideas and relations may arise." So far the claimed results seem similar to those of the "reflective-creative" function. But Babcock asserts even more when she says that first of all one is startled "into fresh views of . . . contemporary reality" and, secondly, is "led to a rediscovery of essential truths, a transvaluation of values, and the affirmation of a primal order."[23]

Babcock's assertion here resembles that of Elaine Jahner in her reading of Vizenor's work and its connection to poststructuralism. In "Heading 'Em Off at the Impasse: Native American Authors Meet the Post-structuralists," Jahner talks about the sacred as a quality that "derives not from qualities intrinsic to the substance but from the relationships that can be observed among entities" and as "the fundamental principle of relationship linking all phenomena. . . . a comprehensive network of relationships."[24] Myth, metaphor, story, dialogue, language, and of course, trickster literature operate "in a sacred manner" when they uncover, access, or enact that "fundamental principle of relationship." Such access is possible through the process, the engagement, invited by a trickster signature.

Many of Babcock's claims about the trickster dynamic seem very much like those of Vizenor. If we compare her descriptions of function and her claims about the effect of trickster tales to his assertions, explanations, and practices, many similarities appear. Vizenor, for example, claims: "Apart from all the bad things anthropologists have said about the trickster, the thing I want to emphasize about him in my experience and in my writing is that he is liberator" (Interview). Babcock writes of "an exhilarated sense of freedom," Vizenor of "liberation." In *The Trickster of Liberty* he claims, "Those people who dread the trickster and the mind monkey must dread their own freedom" (42). In the following passage about MacChurbbs, one of Vizenor's imaginative tricksters whom he describes as "a wise clown, a cosmic jester," note the numerous instances where, as Babcock writes, "hierarchies are leveled, distinctions dissolved, and roles reversed":

> He [MacChurbbs] drew his humor from a moment of knowing the contradictions between passion and reason, between the terminal beliefs of men and women, between cats and dogs, between night and day, between up and down, between words and dreams. He tells fathers they are sons, criminals they are victims, women they are men, saints they are sinners, and he turns the visions and cultural measures of the world around. ("I Know What You Mean," 98–99)

Indeed, throughout the works of Vizenor we find statements about knowledge achieved through apparent contradiction, as in this piece of dialogue spoken by Captain Shammer in the satirical story "Chair of Tears" in *Earthdivers*:

> Balance is not balance, no idea or event is what it is named, there are no places that are known but through the opposites, nothing is sacred but what is not sacred. . . . No thing is in balance but what is confused and in discordance. . . . The trickster seeks the balance in contraries and the contraries in balance; shaman tricksters avoid the extremes, but not with extreme humor or intense manners. (20)

But more important than the similarities between Babcock's and Vizenor's theories about trickster is the way her ideas illuminate Vizenor's methods. They explain how his playful and sometimes convoluted use of language and the unusual action of his plots fulfill the intentions of trickster tales, subverting the confining definitions and institutions of literature and society, working toward liberating and activating the reader's own imaginative powers, and inciting the awareness of a new kind of responsibility to the world, a new identity as earthdivers and "postindian warriors."

"Trickster Founders of This New Earth"

The cast of earthdivers, "postindian warriors," and tricksters in Vizenor's writing include tribal entrepreneurs such as Martin Bear Charme of "Landfill Meditation" and Almost Browne of the story by the same name; his own trickster persona Clement Beaulieu in *Earthdivers* and *Wordarrows*; his imaginative recreations of Naanabozho of the traditional trickster tales; a cross-cultural trickster, Griever, who combines the characteristics of Naanabozho and the Chinese Monkey King; the tribal crossblood Stone Columbus, heir of the great explorer Christopher Columbus; and a family of Anishinaabe tricksters in *The Trickster of Liberty*, whose family roots Vizenor depicts as arising from the imaginative version of his own ancestors' tribal land, White Earth Reservation. Although each of these individual characterizations of trickster does not incorporate all the elements attributed to the figure or fulfill all the dynamic possibilities Vizenor recognizes as inherent in trickster consciousness, they all pursue and achieve some degree of liberation from conventional thinking. They are also "earthdivers" who, like their mythic counterparts, participate in the creation of the place they will call home. But the contemporary earthdivers, Vizenor tells us, "dive into unknown urban places now . . . to create a new consciousness of coexistence" (*Earthdivers*, ix).

Among Vizenor's trickster renditions, his screenplay *Harold of Orange* offers a revealing account of these new places of contact as it tracks the intersections of culture to an urban center and depicts the act of balance and survival undertaken by the tribal characters, the "trickster founders of this new earth."[25] The tale is a playful, imaginative, and humorous account of a scam perpetrated by the "Warriors of Orange" against a group of charitable foundation directors. The tribal tricksters, whose previous miniature orange grove venture was also a hoax, now gain another foundation grant with their proposal for pinch bean coffee, thus duping the establishment a second time. Vizenor's plot line refuses to lie that neatly on the page or on the screen, however. Through the interaction between the Warriors of Orange and the foundation directors, subplots develop and disclose the supposedly dominant action as merely the surface disguise for the true dramatic action: the subversion and symbolic upheaval of established order. Vizenor accomplishes this tricksterlike leveling of supposed distinctions through the revelation that all the characters are co-conspirators playing out a social game.

The narrative functions to a greater or lesser degree in each of the six ways Babcock identifies as characteristic of trickster story. Although the various elements of the drama are inevitably interconnected and their effect cumulative, I isolate them here for illustration. Most obviously, *Harold of Orange* works as entertainment. Consider, for example, an absurd scene in which the leader of the tribal group, Harold Sinseer, performs a farcical naming ceremony in a city parking lot, assigning names by drawing Monopoly cards from a cigar box. Humor arises both from the implied satire and from the multiple incongruities of the scene. Vizenor obviously intends to allude to the panting desire of many to participate in "authentic" Indian rituals and to be adopted into the tribe. He also underscores the patent absurdity of a supposedly sacred ceremony performed in a decidedly profane location by the addition of canned powwow music and elements of a parlor game. He includes the cigar box as a not-so-subtle reminder of stereotyping, exemplified in the cigar store Indian. And finally, through the playfulness of the participants, he mitigates any dullness that might ensue from the heavy-handed symbolism (in much the same way that telling a bad joke as a bad joke allows us again to find delight in it).

Consider this exchange between Harold Sinseer and a foundation board member, Kingsley Newton:

Harold: This is a special name feast prepared by the Warriors of Orange in honor of all the founders and foundations in the New World. . . . Kingsley Newton. . . . The urban spirits have directed me in a dream to select your new name from the cigar box. . . .

Kingsley: Are you serious?

Harold: Who could be serious about anything in a parking lot at a shopping center . . . use your imagination.

Kingsley: By all means. . . .

Harold: Your new name speaks to me from the cigar store Indian Box. (*Shadow Distance,* 316)

As Harold encourages Kingsley, Vizenor might as readily be encouraging his audience, and the lightness of the scene then renders it harmless: it is no hard-line racial attack on white foibles, but a playful jab in the ribs by a trickster companion who might be saying, "Hey, get a load of us," "What a game that was," or "We're really something, aren't we?" The narrative works as entertainment because we are cajoled into seeing ourselves and our actions in a humorous light.

Harold of Orange at first seems ill-suited to the second role Babcock identifies for trickster tales, "myth as social charter," because it tends not to reinforce the most accepted laws, customs, and values of American society, but instead to call them into question or run counter to them. But remember, it is not a tale of mainstream American society but of contemporary tribal society. Therefore it fulfills the role of "social charter" if it tends to reinforce laws or customs of Native Americans. In this case, it reinforces one of the notions most vital in Vizenor's view of Native American culture: survival through wit and humor. It identifies humor as a tool of mediation and a means to achieve balance. It also reinforces the Vizenor truism: "Humor has political significance" (*Heirs of Columbus*, 166). The "Warriors of Orange" engage in verbal play with satiric intentions, assume the poses of the best "simulations" of Indians, and unmask the "manifest manners" of the charitable foundations. They symbolically count coup in the new word wars of foundations and proposals by playing at playing by the rules, always performing their "compassionate trickery" in "the best humor" (*Shadow Distance*, 333).

The screenplay and film also readily function as a vehicle for releasing pent-up negative feelings about the enforced rules and customs of society, as a kind of saturnalian outlet, the third function Babcock identifies. Readers can take great vicarious delight in the rule-breaking performance of the Warriors of Orange, who at every turn subvert the institutional procedures of the granting agency, removing the directors physically and symbolically from the safe, comfortable ground of the boardroom. Verbally, in gestures, and through minor pranks, they disrupt the solemn proceedings. Stage directions tell us at one point, for example, "Two warriors in the back of the room discover the controls for the lights in the board room. . . . The warriors raise and lower the lights according to their mood and interest" (screenplay manuscript, 10). And throughout the action, the tribal element purposely violates or mocks acceptable or proper behavior: Harold mounts a statue in a public park, he climbs on top of artifact cases in a university anthropology display, he eats a daffodil. The warriors are said to "hoot and trill" (*Shadow Distance*, 302 and 317), and all of the warriors clown with the neckties Harold has brought them to wear to the proposal hearing: one is said to "knot a tie on his head like a headband" (screenplay manuscript, 5), and others wear the neckties over T-shirts. They appropriate the "simulations" of the boardroom, but transform them into mock simulations of tribal identity, into simulations of survivance.

This mockery of the symbolic measures of social status also fulfills the "evaluative" role of trickster myth, characterized by Babcock as employing satire and social criticism to bring about a "reexamination of existing conditions and possibly leading to change." The subjects of Vizenor's satire in the film range widely and include the "invented Indian" phenomenon, the commodification of culture, and the distortions of history and the social sciences. Through the voice of Harold, for example, he addresses the issue of the display of Indian remains, a subject that receives a more formal and lengthy debate in "Bone Courts: The Natural Rights of Tribal Bones." In a scene at the university artifact cases, Harold voices a lament about the academic theft of culture: "Those anthropologists invented us and put our parts in these cases . . . now we come to the cities from our past and pace around our parts here like lost and lonesome animals" (screenplay manuscript, 25). Then, trickster fashion, he turns to humor to drive home his point. In a deft reversal he implies that the bones must really be those of a white anthropologist lost in a snowstorm, whose body was discovered years later and mistaken for that of an Indian. The effect, of course, is to challenge readers to reconsider the readily accepted treatment of the remains of "primitive" cultures as museum objects and the implied hierarchy that allows or endorses such practices.

Through satire Vizenor also exposes Indian stereotypes, the moves to position the Indian as exotic other, and the resulting commodification of culture. When one of the directors hesitates in asking a certain question, the warriors run through the list of standard "Indian" questions: "Would you like to meet a beautiful tribal woman?" "How about a hunting guide?" "Sweat lodge ceremonies . . . Purification?" "A shaman, an herbal healing then?" "Leather and beadwork?" "Indian alcoholism?" (*Shadow Distance*, 329–30). In other scenes, the language of both the directors and the warriors, which has been "cut . . . from the centerfolds of histories" (*Shadow Distance*, 313), echoes the false rhetoric of historic encounters and the admonishments the tribes have received over the years. Phrases like "the great white road," "your desire to better yourselves," "a credit to your race" (*Shadow Distance*, 311, 310, 331), and "as long as the rivers flow and the grass grows" (screenplay manuscript, 17), expose the racism or hypocrisy embedded in colonial rhetoric.

But Vizenor's humor is double-edged: by exposing the faulty stereotyping of the Indian, he also unmasks the characterization and pose of the idealized Indian—the noble savage of history's imagination. A romantic ploy of Harold's about his "traditional grandmother" is exploded and his "cultural capital" devalued by Fannie's knowing comment on "the grandmother who had already died about four times that year" (screenplay manuscript, 9). Vizenor's satire leaves the tribal character no place to hide, no safe role to play.

The fifth and, Babcock feels, most important way trickster narratives function is by revealing the artificiality of conventional forms, both literary and social, thus leading the reader to a "sense of freedom from form in general." This revelation is achieved by "juxtaposing two or more incompatible frames of reference."[26] In *Harold of Orange* one frame of reference is provided through the serious, conventional ideas about foundations, their methods, and their intentions. The second, which stems from the subplots of comic intrigue and game playing essentially deconstructs the first.

The foundation's and the foundation directors' ideal of inscrutable respectability is tarnished in various scenes. For example, Fannie is revealed to have been previously romantically involved with Harold, and a comic version of behind-the-scenes bargaining is played out between the two. Fannie isn't taken in for a minute by Harold's scam. Yet, even though she tells him, "This is an important position for me, I have worked for several years to get to this foundation" (screenplay manuscript, 8), she doesn't expose him or his scheme. Indeed, both sides in the story seem at least somewhat aware that they are merely playing a social game, the foundation game, in which they each get what they want—the Warriors of Orange "get a little money," the charitable foundations "get a good name" (film).

Vizenor continues the game motif through the introduction of Monopoly in the naming ceremony, the continued use of these assigned names (like Chance) after that scene, and through the incorporation of a softball scene. Finally, Harold and Fannie engage in their own personal game of intrigue over money he owes her.

The warriors reveal their understanding of the game playing in various speeches. Harold identifies the Warriors of Orange as "tricksters in the new school of socioacupuncture where a little pressure fills the pocketbook" (*Shadow Distance*, 298), and when issuing neckties to his fellow warriors, he says, "Who can resist a skin in a necktie. . . . Neckties are the pressure points in our school of socioacupuncture" (screenplay manuscript, 4). Another warrior speaks of the "cultural bait" (screenplay manuscript, 2) to be used in the scheme, and Harold seems to reveal if not to flaunt his game strategy when he admits to the assembly of directors: "Once we climbed into church basements to better ourselves with those heavy heart and empty pocketbook speeches. . . . The money was good then, but the guilt has changed, and so have we . . . so here we are now dressed in neckties with oranges and pinch beans" (*Shadow Distance*, 311).

In other scenes, the directors, too, seem to broadcast their awareness of both the artificiality of the proposal hearing and the farcical nature of the proposal. One asks, "Could we award him the grant without hearing the rest of his incredible proposal?" (screenplay manuscript, 20). Later, two directors refer to Harold as a "trickster" and a "confidence man," and when one says, "He believes he can stop time and change the world," the other replies knowingly, "With a foundation grant, of course" (*Shadow Distance*, 323–24). All the participants' keen awareness of the gaming serves to expose the false fronts of the rigid social institutions and to call into question the necessity and validity of these and other social constructions. Thus we experience the "exhilarated sense of freedom from form in general" that Babcock describes, which then allows for the reawakening of creative thought and "may well provoke thought of real alternatives and prompt action toward their realization."[27]

Closely related to the trickster tale's unveiling of the artificiality of social forms is the debunking of social hierarchy, or what Babcock calls "the creation of communitas" (the sixth function of trickster narratives), which achieves a community of individuals on relatively equal status. This sense of communitas "prevails in carnival and the marketplace . . . and when trickster appears on the scene."[28] In *Harold of Orange* communitas is achieved both by the presence of the trickster figure, Harold Sinseer, and through the environment of gaming. In a game, as at a carnival or in a marketplace, social status figures insignificantly in the outcome; luck, wit, and strategy figure heavily. Therefore the combatants have equal opportunity regardless of social status—social status is effectively nullified. The trickster, of course, effects the same kind of communitas partly because of his innate ambiguity, his mingling of god/human/animal and good/evil, and his marginal existence outside of, or sometimes in defiance of, the various structures of society and culture. He also enacts this state of communitas through his clowning and his transgression of taboos. "Trickster," Babcock says, "belongs to the comic modality or marginality where violation is generally the precondition for laughter and communitas, and there tends to be an incorporation of the outsider, a leveling of hierarchy, a reversal of status."[29]

In the film version of Harold of Orange, one memorable scene perfectly illustrates both the achievement of communitas through game and the leveling of hierarchy through trickster ambiguity and violation. The softball scene sets the directors against the warriors.[30] Each side wears T-shirts identifying them as "Anglos" or "Indians." In one deft role reversal, the warriors become "Anglos," and the directors "Indians." The ambiguous trickster, Harold, wears several layers of alternately labeled T-shirts. Peeling them off one after another, transforming himself, he becomes at various times a member of each of the opposing teams. Each side also takes on the stereotypic rhetoric of their assumed roles, the "Indian" directors calling the "Anglo" warriors "honkeys," the "Anglo" warriors uttering the rhetoric of manifest destiny: "Rape and plunder if you must but win this game in the name of God!" (film).

Such role reversal, together with the game's establishment of equality, at least imaginatively, achieves the state of communitas. The desired (and, Babcock claims, probable) result is a "fresh view of contemporary reality" and "a rediscovery of essential truth, a transvaluation of values, and the affirmation of a primal order." As the theme song to the film claims, "Trickster changes how everything seems."[31] Having seen the falseness of the constructed social order, the warriors are freed to rediscover for themselves the true nature of reality. The film and screenplay end in expectation when Harold addresses the audience, claiming: "This is where the revolution starts, on a gravel road in the brush . . . At a reservation coffee house in the softwoods . . . Remember, you were here with some of the best trickster founders of this new earth" (*Shadow Distance*, 333). Revolutions and a trickster vision for a new order: these are the same aspirations Vizenor holds for his reader.

Mixedbloods: Myth, Metaphor, Marginality, and Mediation

Social order and the nature of reality, central to most trickster accounts, become the basis of exploration as well in Vizenor's treatment of the mixedblood. In Vizenor's writing the trickster figure becomes nearly synonymous with and a metaphor for the tribal mixedblood, whose symbolic role it is to subvert the artificial distinctions of society. Like the trickster, whose very identity reflects all duality and contradiction, the mixedblood is a marginal character, one who exists on the border of two worlds, two cultures, the white and the Indian. In fact, the existence of the mixedblood resists even that definitiveness. Mixedbloods exist in the place of contact between age-old tribal traditions and contemporary adaptations, as well as in the place of contact between the stereotypic definitions of Indian identity and the reality of Indian existence.[32]

James Ruppert has recognized the position of tribal mixedbloods as mediators whose mediation entails not merely "a middle ground or an alteration between" two bases of understanding or realms of being, but "a dynamic confluence of values and expectations." Likewise, in their discussion of postcolonial literature in *The Empire Writes Back*, Bill Ashcroft, Gareth Griffiths, and Helen Tiffin recognize the position of those poised on the border of two worlds as involving complex mediation that, they claim, must result in hybridization: "Post-colonial culture is inevitably a hybridized phenomenon involving a dialectical relationship between the 'grafted' European cultural systems and an indigenous ontology, with its impulse to create or recreate an independent local identity. Such construction or reconstruction only occurs as a dynamic interaction between European hegemonic systems and 'peripheral' subversions of them."[33]

Central to this understanding of the postcolonial is the recognition that no response to colonial contact can remain innocent of that contact. Even if the "empire" chooses to reject the workings of the "imperial center," their response reflects knowledge of the imperial. Similarly, in Vizenor the notion of "pure" culture is rejected and argued against at every turn. Native Americans may choose tribal tradition over mainstream American culture, but that stance is itself implicated, can only be assumed on the basis of knowledge of both, is formulated in response to the agenda of colonization, and is therefore already in dialogue with or mediating between the two cultures and worldviews.

The metaphor of the mixedblood itself represents a confluence in Vizenor, standing as it does not merely for the conditions of race but also for the mixed conditions of culture, spiritual values and traditions, sites of knowledge and truth, and personal and social motives, as well as for the mixed conditions of literary traditions. Ruppert characterizes Vizenor's writing as "mediational discourse" that, like the work of many other Native American writers, "strives to bring the oral into the written, the native American vision into contemporary writing, spirit into modern identity, community into society, and myth into modern imagination." As mediators, he claims, Native American writers are participants "in two literary and cultural traditions—white and tribal" and "use the epistemological structures of one to penetrate the other." The texts of such writers as Vizenor both depict and are themselves that "dynamic confluence" Ruppert speaks of. "The post-colonial text," claim Ashcroft, Griffiths, and Tiffin, "is always a complex hybridized formation. It is inadequate to read it either as a reconstruction of pure traditional values or as simply foreign and intrusive."[34]

Key in Vizenor's imaginative rendition of the mixedblood condition, as well as in his literary method, is his use of trickster and the trickster dialectic. In both his early prose collection *Earthdivers* and his more recent novel *Griever*, Vizenor self-consciously links the two.

As Louis Owens has noted, Vizenor's dedication in *Griever* "to Mixed-bloods and Compassionate Tricksters" essentially merges these figures.[35] His preface to *Earthdivers* likewise underscores the identification of one with the other: "The earthdivers in these twenty-one narratives are mixedbloods, or Métis, tribal tricksters and recast cultural heroes, the mournful and whimsical heirs and survivors from that premier union between the daughters of woodland shamans and white fur traders" (ix).

This passage, when informed by an understanding of the mythic, also identifies the role of the mixedblood trickster by the application of the epithet "earthdiver." Like the characters in *Harold of Orange*, these mixedblood tricksters are "founders of this new earth." Later in his preface, Vizenor again implies the correspondence between tricksters and earthdivers, again identifies their role, and also implies an important association between the function of tricksters and writers: "Earthdivers, tricksters, shamans, poets, dream back the earth" (xvi). The mixedblood trickster earthdivers of the collection, and by implication the writers, find or create new and sometimes foreign spaces for survival; they "dive into unknown urban places now . . . to create a new consciousness of coexistence" (ix), "search" for "a few honest words on which to build a new urban turtle island" (xi), and "speak a new language, . . . and in some urban places . . . speak backwards to be better heard and understood on the earth" (xvi). The trickster, the mixed-blood, the earthdiver, Vizenor employs as metaphors for the mediation that ultimately constructs a new Native American personal (or more likely tribal) and literary identity. They are the "postindian warriors of survivance" of Vizenor's *Manifest Manners*. "The best stories," writes Vizenor, "are survival trickeries on the borders" (*Interior Landscapes*, 73).

This mediative rendering of a new existence is central to an understanding of the mixedblood trickster in Vizenor as is the permanence of the trickster, mixedblood state.[36] In Vizenor the mixedblood trickster marginality is a type of existence, not merely a phase of existence; it is a state of being as well as a way of being. This distinction becomes important in understanding the political and social conditions of mixedblood identity, and it becomes apparent in the plots and characterizations of Vizenor's trickster fiction.

While most mixedblood protagonists in Native American fiction find themselves in a state equally as ambiguous as those of Vizenor's fiction, they differ in their response to that ambiguity. The depictions of mixed-bloods by most contemporary Indian authors treat their condition as temporary, as a phase that, by nature, entails the possibility of change, the possibility of resolution of the ambiguous state. Abel in N. Scott Momaday's *House Made of Dawn*, the nameless protagonist in James Welch's *Winter in the Blood*, Tayo in Leslie Silko's *Ceremony*, Lipsha in Louise Erdrich's *Love Medicine*, Ephanie in Paula Gunn Allen's *The Woman Who Owned the Shadows*, Tom Joseph in Louis Owens's *Wolfsong*, Cecilia in Janet Campbell Hale's *The Jailing of Cecilia Capture*, all enter the fiction in a confused state of identity, progress through phases (sometimes ceremonial phases), and thereby emerge in a less marginal space (sometimes returning to a physical center, sometimes to a spiritual, ancestral, or communal center). Most mixedbloods in Native American literature (read marginal characters) have desired and sought this resolution of ambiguous identity that results from movement to one side of the border or the other (most usually back to a tribal center of culture). Therefore, unless and until they reach that resolution, they exist in and are depicted in a tragic state.

But Vizenor's mixedblood characters (read tricksters) seldom seek or desire resolution for their ambiguous or marginal state. Rather, they celebrate that state, create from it new mixedblood identities, and exist in and are depicted in a comic mode. Both Louis Owens and Alan Velie have noted Vizenor's positive, celebratory rendering of the mixedblood, wherein the marginal state becomes a position of power.[37] Owens also discusses the "acts of recovery" central to most Indian novels and the "re-constructions" of identity built of the past, the traditional tribal culture, the original place of community, and so on. He contrasts these attempts with those of Vizenor, who instead deconstructs "the verbal artifacts of Indian—or mixedblood—identity."[38] But Vizenor's decon-struction of what he sees as stereotypic and invented Indian identity serves the ends of another kind of construction, the construction of new authentic identity, existing though it might at the intersections of cultures and surviving though it does by a constant struggle for balance.

He deconstructs notions of a lost past in order to construct an existence in the present and a vision for the future.

The complications of Vizenor's trickster signature extend not only to the plots of his work but also to the methods and even to the very act of writing itself. Poised between oral and written cultures, between tribal languages and English, Native American writers again enact the polygenic role of the mixedblood. Ashcroft, Griffiths, and Tiffin have acknowledged this "intersection" as involving, "not simply . . . two different languages, but . . . two different ways of conceiving the practice and substance of language." Owens, too, has recognized the troubled position of Native American writers who "attempt to recover identity and authenticity by invoking and incorporating the world found within oral tradition—the reality of myth and ceremony—an authorless 'original' literature," but who, "through the inscription of an authorial signature," place themselves "in immediate tension with this communal, authorless, and identity-conferring source." Finally, the indigenous writer, by acquiring and employing literacy in the language and literary forms of the colonizer in order to promote, preserve, or serve her culture, may actually contribute to its marginalization or more rapid demise.[39]

As Chapter 3 has shown, Vizenor responds to these literary quandaries in trickster fashion, employing both balance and subversion. He achieves a balance of form and expression by investing the written with elements of the oral and using Anishinaabemowin along with English. He subverts the literary and grammatical standards, not only by deliberately running afoul of the rules, but also by overtly challenging them through plot and dialogue. While further attention will be given to Vizenor's methods in the following chapter, here I offer a discussion of one work that embodies the mixedblood quality of Vizenor's trickster signature, the short story "Almost Browne," from *Landfill Meditations* (1–10).

By the very name "Almost Browne" Vizenor blatantly announces his protagonist's mediative position and foreshadows his narrative's mediational discourse. The protagonist comments on his identity, saying, "I was born in the back seat of a beatup reservation car, almost white, almost on the reservation, and almost a real person" (6). The doctor who signs Almost's birth certificate calls him "one more trail born halfbreed"; the narrator tells us, "Almost was born to be a trickster" (3), and later calls him a "crossblood trickster" (5). If the reader needs further indication of the protagonist's marginal position, Vizenor's fiction supplies it in ready abundance. Almost, we are told, lived in the back seat of abandoned cars; he lived "on the border between two school districts, one white and the other tribal"; and "each school thought he attended the other, and besides, no one cared that much where he lived or what he learned" (5). Almost's best friend is "a reservation consumer" named Drain, the son of white immigrants. Almost serves as mediator between Drain and tribal culture, "telling stories that made the tribe seem more real" (5). These physical details clearly create a setting of border existence within which mediation takes place.

Vizenor's plot, for example, playfully enacts mediation between the oral and the written traditions. Almost teaches himself to read from "almost whole books," books whose edges have been burned. He "pictures" or "imagines" the rest of the words, and they become "more real in . . . imagination." "Finally," he says, "I could imagine the words and read the whole page, printed or burned" (8).

Vizenor also comments on the origin and existence of words outside the static written tradition, on the authenticity of the oral and the actual, on the presence and power of sound and language, and on the "almost" quality of mere words:

> Listen, there are words almost everywhere. I realized that in a chance moment. Words are in the air, in our blood, words were always there, way before my burned book collection in the back seat of a car. Words are in snow, trees, leaves, wind, birds, beaver, the sound of ice cracking; words are in fish and mongrels, where they've been since we came to this place with the animals. My winter breath is a word, we are words, real words, and the mongrels are their own words. Words are crossbloods, too, almost whole right down to the cold printed page burned on the sides. (8)

Almost delivers other lessons about words during the course of the story, distinguishing, for example, between the real world and the images on menus, and claiming that "the men who rule words from behind double doors and polished benches" miss "the real words" (9).

He also offers a critique of the educational system, seeing classrooms as "nothing more than parking lots . . . places to park a mind" (7) and claiming to receive his true education outside of school: "Nature was my big book, imagination was my teacher" (7).

Vizenor's subversion of the written literary tradition and the educational system continues as Almost and Drain engage in selling blank books, finding their best customers near the university. They are told by one professor who supports their business that "blank books made more sense to him than anything he had ever read" (9). Each book also contains a single pictomyth, a different pictomyth in each book, and each on a different page. Almost believes the almost-blank-book business succeeds because "college students were tired of books filled with words behind double doors that never pictured anything" (10). But Almost and Drain's book selling at the university is banned, and they turn to a mail-order business. They add a signature to each book, including forged signatures of tribal leaders, presidents, and famous authors.

The trickster movements in this tale seem infinite as the text works to undermine the authority of the written, play with notions of literary censorship, challenge modernist conceptions of artistic closure, question definitions of literacy, attack the conformity of literature, and question the privileging of a single literary interpretation. The form of Vizenor's story is also stamped with a trickster signature. It literally offers two versions of the same story, the first account given in third person omniscient, the second in first person. Vizenor thus establishes a literary dialogue or enacts a discourse wherein the two voices of the story can enrich one another. But this discourse comes about only through the engagement of the reader, who must take up the role of trickster mediator.

Enacting Trickster

Always an ambiguous character, a shape-shifter, an amalgam, trickster remains difficult to pin down, as does Vizenor's trickster literature. Both overturn ideas, challenge the status quo, and upset the accepted structures of society as they wend their way through every kind of bizarre experience imaginable. Through this kind of trickster consciousness, Vizenor attempts to "kick the sides of boxes out," to break through the prison of static words and encourage an individual effort at imagining more healthy alternatives ("Gerald Vizenor, Ojibway/Chippewa Writer," 168). By upsetting the status quo, bringing it under scrutiny, and questioning its authority or necessity, Vizenor invites the reader into the dialogue, encouraging us to find our own answers or alternatives. Thus the reader is ultimately liberated from the text and becomes involved in life. This liberation, this vitality, Vizenor feels, is the ultimate benefit of trickster consciousness. "Trickster tales," he says, "are discussion in the best sense of the word. It's engagement, in the most simple way people talk together or they confront each other. It's imaginative. It has to do with the mind. It's a discourse. It's communal, it's liberation, it's enchanting, it's lusty, it's contradiction. . . . It's life, it's juice, it's energy. . . . But it's not a theory, it's not a monologue" (Interview).

Because the goal of Vizenor's trickster tales is liberation, the stories work best "in places where there are severe contradictions and repressions" (Interview). To date, the settings Vizenor has found appropriate include both the urban and the woodland tribal reservations, China, the academic community, and the imagined futuristic world of *Bearheart*. In all of these settings, in each of his individual stories, Vizenor, in his role as a teacher of survival in the contemporary word wars, emphasizes the healing power of trickster consciousness:

> We can be prisoners, and we are, in our bodies. But we can liberate our minds. Tribal people were brilliant in understanding that a figure, a familiar figure in an imaginative story, could keep their minds free.
> . . . I'm going for trickster consciousness because it's an ideal healing, because it disrupts the opposites and that creates the possibility for discourse that's communal and comic. (Interview)

In his role as wordmaker, Vizenor deftly blends tradition with innovation. His writing clearly reflects the mythic tradition of tribal trickster narrative, but he applies it to contemporary conditions and links it with contemporary theory. To embody tribal ideas of trickster in written form without relegating them to a static state, he centers his energy on inviting involvement, creating momentum, eliciting response—he centers his energy on breaking out of print. He infiltrates the narrative structure with the trickster aesthetic. Through the engagement with trickster consciousness, a reader should experience liberation and healing.

But the movement is not only from author to reader, from writing to reading. The intended movement is from author to reader to actor, from writing to reading to experiencing. The thread from Vizenor's prose intends to extend beyond print to life. As wordmaker, Vizenor seeks to engender survival, and the key to survival is vitality, life, continuance. In *The Trickster of Liberty*, Vizenor first pictures the invented Indian memorialized on a coin and then appropriates, subverts, and radically transforms that static invention when he likens the trickster to "a warrior on a coin that never lands twice on the same side" (xviii). He thus symbolically vivifies the Indian identity, picturing it in an endless process of transformation, engaged in a trickster dynamic. The world keeps on turning, trickster keeps on shifting, Vizenor keeps on writing. The mixedblood trickster earthdiver survives, "a metaphor in a timeless tribal drama" (xv).

6

Reanimating the Dead Voices
Strategies of a Revolutionary Style

*Whatever is felt upon the page without being specifically named there—that,
one might say, is created.*
—Willa Cather, "The Novel Demeuble"

*I thought that if I could put it all down, that would be one way. And next
the thought came to me that to leave all out would be another, and truer, way.*
—John Ashbery, *Three Poems*

I n a self-portrait published in 1980, Vizenor writes, "I will not be
pinned down" ("Gerald Vizenor, Ojibway/Chippewa Writer," 168).
In an interview given that same year, he comments, "I think writing
ought to push consciousness."[1] In a 1987 interview, he says, "Literature
ought to confront the comfortable values of authority. What other good
reason is there for literature but to heal ourselves?" (Interview). In the
interface of these statements we find important keys to understanding
the purpose and the strategies behind Vizenor's revolutionary style.
Knowing well that "listeners bring the experience of a story back to
life," Vizenor resists the "dead voices" of the written and pursues the
reanimation of text by engaging his audience in the literary process
("Tribal People and the Poetic Image," 18). He employs a deliberately

ambiguous style in his writing, creating a sense of indeterminacy that requires the audience to eke out meaning. He brings the postmodern to Native literature, practicing "postindian turns," and his difficult style resists what he calls the "consumer mentality of the arts" as he challenges "tribal simulations," "manifest manners," the "ruins of representation," and all "comfortable values" of contemporary society in order to liberate consciousness, to "push the consciousness" of the reader.[2] This chapter looks in detail at many of Vizenor's dialogic techniques and explores the revolutionary bent of his methods and his message.

Theories of Ambiguity

The English language, especially as it is written, Vizenor claims, often "possesses experience, rather than showing how experience is present" (Interview). It reflects many conventional ideas he sees as false constructs of society. He claims, for example, a relationship between our rhetorical patterns and a worldview of cause and effect: "We . . . demand from our experiences the causes. We don't accept things as chance. We say: 'What's the meaning of this?' 'What's the cause of that?' " (Interview). But, Vizenor insists, reality or truth is more complex. There isn't any such thing as "fact and objectification," there is only "story . . . [which] depends upon who, when, what the circumstances are of perception and what the values are of the perceiver" (Interview). In a similar manner, our very grammar dictates structured oppositions, our linguistic patterns reinforce a view of the world as oppositional binaries:

> Most events or issues are presented with two sides. Seldom do we get any other complex points of view. So we have a perfect binary. We have this, and then on the other hand, . . . the Republicans and the Democrats, night and day, men and women, up and down, black and white, good and evil, Indians and whites, civilization and savagism. These all end up being pretty comfortable, recognizable binaries, either/ors, opposites. But they don't really absorb each other, do they? We hold them as opposites . . . force them to continue the dialectic. (Interview)

Vizenor challenges the validity of such opposites and decries the truth of any view that separates experience in such a way. Like John Berger, he claims, for example, that love and hate are not truly opposites. Both are passionate emotional responses, and the opposite of both or either is "to separate."[3]

To combat these and other tendencies of language to replace experience, Vizenor consciously employs restraint in his writing. As the reader-response theorist Wolfgang Iser also notes, "Any 'living event' must to a greater or lesser degree remain open"; and "The inherent non-achievement of balance is a prerequisite for the very dynamism."[4] Because Vizenor clearly recognizes the efficacy of the open text, his writing seeks, through various means, a sense of indeterminacy. Not only do his individual works ultimately exhibit a lack of closure or failure to resolve issues, but from start to finish the way he writes exhibits an allusiveness and ambiguity.

As William Empson so persuasively demonstrates in *Seven Types of Ambiguity*, the term *ambiguity* itself admits of multiple stylistic possibilities. In my discussion of the indeterminacy in Vizenor's work, I accept as my starting point Empson's definition of ambiguity as "any verbal nuance, however slight, which gives room for alternative reactions to the same piece of language" and his statement about the various possible intentions of ambiguity as "an indecision as to what you mean, an intention to mean several things, a probability that one or [the] other or both of two things has been meant, and the fact that a statement has several meanings." The use of ambiguity obviously opens a text to the reader. Terry Eagleton has commented on the relationship between Empson's notion of ambiguity and reader-response aesthetics: "Empsonian ambiguities . . . can never be finally pinned down: they indicate points where the poem's language falters, trails off or gestures beyond itself, pregnantly suggestive of some potentially inexhaustible context of meaning. Whereas the reader is shut out by a locked structure of ambivalences, reduced to admiring passivity, 'ambiguity' solicits his or her active participation."[5] Vizenor's use of ambiguity functions in exactly this way: by refraining in numerous ways from pinning meaning down, he engenders active reader participation.

Two other specific discussions of ambiguity I find particularly helpful in illuminating the dynamics behind the indeterminacy in Vizenor are Chris Anderson's *Style As Argument: Contemporary American Nonfiction* and, to a lesser degree, Frederick R. Karl's discussion of minimalism in *American Fictions, 1940–1980*. Karl discusses the "less is more" claim as it applies to literary works, explaining how absence insinuates presence and incites the reader to search for what is left out. In minimalist fiction, Karl says, the writer often "makes as his point of reference not the line he develops but the beyond; what is not as dominant as what is, and possibly more significant" and he tips the reader off "that the artist is conscious of what is being omitted." The reader, in her turn, "is aware of the spaces between words, the pauses between breath, the silence between noises," and in her awareness she begins to look for meaning in the absent parts. The work of Vizenor frequently functions in the way Karl describes. Elaine Jahner, for example, notes in her discussion of Vizenor's work that "what is absent remains an affecting presence."[6]

The thrust of Anderson's book involves "the effort to convey in words the inexplicable energies, intensities, and contradictions of American experience." Although Anderson's analysis centers on the works of four contemporary literary journalists, he makes important points about the implications of the choice to either attempt to or refrain from putting something into words, and about the ways in which style itself conveys or implies meaning. About the writers he analyzes, Anderson notes:

> Each define their subjects as somehow beyond words—antiverbal or nonverbal, threatening or sublime, overpowering and intense or private and intuitive—and then repeatedly call our attention to the issue of inexplicability throughout their descriptions and expositions. A self-consciousness about the limits of language is the structuring principle of their work. Wordlessness can be positive or negative in these texts, energizing or threatening. It can be personal or communal. It is something to fight and something to claim. Yet, whatever its nature, it generates a rhetorical challenge for the writer . . . [who] must push language to its limits, explore the edges of expression, intensify and expand the power of words to reach the level of a sublime and inexplicable object.[7]

Of course, Vizenor, too, is "self-consciousness about the limits of language" and strives to "intensify and expand the power" of written words. Indeed, a great deal of what Anderson says could as readily apply to Vizenor. He offers much helpful terminology and a detailed analysis of the implications of the various stylistic devices. Many of the specific stylistic tools he isolates in the body of his book are likewise found in Vizenor's writing. The rhetorical strategies identified in Anderson's book that also accompany Vizenor's hidden discourse of ambiguity include: deliberate attempts by the author to "work against readability," thus forcing the reader to contemplate the "surface of language" and the "complexity of the experience it seeks to describe"; the "grammar of radical particularity," in which the author uses one or more very concrete images, sometimes juxtaposing incongruous images, and then refrains from revealing their significance, connection, or underlying meaning; the "rhetoric of gaps," which includes everything from avoiding conjunctions to including actual physical blank space in the work; the "rhetoric of process," which presents the material in a way that makes "thinking and writing seem simultaneous" and creates a sense of spontaneity; and the undermining of conventional technique while revealing the reason behind this action—the incapability of conventional language to capture the true nature of reality. Empson's work also isolates and provides examples of the various uses of ambiguity, although the terms he employs to characterize the rhetorical dynamics differ. What he calls a "fortunate confusion" ("when the author is discovering his idea in the act of writing"), for example, parallels Anderson's "rhetoric of process."[8]

Indeed, the aforementioned critical discussions are by no means the only ones applicable to Vizenor's work, but they do provide pertinent theory and a vocabulary for understanding and evaluating his methods. Ambiguity takes a wide range of forms in his writing, and the strategies behind these various modes of indeterminacy vary.

A Rhetoric of Gaps

Perhaps the most recognizable means of implication in a text is simple absence: the use of ellipses, blank space in the text, the failure to complete thoughts or sentences, and a lack of closure of the work itself. These tools of indeterminacy are examples of what Anderson calls the "rhetoric of gaps." Iser talks about the purpose for such reader-response techniques, explaining that modern texts exploit omission to "make us aware of the nature of our own capacity for providing links."[9]

Vizenor frequently employs each of these techniques. We see his use of ellipses and incomplete sentences, for example, in a scene from "Mother Earth Man and Paradise Flies" (*Wordarrows*, 89–103) in which Zebulon Matchi Makwa is singing on the shores of Mille Lacs Lake. Vizenor conveys the desperation, the driven quality of his song chant partly by the use of ellipses, which indicate its continuation despite the other actions occurring around Matchi Makwa:

> "Our women are poisoned part white," wailed Zebulon Matchi Makwa down to the dock through the pale poplar and pine part drunk on reservation wine. "Part peeled at night ho ho ho ho buried deep down where the dead turn around and around. . . ."
>
> Tame deer waited near the salt blocks.
> Fisherman cast their lines and lures near shore.
> "Our women are poisoned part white. . . ." (89–90)

The ellipses might also indicate Matchi Makwa's voicelessness, his inability to express his pain. Later in the scene, Vizenor writes: " 'Our women are poisoned part white . . . too much,' he wailed over and over on his stout tongue" (90). Whether the ellipses indicate continual singing by the character, convey the pregnant quality of his repeated chant, imbue the other actions of the scene with his haunting presence, or allude to things that cannot be verbalized, they invite the reader to participate in the imagination of the scene and to follow through the probable implications of Matchi Makwa's words. Vizenor uses ellipses throughout his work to create the deliberate gap that is an invitation to imagine story.

Another fairly conventional form of indeterminacy that appears frequently in Vizenor's writing is the lack of closure in a plot line. We find a classic illustration in his novel *Griever: An American Monkey King in China*. Vizenor refrains from closing the novel, but instead has the protagonist leave the scene where the main action of the novel took place by means of an ultralight airplane, presumably on his way to new adventures. Vizenor might well be professing his own feelings when he writes of the mind monkey: "nothing bored him more than the idea of an end; narrative conclusions were unnatural, he would never utter the last word" (128). He offers the dramatic basis for his own open-ended account when he recalls that "Monkey became immortal when he ate the peaches; there were no end to his stories" (128). This lack of closure not only aligns itself with contemporary techniques of indeterminacy but suits the traditional Native American storytelling style, especially as practiced in the telling of trickster tales, and likewise fits the Chinese stories about the Monkey King. As Jarold Ramsey has commented, the "Western tradition" of literature usually involves "tragic fictions, ending in the heroic death of the protagonist: 'the rest is silence,'" while the tribal tradition involves "an endless story whose episodes are still unfolding."[10]

In addition to actual absence in the text, the rhetoric of gaps can involve implied absence, suggestion of a connection to something beyond the text, or an obvious allusion to another level of meaning. From simple puns to sophisticated associations, these forms of ambiguity also fill Vizenor's work. One signature device in his work is the frequent use of allusive titles or names. For example, he entitles a chapter in *Bearheart* "Green Machines" (15–18). The action of the chapter involves two rigid government officials who come to interrogate the protagonist of the book, Proude Cedarfair. The two ride "green fenderless machines," so, on a strictly literal level, the title refers to these bicyclelike "pedal machines." But because the story reveals the robotlike actions of the officials and their mission of obtaining part of the cedar forest for government timber use, on a symbolic level the title identifies the officials as "green machines"—government moneymaking machines. The double entendre of Vizenor's titles, like many of his character names—Captain Shammer, Little Big Mouse, Jordan Coward, Matchi Makwa, Trickster of Liberty, Father Mother—involve blatant allusions or symbolism and allow the reader a playful entrance into the text. "The name," Vizenor says, "has its own invitation" (Interview).

Another stylistic device Vizenor employs to invite response is what Anderson calls "the grammar of radical particularity." In this strategy, the writer verbally "isolates the ironic or symbolic or evocative image," "shows" but doesn't "tell" his message.[11] As readers, we receive cues meant to arouse our own capabilities of reflection and analysis.

In a scene from *Griever*, for example, Vizenor describes in elaborate and vivid detail the butchering of chickens in a street market. This excerpt from one long, descriptive paragraph almost clinically presents the particulars of the scene: "With one hand the cutthroat turned the chicken upside down; he laced his fingers around the neck, leg, and one wing of the hen, and with his other hand he whished a stained blade beneath the neck feathers. Dark blood splashed in a metal basin on the wooden counter. Blue flies circled the blood soaked feathers. The bird blinked once, twice, three times, wild near the end" (35). But Vizenor refrains from analyzing the action. Although he presents the particulars, he provides no generalizations about meaning.

In a new paragraph, he follows the graphic description with a single bland statement about the vendor's action after completing his gory tasks: "Cutthroat drank warm chicken blood" (35). Though obviously intending to reveal something about Cutthroat's callous character and his indifference to the fate of other creatures, Vizenor leaves to the reader the job of arriving at those conclusions.

Vizenor's rhetoric of gaps often proceeds in this fashion. By giving elaborate or exaggerated attention in the text to one element or one form of writing, he creates an awareness of, and thereby alludes to, another absent element or form. Here the stark details advertise the absence of commentary. Thus, behind Vizenor's use of lengthy detailed description and his use of short, often flat, one-sentence paragraphs stand similar intentions, operates a similar dynamic. Both of these kinds of writing prove themselves to be minimalistic statements carrying heavy implications.

Vizenor self-consciously uses both techniques, often playing them off one another for effect as in the scene from *Griever*. "I'll understate," he says, "and then some description is very detailed. I do that sometimes for contrast" (Interview). Actions and gestures in particular suit the vehicle of radical particularity because they make their own statement. In describing a character, Vizenor often centers on "a tick or gesture to reveal the truth of it" and employs detailed description in scenes where he feels "the action carries it" (Interview). But he distinguishes between the brand of detailed description that exercises a kind of restraint and the brand of description that works to possess, capture, or pin down everything in words. People who write with the latter intention only succeed in "obliterating" the object of their description: "They steal it with words," he says. "They have to know the latin word for the name of the leaf. In so doing, they finish it off" (Interview).

Vizenor prefers to proceed by suggestion, without bluntly categorizing or evaluating. "Usually, the words which carry the most value," he claims, "are lucid, elliptical, but you don't really state it. . . . The reader finishes it" (Interview). By this restraint the reader's own imaginative powers are liberated. Wolfgang Iser has commented on the relationship between indeterminacy or what we are calling a rhetoric of gaps and the opportunity for reader response:

> With a literary text we can only picture things which are not there; the written part of the text gives us the knowledge, but it is the unwritten part that gives us the opportunity to picture things; indeed without the elements of indeterminacy, the gaps in the texts, we should not be able to use our imagination. . . . The moment these possibilities are narrowed down to one complete and immutable picture, the imagination is put out of action.[12]

Frequently what remains unwritten in Vizenor's work is the very point he hopes to make. He provides the means to arrive at a conclusion, but refrains from bluntly stating that conclusion, leaving the discovery of meaning to the reader. For example, he often employs unusual juxtapositions of content, sometimes of contradictory elements or ideas, to compel his audience to ponder the connections or relationships for themselves. Another type of radical particularity, these juxtapositions may involve a few lines of text played off against the preceding lines, or an entire story placed within the context of another through juxtaposition. As the complexity of the intersecting ideas or actions increases, so does the degree of indeterminacy.

"The Shaman and Terminal Creeds," a chapter in *The People Named the Chippewa*, for example, illustrates a fairly complex type of juxtaposition (139–53). This chapter consists of one section that gives information and tells stories about tribal shamans and healers; one section that recounts the burial of John Ka Ka Geesick, who is identified as a tribal shaman; and a third section, which tells the story of Cora Katherine Sheppo, who professed to following "traditional Indian religion" but murdered her grandson because her beliefs told her he had been "spawned by the devil." The three sections obviously intersect around the general topic of shamanism, but more significantly, the first sections provide the stabilizing context needed for evaluating or dealing with the horrendous wrenching of tradition depicted in the Sheppo story. By giving the Sheppo story alongside that of the 124-year-old shaman Ka Ka Geesick and alongside a tradition dating back before white contact, Vizenor also gives the reader the tools to put the Sheppo tragedy in perspective. It emerges, then, not as a symptom of a dangerous religion, but as the story of a warped individual interpretation of that religion. When asked about his strategy, Vizenor says he used a "narrative approach to put it [the Sheppo incident] into a context critically" (Interview).

Vizenor's immersion of events, ideas, and characters in a critical context that he believes will illuminate them has become a trademark of his style. Sometimes factual, sometimes fictional, sometimes both together, scenes and quotations fill Vizenor's work as he juxtaposes the words or ideas of one writer or theorist against those of another, letting the context itself support, incriminate, or interrogate the ideas presented. *Manifest Manners* may be the best example of this technique, containing as it does innumerable instances of Vizenor's refusal to verbalize his interpretation or to offer commentary. His statements about Native American authors and literature, for instance, describe various works and eras, often letting their textual proximity to one another provide a mutual context for evaluation.

In one section he offers descriptive passages about Paula Gunn Allen's work in *The Sacred Hoop* and *Grandmothers of the Light: A Medicine Woman's Sourcebook* and refers to her as "the most honored postindian warrior of simulations in literature" (21). Next he reports her accounts of channeling by means of a crystal skull, taking quotations from her own writing; juxtaposes those accounts with comments from Mark Jones's *Fake: The Art of Deception* on the conflicting stories about the origin of the skull; and then suggests a connection between Allen's Crystal Woman and the responses aroused by Lynn Andrews's fictional accounts of the medicine woman Agnes Whistling Elk. Vizenor attacks Andrews's "racialism" and calls her "the headmost simulator of manifest manners and ersatz spiritualism in the literature of dominance" (23). Although he never straightforwardly criticizes Allen, the context in which he places her work issues an indictment.

Griever: Allegory and the Indeterminacy of Baroque

Vizenor's practice of creating context by means of juxtaposition becomes a tool of allegory in *Griever*. The novel is the tale of the escapades and entanglements of a mixedblood trickster from White Earth Reservation who, when he travels to communist China as an exchange teacher, criticizes and sabotages the country's political strictures. An episode involving a Peking nightingale offers a satiric perspective of the larger action of the novel and, beyond that, of human action in general (32–33).

The nightingale tale focuses on liberation, as do many of the other individual incidents in the book and as does the book in toto. Specifically, Vizenor tells the story of Griever's attempt to free a caged nightingale and of the bird's fear and ultimate return to her cage. Vizenor's description of the action—"The babbler flew back to her secure keep in the dead tree" (33)—by inclusion of the word "dead," implies a negative judgment of the bird's action, as does the warning delivered by Griever: "When a bird gets too big, it breaks the cage" (33). With the more expansive action of the novel involving Griever's attempts to liberate the Chinese people both mentally and physically from bureaucratic controls, readers can assume an implicit connection between the two stories. Vizenor provides a subtle clue that reinforces this connection. Just as Griever notes early in the novel that the Chinese built oversized facilities for the Americans because they "must have imagined we were huge barbarians" (16), in the nightingale scene he likewise imagines that the bird sees him as oversized, as "the barbarian" (32), and as "the monster" (33). By thus linking the reactions of the nightingale with those of the Chinese, he implies that the nightingale story is meant to illuminate the general plot of the novel. This allegorical episode works to spotlight the resistance to liberation exhibited by many of the novel's characters and to liken their responses to the bird's fear of the unknown.[13]

Throughout the novel Vizenor also draws both visual and social parallels between the Chinese and tribal people—linking the tribal trickster and the monkey king (34), noting similarities between one old Chinese woman and his own grandmother (41–42), and mentioning the *shibajie*, fried twists of dough that call to mind tribal fry bread (28). The lessons of liberation, by extension, thus become universal. The story of the nightingale has far-reaching implications as allegory, illuminating the satiric intentions of the book.

In addition to employing allegory, simple inferences, and directed allusions, *Griever* also includes a fine example of the more complex and less reducible kinds of ambiguity in Vizenor's work, an indeterminacy like that Umberto Eco compares to the Baroque form. In "The Poetics of the Open Work" Eco notes that to some degree all art requires response and is therefore "open"; but he makes an important distinction between works that "never allow the reader to move outside the strict control of the author" and those that make "a deliberate move to 'open' the work to the free response of the addressee." The two categories of works, he claims, also involve "different visions of the world." The controlled response reflects "an ordered cosmos, a hierarchy of essences and laws which poetic discourse can clarify at several levels, but which each individual must understand in the only possible way, the one determined by the creative logos." The contemporary open work, which frees the reader from the control of the author, instead reflects "a world in a fluid state which requires corresponding creativity on his [humankind's] part." Eco compares the liberation of the latter kind of text to the dynamic quality of the baroque form, which, he says, "never allows a privileged, definitive, frontal view; rather it induces the spectator to shift his position continuously in order to see the work in constantly new aspects, as if it were in a state of perpetual transformation."[14]

Vizenor's writing has clearly developed in the direction of invoking free responses on the part of his readers. In his effort to ultimately liberate the reader from the written, he often creates a text of self-generating ambiguity that mirrors the irreducible plurality of authentic experience. One example that convincingly illustrates this baroque quality and Vizenor's power to arouse the dormant imaginative energies of his readers involves his use of the word "luminous" and the quality of luminosity in *Griever*. The word on a denotative level means "emitting light, especially self-generated light."[15] Vizenor employs the adjective at various times throughout the book, allowing the context to imply connotations that build until luminosity becomes an evaluative quality in the minds of the reader, signifying an indwelling, spiritual power or near-visionary status. An analysis of the gradual formation of ideas about the signification of "luminous" shows the active reading process at work—what Wolfgang Iser calls the making and breaking of literary "gestalts" or configurative meanings of the text. But the mirage of ultimate or definitive meaning in the text (as in life) is always in infinite regress. The work remains open because it invites the reader, in the words of the Belgian composer Henri Pousseur, into "the midst of an inexhaustible network of relationships."[16]

The complicated network of relationships surrounding luminosity in Vizenor's novel begins with the first appearance of the word "luminous" when Griever describes a dream he had: "we were at a glacial stream with luminous animals and birds" (14). Subsequent descriptions of dreams include additional mentions of luminosity: "a luminous man" (16) and "luminous stones" (17). Reader conjecture that luminosity is linked to dream experience is soon confirmed: "Griever lectures, with his hands in constant motion, that we are 'luminous when we dream.' Imagination, he believes, 'is what burns in humans. We are not freeze-dried methodologies. We remember dreams, never data, at the wild end'" (32). In addition to linking luminosity and dreams, Griever's explanation makes another connection when it links by juxtaposition luminosity and dreams with "imagination." Imagination seems to have visual presence as luminosity—it "burns in humans."

The parade of associations lengthens yet further when luminosity is likewise linked with shamans and transformation. Again describing a dream experience, Griever says he is drawn to a "bright light which seemed at first like a star" but which is actually "a fire on the balcony of the apartment, a fire bear, a shaman" (16). The movement from bright light (luminosity) to star to fire to fire bear to shaman might parallel the movement of Griever's personal imaginative power, in which he moves from viewing the presence in merely conventional and physical terms to apprehending its spiritual quality or essence. It might also imply the imaginative power of transformation. This notion of transformation is reinforced later in the passage when Griever says, "I reached for the bear, to be the bear, the fire" (16). In any case, a link has been forged between luminosity or light, imagination, dreams, and some sort of spiritual power.

We see luminosity and the power of transformation linked again in the climax of a series of encounters between Griever and a mute child. In China, which Griever calls "a one-child nation" because of harsh population control dictums, he meets the child whose "eyes held the pale light" (58), and who had "a pale blue light around his head and chest" (59). Contact between the two culminates in Griever's transformational experience. He says, "When the light passed through me, I became the child, we became each other" (59). The encounters and the transformation take on further significance when Griever learns that the mute child is "Yaba Gezi, the mute pigeon. . . . Child from old stories" whom "no one sees" (60–61). Taken together, these passages insinuate that Griever's experience is otherworldly and that only through the grace of some unusual power or transcendence could he have known the child's presence.

The text continues to offer clues linking luminosity with power and persons of power. For instance, it associates luminosity with the traditional Chinese figure of the Monkey King, whom Vizenor portrays as paralleling the tribal trickster, and with Shitou, the stone shaman, whose power is admired by Griever. The quality of luminosity is also linked with Hua Lian, an old blind woman with a "sixth sense" (112) who carries a horsehair duster, which, we are told, is "a token of refinement" in the classic Chinese opera, something carried by "exalted persons" (120). And luminosity figures into Griever's story of the vivification of carved animal figures: "We carved animals and bird figures from luminous punk . . . and then we became luminous bears and wheeled through the trees and liberated the animals and birds" (93). Here again, luminosity appears to be the physical manifestation or outward sign of inner power.

In the final scene, which deals with luminosity as the herald of power, the indwelling power is shown to defy conventional boundaries of life and death. Griever and his companions are drawn to a pond in which the "water holds a blue light" (224). There they discover that the light emanates from the bones of murdered children. Even here, Vizenor gives no straightforward or definitive statement about the manifestation of the light, but leaves the way open for interpretation, saying only, "The blue light was a court to a secret place, a shared dream that carries voices over a cataract" (225). Put in the context of the knowledge the reader has amassed throughout the story, the blue light would seem to stem from the spiritual power of those physically dead, and to serve as messenger. This reading is reinforced by one of the final lines in the text, "You can't wrap fire in paper" (235). The power of the dead children still burns, destroying the physical "wrap" or boundary of death, and signals to the living for discovery. The blue light is "a court," a beacon marking the entryway to a much larger realm or reality, a place as yet secret and unbreachable. But the radiating light is the marker for the place of communion or communication with that other realm.

Only by actively working with the clues provided can the reader begin to unravel the significance of luminosity in the text. More significantly, each discovery of a relationship between passages that seem to point to the possibility of defining meaning is further altered by another discovery. Ultimately, the suggestive nature of Vizenor's writing in *Griever* not only necessitates involvement within the text itself but, through allusion, also opens possibilities for interaction with ideas outside the text proper, most obviously with other works of Vizenor's that likewise involve luminosity or employ the phrase. In the stories from *Landfill Meditation*, for example, auras and luminosity again appear (see especially "Luminous Thighs," 180–201). Beginning with the early "reexpressions" of tribal songs in *anishinabe nagamon* and continuing throughout his works, Vizenor includes frequent reference to the *migis* shell, a sacred white seashell used in *midéwiwin* ceremonies and described as reflecting light.[17] Vizenor's repeated use of the term "luminosity" in a Chinese setting might also signal a satiric critique of the common racial stereotyping of Asian women, since, as Shirley Geok-lin Lim has pointed out, "luminous" is one of the trite words characteristically used to describe the Chinese feminine ideal.[18]

Finally, and perhaps most significantly for this text and for the Vizenor canon, Vizenor's use of the term "luminous" or the quality of luminosity may imply a connection to Ernest Fenollosa's description in *The Chinese Written Character* of a phrase "charged, and luminous from within"; or to Ezra Pound's notion of "luminous details."[19] Since Fenollosa and Pound both are describing a method of poetic expression, Vizenor's allusion has multiple implications about the inherent power of words, particularly in a work such as *Griever*, which has much to do with language. Many scenes from the novel take on additional significance. For instance, Hua Lian, who, as I previously noted, is associated with luminosity, engages in various conversations with Griever about language and the power or lack of power of words. *Griever* might then be read as metafiction; and the "network of relationships" further expands.

In this example of self-generating ambiguity, Vizenor refrains from exercising ultimate control over the readers' responses. Apparently *what* they imagine is of less significance to him than *that* they imagine. If they imagine, then his words have brought them liberation from the text. "Imagination," he says, "is so rich there shouldn't be any story that's limited by the text. And even a published text is not a limited story. The healthiest way to read is to look upon this as a possibility of the story."[20]

Educating the Audience: A Rhetoric of Process

Yet Vizenor obviously writes to express ideas as well as to induce thinking or imagining. He frequently speaks of his desire to develop a "dialogue" with the reader, which presupposes Vizenor's stating his ideas in the exchange. So how can he express his beliefs or ideas without editorializing in the way that makes writing static? How can he comment without writing commentary? How can he fulfill his desire to "educate an audience so [he] can write for them" (Interview)? Vizenor speaks of his dilemma: "I face an unusual problem here. I'm working in a kind of literature—if you like we can call it trickster fiction—that doesn't exist. . . . The problem for me is that I have to educate an audience to understand what I am doing so I can do it" (Interview).

Such an ambition seems to place Vizenor in a catch-22 situation. If we acknowledge that at times in his writing Vizenor does want to guide the reader through a thought process or he does want us to read in a certain way or arrive at specific conclusions, how can he accomplish this without violating his own principles of open text? Eagleton indicates an answer: "Literary texts are 'code-productive' and 'code-transgressive' as well as 'code-conforming': they may teach us new ways of reading, not just reinforce the ones with which we come equipped."[21]

What Eagleton suggests, Vizenor has also discovered: through his method of writing he can teach a method of reading or thinking. To a certain degree, each of the kinds of ambiguity employed by Vizenor in his writing works toward this end. But specific styles of ambiguity allow him to more readily present his own ideas or guide the readers' thinking while still maintaining their role as participants. Employing what Anderson calls a rhetoric of process, he teaches his readers a new way of thinking or writing by involving them in the act of thinking or writing as it happens. He displays the process itself; his writing becomes the process.

In the autobiographical "I Know What You Mean, Erdupps MacChurbbs," for example, he playfully introduces the reader to a new way of apprehending reality by tracing his own gradual awakening to or initiation into awareness of this enlightened view (77–111). The character MacChurbbs, not Vizenor, plays the role of teacher, thus absolving Vizenor from didacticism. Vizenor relates his own imperfect path to understanding the concepts MacChurbbs teaches him, thereby establishing a rapport with the equally fallible reader. This rhetoric of process also gives him the tool he needs to confront or undermine whatever errors in the reader's thinking he might anticipate. But because his position as novice puts him on a par with his readers, he can achieve his purpose by portraying MacChurbbs admonishing him. The reader learns his lessons painlessly through Vizenor's autobiographical rendition of himself. Vizenor avoids the role of educator by performing as storyteller: he merely tells us the story of his own education. His tale enacts mediation between us and our own ignorance and makes the learning a shared or communal experience.

Vizenor's autobiographical account accomplishes its didactic intentions in various ways. At times we get our lessons straight through the voice of MacChurbbs, as when he counsels Vizenor: "free yourself from the customs of civilized measurement. . . . We are so big and so little at the same time. You have learned only one way to measure the world" (96). At other times Vizenor becomes our voice, asking the questions we might ask, and we learn the answers with him:

> "There are so many of you," I said, trying to blink away the many images of his stern face. "Which one of you is real?"
> "The one you see."
> "But I see you everywhere."
> "Then you must be everywhere to see me everywhere." (97–98)

In still other instances, we learn vicariously through Vizenor's errors. During a conversation MacChurbbs warns, "I will disappear when you think about what you will be in the future, but are not now, by the measures of the past" (97). But when MacChurbbs asks Vizenor who he will be, Vizenor answers, "A famous writer," and MacChurbbs "snaps into dust before his eyes" (97). Vizenor writes, "I had been tricked by my own thoughts and felt stupid" (97). Vizenor errs; we learn. He relates the faulty thinking of his persona so that we may recognize the folly of our own erroneous thinking. He saves us from mistakes by making them for us—in story. He teaches us how to think by learning how himself—in story.

Vizenor frequently takes advantage of the "code-productive" possibilities of a rhetoric of process. By cuing his reader through questions, for example, he directs the audience's attention to issues that need examination, demonstrates something about the techniques and positive results of inquiry, and provides the reader with practice in formulating questions. In other instances, Vizenor offers variable (usually contradictory) points of view through two or more characters. Representing a dramatization of a debate on an issue can aid him in making his point and undercutting opposing points of view. Or in instances where Vizenor's primary goal is to teach the validity of multiple points of view, his dramatization helps to broaden the reader's perspective.

In the prologue to *The Trickster of Liberty*, in order to introduce his reader to some of the issues surrounding the trickster figure, Vizenor employs two of these tactics: cue questioning and the presentation of debate through dialogue (ix–xvii). In this instance he hopes to eliminate fallacious theories from the minds of his readers by exposing the weaknesses of those theories. The following conversation between Sergeant Alexina Hobraiser and an anthropologist illustrates his use of oppositional dialogue:

> "*Alexina*, why did you disown your given name?" asked the anthropologist. "Worried about being identified as a woman?" He smiled and opened his narrow hands over a notebook.
> The sergeant turned to the window, pretended not to listen. "The trickster is never in a name, tribal tricksters are in our consciousness."

"You mean illusions," he countered.

"The sunrise is an illusion, the ocean is a trickster, and both are healers," said the sergeant. "Cesar Vallejo wrote that consciousness is that 'historical relationship between boat and water.' Our trickster is imagination, the humor between our minds and bodies, boats and water." (xii)

"Vocation of Violator": Transgressing Old Codes

Another way that Vizenor uses his writing to teach us new ways of thinking is to deliberately violate the accepted rules, both the rules of grammar and the rules of society. His "vocation as violator,"[22] his undermining of conventional codes, is one more tool of liberation.

Code transgression in Vizenor's style of writing becomes a message in itself. For example, he often employs an aggregative style. By stacking visual images or running together ideas, he simultaneously reflects a process of thinking, teaches a way of understanding the world, and makes a revolutionary statement. Vizenor explains this process: "The first reference to action or description, is usually the obvious or categorical one. Then, I think, I break it down by additions or expand on it. I make it broader, expand the possibilities of it or even contradict it, which, I believe, expands it. . . . So that the image, the event, the action, or description is broader than what is grammatically allowed."[23]

Vizenor's aggregative style is at work in the following statement: "The University of California at Berkeley is a material reservation, a magic snapshot separation from the sacred, and, at the same time, this fantastic campus is a sweet place in the imagination, like an elevator filled with androgynous talebearers moving to the thirteenth floor in search of new spiritual teachers" ("Word Cinemas," 389). Although his description begins with a definite, evaluative statement, the sentence, taken whole, affects us as an enumeration of qualities rather than ultimate evaluation. Vizenor achieves this change of feeling through his use of visual images, his deliberately difficult prose, and his contradiction of his own original statement. The sentence functions as if Vizenor were in the act of formulating his own diverse thoughts about the campus, remembering his varied experiences and reactions. So although he begins with a definitive statement, ultimately he works against definition. The last phrase, for example, completely negates the possibility of narrow evaluation by moving the attempt at definition to the realm of the visual image. By asking readers to envision "an elevator filled with androgynous talebearers moving to the thirteenth floor in search of new spiritual leaders," Vizenor invokes their imagination. The provocative phrase is filled with dormant possibilities waiting to be envisioned. The sentence, by reflecting Vizenor's own thinking process, has taken the reader from the simplified judgmental perspective of the opening phrase to a perspective that celebrates the inherent multiplicity of experience. The style of the sentence itself both teaches plurality and takes a stand against the grammar of definition.

Other elements of Vizenor's rule-breaking style likewise become not only the means of transmitting a message but also the message itself. For example, Vizenor's habit of coining words makes a statement about his feeling regarding the inadequacy of written language. Since words that can completely express what he intends do not exist, he can, by creating his own words or phrases, endow them with whatever implications of action or meaning conventional words lack. Vizenor's neologisms include "holotrope," "holosexual," "socioacupuncture," "word cinema," "visual dreamscape," "wordarrows," "dead voices," "landfill meditation," "natural tilt," "manifest manners," and many others. Sometimes Vizenor explains his new word or the new use of an old word. At other times, he requires readers to put together the meaning for themselves based on the context and implications of repeated uses. But even when offering a definition, he remains cautious about creating too much confinement with language. For example, he explains "holotrope" as "the whole figuration; an unbroken interior landscape that beams various points of view in temporal reveries" (*Trickster of Liberty*, x). His "definition" remains ambiguous. Such practices emphatically express Vizenor's belief that words should open up, not close down, possibilities.

We see a similar attempt to expand possibilities in Vizenor's frequent pronoun and identity switching, which implies androgyny or transformation. Almost signaturelike in style, this form of indeterminacy again transgresses accepted grammatical rules and the vision of the world reflected by those rules. In *Griever*, for example, Vizenor changes the pronoun reference for Griever when he describes a sexual encounter the trickster/mind monkey has with a character named Sugar Dee.[24] Until this point, Griever has been referred to as "he." Here however, we are told, "He became a woman," and the pronouns become "she" and "her" (55). In another scene in the novel, Griever takes on a series of identities, including the identities of actual Chinese political prisoners, thus emphasizing both transformation and the deep kinship that links human experience. In succession, Griever identifies himself to authorities as "White Earth Monkey King," "Wei Jingsheng," "Sun Wukong," and "Fu Yeuhua," thereby forging a symbolic link between himself as trickster and other revolutionaries, and between the fictional, mythical, and historical realities (151–52).

In the novel *Bearheart* we find many examples of the kind of suggestive language that more strongly emphasizes the tribal ideas of transformation or identification with natural beings and elements. For instance: "The cedar became his source of personal power. He dreamed trees and leaned in the wind with the cedar. In the winter he stood outside alone drawing his arms around his trunk under snow. He spoke with the trees. He became the cedar wood" (3). Vizenor's code-transgressive texts succeed in opening up the possibility for new ways of thinking and understanding the world.

One of the frequently criticized aspects of Vizenor's writing stems from his blatant violation of the "polite" limits of language, his relentless transgression of verbal mores regarding the graphic description of sex and violence. *Bearheart*, for example, has aroused vehement reactions from the time it was circulated as a manuscript all the way through its second publication: the manuscript was repeatedly "lost," typesetters were so upset by the book that businesses rejected the job, students protested its use in classrooms, and reviewers and scholars have blasted Vizenor for its graphic quality.[25] Kenneth Lincoln, for example, has characterized *Bearheart* as "carnage, cocksucking, and throwaway dirty talk," and after discussing both *Bearheart* and *The Trickster of Liberty*, he asks, "So why all this funny talk, fellatio, cryptic comedy, and mindless violence?"[26]

Over the years, Vizenor has offered several answers to Lincoln's question. He attempts to break down what he sees as civilized illusions with uncivilized language, to state what good taste dictates should not be stated, partly to force a recognition of our own most basic energies. In this aspect, Vizenor's writing can be likened to that of T. S. Eliot, who also sought potent sensory language that would connect people to such universal experiences as birth and death. Terry Eagleton describes Eliot's goals this way: "He must select words with 'a network of tentacular roots reaching down to the deepest terrors and desires,' suggestively enigmatic images which would penetrate to those 'primitive' levels at which all men and women experienced alike. Perhaps the organic society lived on after all, though only in the collective unconscious; perhaps there were deep symbols and rhythms in the psyche, archetypes immutable throughout history, which poetry might touch and revive."[27]

Bearheart contains many examples of Vizenor's similar attempts to reach beneath the civilized surface of language and awaken an awareness of life's elemental forces. The book deals with a nationwide oil shortage and the resulting upheaval of social structures and other measures that previously defined civilized life. It depicts the cross-country journey of a group of "pilgrims" and their struggle for physical and spiritual survival, their attempts to satisfy their most basic needs and raw urges. Among the many jarring scenes in the text are descriptions of the various physical deformities of the characters who inhabit the novel, the torture unleashed on tribal people when the gasoline runs out, the pilgrims' stay with a group of former priests who have been forced to eat the flesh of their own dead to survive, and the strange and sometimes violent sexual encounters at the Scapehouse on Red Cedar Reservation. By destroying the buffer zone of organized society in the novel, Vizenor shows human beings grappling with the basics of life and death, good and evil, and we are obliged to see the characters' actions in the light of altered circumstances. Indeed, one of Vizenor's attempts throughout the book is to force readers to reconsider their own "terminal beliefs," the inflexible ground rules that color the way we look at the world. By unmasking all rules, revealing their true nature as fragile social constructs, he encourages readers to relinquish their moral props and to reevaluate things on their own merits.

Vizenor's technique also proceeds from a revolutionary purpose. Seeing the way we buy and sell violence as passive entertainment in our society, he writes to disrupt that pattern, which, he believes, sustains our distance from the actual ills of society. In Brechtian fashion, he tries to unsettle the reader with his writing, to deny the reader satisfaction in the text in order to force us to arrive at resolution outside the text. Vizenor talks about these tactics in *Bearheart*: "I am not approaching any bourgeois reader with comfort. If I have an objective . . . I would, with this book, choose to confront the bourgeois expectation of the American audience. . . . I think literature ought to engage, upset, confront, disrupt, liberate people from their reading habits which reflect their worldview and compulsive behavior, inhibitions, . . . religion, whatever, as the great life, as civilization. They ought to be tested, disrupted, and confronted" (Interview). *Bearheart* violates our social and moral taboos with brazen depictions of sex and violence in a deliberate effort, Vizenor tells us, to arouse reader response.

Louis Owens suggests that the objections to *Bearheart* may actually stem from unacknowledged resistance to Vizenor's disruption of the romantic and static definition of "Indianness." The novel, which contains "transsexual Indians" and Indians capable of "cowardice as well as courage," capable of "greed and lust as well as generosity and stoicism," is, Owens claims, an "essential corrective to all false and externally imposed definitions of 'Indian.'"[28] These transgressions of comfortable stereotypes typify Vizenor's vocation as violator.

The Trickster of Liberty is another perfect example of his inversion of romantic expectations. Populated by urban Indians, mixedbloods, and cross-cultural tricksters, the novel relates the zany stories of three generations of White Earth tricksters and their extended family. Accounts of characters such as Mouse Proof Martin, who takes his name from the words on an organ and collects lost and autographed shoes, violate expectations about sacred naming ceremonies and traditional lifestyles.

The Trickster of Liberty also exemplifies another code-transgressive quality of Vizenor's writing: its violation of conventional form and genre classifications. Because, as Lincoln explains, "the world of experience does not lie flat on a page, or always justify its margins, or behave only according to conventional rhyme and meter," Vizenor has come to rely for part of his effect on antiform as the more successful conveyer of experience.[29] Though purported to be a novel, *The Trickster of Liberty* is an extremely episodic work made up of seven sections, each containing two or three stories devoted primarily to the exploits of one of the tribal tricksters. It relies for part of its form on a genealogical structure, tracing the offspring and family relationships of Novena Mae Ironmoccasin and Luster Browne. It resists a conventional plot line, repeating characters and stories from previous works, adding to them new episodes of confrontation, and centering them all loosely around its theme of trickster liberation.

This violation of form and genre typifies all of Vizenor's work, as the many discussions from previous chapters have also shown. One reviewer, for example, commented on *Manifest Manners*, saying, "Vizenor exhibits his imaginative literary and cultural criticism and refuses to conform to the limits of the essay genre. In some cases the essays may be better thought of as critical poems, engulfing the reader in a swirl of images and linguistic play." Another says of *Dead Voices*, "There is a price to be paid . . . for the use of multiple, shape-shifted narrators: the novel loses its narrative impulse and fictive appeal and reads more like a moral allegory."[30] Vizenor's violations, whether stylistic or moralistic, all wend their way toward liberation from old codes.

Language Falls Apart: Mythic Metaphor

Vizenor's use of metaphor likewise becomes a kind of liberation, a strategy of indeterminacy. Ironically, he employs language in order to move beyond it, to escape from language into the realm of experience. Behind his understanding of the particular ambiguity of dynamic metaphor lies rather sophisticated literary theory.

Vizenor discusses the power of metaphor and his own uses of it in the preface to *Earthdivers*, linking his ideas to Karsten Harries's "Metaphor and Transcendence" and Donald Davidson's "What Metaphors Mean" (xvi–xvii). He uses a quotation from Davidson to explain the dialogic quality of metaphor: "Understanding a metaphor is as much a creative endeavor as making a metaphor, and as little guided by rules. . . . We can explain metaphor as a kind of ambiguity; in the context of a metaphor, certain words have either a new or an original meaning, and the force of the metaphor depends on our uncertainty as we waver between the two meanings" (xvi–xvii). Quoting from Harries, he prepares to claim yet more about the inherent power of metaphor. Keenly aware of society's increasing indifference to language, Vizenor seizes upon metaphor as a means to counteract that complacency. As Harries explains: "We understand things without having made them our own. The adequacy of words is taken for granted, their origin forgotten. There are moments when the inadequacy of our language seizes us, when language seems to fall apart and falling apart opens us to what transcends it. . . . As language falls apart, contact with being is reestablished" (xvi).

Vizenor thus uses metaphor to create those moments "when language falls apart and falling apart opens us to what transcends it." His characters "speak unusual languages" and sometimes "talk backwards" in order to push language to the point of disintegration and thus to transcendence and contact with the nonverbal essence of reality. For example, in describing his métis earthdiver characters, he explains that they "speak a new language, their experiences and dreams are metaphors" (xvi). This understanding of metaphor has obvious similarities to Vizenor's philosophy of haiku and to his understanding of myth, in that all three—metaphor, haiku, and myth—operate within one realm of reality, the physical, with the express intention of providing us access to another, primal or spiritual, realm.

Joseph Campbell's intriguing discussion of this process in *The Inner Reaches of Outer Space: Metaphor as Myth and as Religion* offers helpful insights on the theory of metaphor. Basically, Campbell claims that humankind has an intuitive connection with and knowledge of the whole of nature, but that this intuition generally remains dormant while people give their attention not to the transcendent reality but to their ethnocentric existence. The goal of artists, like that of mystics, is to achieve a state of epiphany, a moment of knowing the essence of life. Using various tools, including mythology and metaphor, artists hope to make the path to epiphany available to every person. They employ the recognizable ethnocentric imagery but make these images "transparent to transcendence," implying or connoting the primal, intuitive experiences of truth. The way of proper art, according to Campbell, "is of recognizing through the metaphors an epiphany beyond words" wherein "the imagery is necessarily physical and thus apparently of outer space" while "the inherent connotation is always, however, psychological and metaphysical, which is to say, of inner space."[31] But to understand metaphor, Campbell explains, the reader must get beyond the words themselves, to see them as mere symbols.

Clearly, Vizenor's intentions are similar. Words to him must always be "dissolved" into meaning. His writing self-consciously strives to make language fall apart, causing the reader to activate the metaphor. In his frequent use of deliberately difficult language, for example, lurks Vizenor's hidden aim: to compel the reader to ponder the text as language and thereby become more ready to dismiss the words themselves in favor of the experiences they invoke.

Elaine Jahner's discussion of Vizenor's use of metaphor helps clarify the particular kinds of experiences he hopes to invoke. She claims that the literal language of metaphor is only a means of using the physical present to recover an understanding known in the past: "All human knowledge is partial and always metaphorical, in the sense that one term of the metaphor derives from direct observation, the other from remembered observation—from tradition. . . . While partial, and in some sense, indirect, learning gained through the process of metaphor is valid even though metaphor is never reducible to the literal."[32]

The aforementioned observations about metaphor (particularly those theories of Campbell and Jahner), taken together with the philosophy and intentions Vizenor expresses in his work, tend to construct a three-level metaphor or tripartite referential system. Vizenor enlists things in contemporary life in order to allude to the tribal beliefs. Yet he invokes tribal tradition not as an end in itself, but as a metaphorical representation of the primal connections. For example, he uses the "metaphor of the Métis earthdiver" to recall the "traditional earthdiver creation myth" (*Earthdiver*, x).[33] The tribal myth itself, he claims, "centers on the return to the earth," a return to primal connections and to the intuitive knowledge of creation (x–xi).

The ultimate goal, then, of Vizenor's metaphors is to bridge the boundaries of conventional references and conventional understanding and arrive at another arena of meaning. He says of this attempt, specifically as it pertains to the earthdiver metaphor, "The mixedblood earthdiver is a metaphor in a timeless tribal drama. Turtle island is an imaginative place; not a formula, but a metaphor which connects dreams to the earth" (xv–xvi). What Vizenor hopes to arrive at through his metaphors Jahner calls "the sacred"; Campbell would call it "epiphany." Vizenor puts it yet another way: he attests that his persona in *Earthdivers* "captures some light from the written images of his experiences" (xx). A knowledge of the sacred, an epiphany, capturing some light—each of the phrases points not to the words themselves but to what lies beyond them. This referential quality is both the ambiguity and the power of Vizenor's metaphors.

Dead Voices: A Network of Critical Subtexts

Metaphor is one means by which Vizenor's work seeks an expansion beyond the literary page into the realm of experience. Another is intertextual dialogue. By weaving his own works into a web of active connections, Vizenor invests them with a network of critical subtexts that add richness and vitality to the written text. *Dead Voices: Natural Agonies in the New World*, for example, comes alive, is reanimated (as all Vizenor's works are) through the agency of a reader, a reader thrown into dialogue first with the novel and then, by virtue of the allusiveness of the text, with an entire network of interconnected stories and ideas. The book, which in principle privileges the ear over the eye, invites the reader to become a listener and a speaker, a part of the living stories and ongoing conversations, the seeds of which are planted in the novel. Like the novel's shaman sprite Erdupps MacChurbbs, we are invited to "read books to hear voices on the page," voices that cannot be fully printed or bound neatly between the pages of any single book (131).

Dead Voices takes as epigraphs quotations from Samuel Beckett's *The Unnamable,* John G. Neihardt's *Black Elk Speaks,* and Maurice Blanchot's *The Writing of Disaster,* and the voices of these authors are among those we "hear on the page." The text, for example, echoes Beckett's "nothing to be done" and "I can't go on, I'll go on." It employs a twist on Black Elk's notion of shadow. These works, then, become a part of a large network of texts with which *Dead Voices* engages in dialogue. Readers overhear and participate in dialogues by virtue of their own familiarity with the subtexts. From a subtle rhythmic echo of Thomas Wolfe's

A Stone, a Leaf, a Door in a phrase such as "a bear, a bird, a stone," to the retelling of the Ojibway creation story, to the many echoes of Vizenor's own earlier works, the kinds of connections vary (25, 109).[34] Among the subtexts, three theoretical works invoked in the premises and the theories of the novel seem particularly significant: Daisetz Suzuki's *Zen and Japanese Culture*, Valentin Vološinov's *Marxism and the Philosophy of Language*, and Walter J. Ong's *Orality and Literacy*.

Vizenor's own involvement with haiku (discussed at length in Chapter 4) includes an acquaintance with Suzuki's work. Indeed, in his own discussions of haiku, he quotes from *Zen and Japanese Culture*. Among Suzuki's statements on Zen and haiku, the following characterizes his stance and how it informs Vizenor's work in *Dead Voices*: "The Zen masters have the saying, 'Examine the living words and not the dead ones.' The dead ones are those that no longer pass directly and concretely and intimately on to the experience. They are conceptualized, they are cut off from the living roots. They have ceased, then, to stir up my being from within, from itself."[35] Philosophical and verbal links abound between Suzuki and Vizenor's work, and the most basic premise for the novel aligns itself with Suzuki's statement: language must remain connected to experience or become "dead." In the rhetoric of *Dead Voices* Vizenor reiterates this message. For example, the narrator of the novel, Laundry, claims that Bagese, the storytelling trickster woman/bear, taught him to "see the real world in stories" and told him, "The secret . . . was . . . to see and hear the real stories behind the words . . . not the definitions of the words alone" (142, 7).

Vizenor depicts the detachment of language from experience, the conceptualization that Suzuki warns against, as the plague of modern culture. Universities are among his targets. He writes of the "dead voices of education" and the "wordies" who have lost contact with the living roots of language, who "hear nothing but dead voices at the university" (88, 132). Laundry, who essentially becomes Bagese's pupil, is a lecturer on tribal philosophies at the university, but the old woman tells him that "even the most honored lectures" are "dead voices" (7). Vizenor uses scenes at a child care center and a university laboratory to illustrate his claims. Describing the return of the children to their schoolroom, for instance, he writes that they were locked "back into their cages"

(94). In his critique of the university laboratory, his comments on the blonde biologist and the effect of her studies on the praying mantis can be understood by allusion to describe the relationship of anthropologists to native peoples: "We would exist the way she discovered and studied praying mantis. We were no longer the mantis of our stories in the city, we were laboratory mantis. Our stories would die at the end of their studies, and we would end in the dead voices of the wordies" (83).

Anthropologists and the educational system are but two of the many aspects of modern society Vizenor accuses of creating the dead voices of civilization. Yet the novel also suggests we can still reclaim our basic connections to the life of story and to the earth from which story comes. The primary action of the book demonstrates the possibility of connection through living words. Vizenor uses a "wanaki" game, his fictional adaptation of an Ojibway dish game, to illustrate imaginative connection. In the game, the player selects a tarotlike card, which bears a picture of a creature, such as a bear, beaver, flea, or trickster. Through imagination and meditation the player experiences that identity for a day and tells stories of the creature's adventures using the plural pronoun "we." The object of the game is the object of Vizenor's work: reconnection with life through imaginative story. Although *wanaki* means "a place of peace," the wanaki game becomes Vizenor's "war with loneliness and human separations from the natural world" (29).

The language of Vizenor's novel gives us other indications that words can indeed still connect us with being. One trickster crow, for example, is described as having "bounced out his stories for the children" (90). His words are action. In another passage Vizenor writes, "We heard the best glances in the poplar and birch" (87). Here and in clever reversals like "catch my ear" and "more than meets the ear," the author clearly emphasizes the oral. Understood in their dialogic relationship with Suzuki's work, however, these phrases carry additional signifi-cance. They can be seen to have as much to do with the reconnection of words with experiential reality. "Heard the best glances in the poplar and birch" is a startling image, one that we must enter to understand, just as we must enter haiku. We can move beyond the words to a moment of knowing the feeling of a tree that looks its story to you, to a fuller, less conceptualized experience of reality where senses are intermingled, not isolated. The unusual phrase is the pounding on the head that Bagese gives Laundry in the novel to liberate him from the dead voices, it is the physical reality thrust upon students of Zen when they are trapped in concepts, it is the moment of imbalance that liberates the reader from the text and demands active response.

Vološinov, like Suzuki and Vizenor, also distinguishes between dead and living words, characterizing "dead language" as that which "is permeated through and through with the false notion of passive understanding, the kind of understanding that excludes active response in advance and on principle." Clearly Vizenor's "dead voices" have much in common with Suzuki's "dead words" and Vološinov's "dead language." Much else in Vološinov's work also seems a part of Vizenor's subtextual dialogue in the novel. Vološinov speaks of the "dead, written, alien language," the "isolated, finished, monologic utterance," and contrasts them with "true understanding," which, he says, is "dialogic in nature." "Meaning," he claims, "is the effect of interaction between speaker and listener," since a listener is, after all, "not a mute, wordless creature that receives an utterance, but a human being full of inner words."[36]

Dead Voices both expresses and illustrates an understanding of language as dialogic relationship. The conversations of the novel extend, not only between Vizenor's text and the recognizable subtexts, but to the reader as well and to what Vološinov has called the reader's "inner words." Like Vološinov, Vizenor has acknowledged the existence of these inner words, calling them in previous works "words in the blood," writing of them in *Dead Voices* as an "inner sound in their stories" and "stories in the blood" (127, 88). Surviving the "dead voices," Vizenor makes clear through the action and dialogue of the novel, comes with remembering these "stories in the blood."

Another critical voice invoked in the novel, Ong's, also addresses the limitations and stultification of text and the conceptualization of words. His emphasis, though, is on the differences between oral and written, a central focus of Vizenor's in *Dead Voices*. Ong writes, for example, "The shift from oral to written speech is essentially a shift from sound to visual space," and "Sound resists reduction to an 'object' or an 'icon'—it is an on-going event."[37] Vizenor sets up an opposition between eye and ear in *Dead Voices* with the clear intention of breaking open the confined visual space of text. Placed in dialogue, *Dead Voices*, like sound, like the oral tradition, like story, becomes an "on-going event."

Within the novel itself, Vizenor illustrates the continuum of the storytelling tradition when he juxtaposes and interconnects the traditional Ojibway creation story with a new version:

> She had a new version of creation that turned the great flood into a sewer of anthropologists.
>
> When the very first trickster was up to his nose in the great flood he asked some animals to dive down and come back with a few bits of sand so she could start a new world. The beaver and others dove down and one of them came back with enough for the trickster to make a new world.
>
> Naanabozho told the new stories of creation in the city. "The last time we had to dive through shit shaped anthropologists to find the remains of the tribal world and create a new one," said the trickster. (109)

As the creation of story and the creation of our own world are aligned in the account, both are shown to be ongoing, and the dialogue Vizenor sets up and encourages through *Dead Voices* has finally to do with life, not just with literature. Story networks with experience, live voices speak to being.

In a playful revision of a magician's cant, we might claim that in *Dead Voices* the ear is quicker than the eye. To the degree that *Dead Voices* succeeds in achieving an active connection with the reader and with a network of critical subtexts, it is alive, quick, quicker than the text that caters merely to the eye, and not to the ear, the oral, as well. The magic of Vizenor's *Dead Voices* is the disappearance of the text from the page, the levitation of the words, which float between writer and reader, between concept and experience.

Revolution and a Literary Ghost Dance

The dialogic quality of Vizenor's style clearly harbors supraliterary intentions, seeking to connect with experience. The style itself also embodies revolutionary intentions, the same intentions as the rhetoric of his satire—to incite action, to undermine the existing social paradigm.

Vološinov has claimed a significant relationship between writing style and social structure. As James Thomas Zebroski notes, "Vološinov argues that style is a political act. . . . Style evokes and can help reproduce existing social-class relations." Vološinov identifies two basic styles of writing: the linear or monologic, associated with the ruling classes, and the dialogic or pictorial, associated with the under- or working classes. The first, in Zebroski's words, "draws hard, clearly demarcated boundaries" and "tends to move toward purity and unity." The second is "a mixture of popular and unofficial genres, full of voices of other people, full of reported speech"; it "infiltrates boundaries and blurs established genres," "tends to mix texts and their authority," and often results in "a hybrid language."[38]

As each of the foregoing chapters has shown, the statements, plot, and style of the Vizenor canon clearly align themselves with the dialogic or pictorial writing of the under- or working classes. Vizenor's trickster discourse consistently "infiltrates boundaries" between races and social classes; between fact, truth, and fiction; between imagination, reality, and hyperreality. All of Vizenor's work "blurs established genres" as he crosses and recrosses the theoretical lines between prose and poetry, history and narrative, autobiography and fiction, theory and story, oral and written. Amass with "the voices of other people," contemporary and historical Native Americans from Chief Joseph to N. Scott Momaday, filled with the "reported speech" of scholars, peasants, and politicians from Ronald Reagan to Marlene American Horse to Larzer Ziff, Vizenor's works definitely "mix texts and their authority." And his work, more than any other Native author writing today, has created its own "hybrid language."

Although writing differently does not always mean writing against, in Vizenor's case he both theorizes and employs a dialogic style because he recognizes the power theory holds in the literary arena. In her discussion "Rethinking Modernism: Minority vs. Majority Theories," Nancy Hartsock writes of "those who have been marginalized by the transcendental voice of universalizing theory" and insists that we should neither "ignore" the knowledge/power relations inherent in literary theory and canon formation nor merely "resist" them; rather, we must "transform" them.[39] Vizenor's is an extremely self-conscious attempt to challenge the enshrined monologic style, to "transform" it through theory and through practice. In "Almost Browne," for example, through the action of the story (the reading of half-burned books that require active response, the selling of blank books and pictomyths, the rejection of educational indoctrination, etc.) and the dialogue of the characters, Vizenor offers a critique of the enforced teaching of the linear, monologic style of literacy and himself employs a dialogic pictorial style. He thus moves to impeach the ruling form.

Given Vološinov's claim of the political intentions of style, Vizenor's literary style can also be read as a denunciation of the existing social paradigm and a move to dismantle it. His own professed intentions, to "push consciousness," to "confront the comfortable values of authority," support such a reading as does his metaphor of a literary ghost dance. In *Manifest Manners* Vizenor recalls the ghost dance religion and how its rapid spread across the plains was aided by the tribes' mutual enforced knowledge of the English language. The ghost dance was the "religion of renewal," meant to unite Indian people with their dead ancestors, to revive the dying culture and the natural world to which it was tied (105). Vizenor suggests that English might once again be used to invoke tribal renewal, this time through the literature of "tribal poets and novelists" (106). The "new ghost dance literature" of "contemporary postindian authors" might accomplish a social revolution, "liberate readers," and "enliven tribal survivance" (104, 106). Through "imagination and performance of new stories," the new ghost dancers, the "postindian warriors of postmodern simulations," can, Vizenor claims, "undermine and surmount" the "manifest manners of scriptural simulations" and the "literature of dominance" (17). Moves to "undermine and surmount" are the revolutionary moves of Vizenor's own ghost dance literature.

Vizenor's dialogic style, then, both engages his reading audience in discovering his revolutionary message and becomes itself a revolutionary act that might implicate the reader, since, as Iser claims, the reader's participation inevitably results not only in the expansion of the literary text but also in the expansion of the individual's own thinking. Iser identifies a quasi-moral dimension in the active process of reading, saying it not only helps to formulate the literary text but also "entails the possibility that we may formulate ourselves and so discover what had previously seemed to elude our consciousness."[40] Vizenor's writing works deliberately to feed this kind of self-formulation on the part of the reader. His writing is political; his goal, to disrupt our present beliefs and liberate us from conventional views. By combining revolutionary content and revolutionary style, he forces us to think in new ways and thus to develop our own power for revolutionary thought. From first to last, from the captivating imagery of his haiku to the brutal descriptions of *Bearheart*, Vizenor writes with the reader in mind, because, for him, writing succeeds only if it ultimately acts as a tool of liberation from any and all texts, if it awakens creative powers, works to "push the consciousness" of the reader, and causes us to "reformulate ourselves."

Conclusion

"The Almost World":
Finding a Place on the Printed Page

The tribal singer had the eyes of the animals, the legs of the birds, the wings of the spirits, the heart of the bear and the breath of the wind. He was the breath and touch of the woodland and prairie and desert. . . . Today we sing what we believe others have believed and trust the past for the future. Our songs of peace and timeless myths may bring all men together with a good energy to live.
    —Gerald Vizenor, "Visions of Eyes and Hands"

The Anishinaabeg had an oral tradition, yet Vizenor works in a written medium. The Anishinaabeg spoke Anishinaabemowin, while Vizenor writes in English, employing words or phrases from the tribal language now and then.[1] The Anishinaabeg were a woodland people, but Vizenor has spent more than half his life in metropolitan areas. The list of contrasts goes on. But despite these disjunctures, the work of mixedblood writer Gerald Vizenor seeks and achieves a tribal connection.

Having written his way through thirty years, through poetry, fiction, journalism, history, myth, autobiography, essays, and his own adaptations of each, in every endeavor Vizenor has emulated the Native American oral tradition because "tribal words have power in the oral tradition" (*The People Named the Chippewa*, 24). All the while, the mixedblood writer has remained hyperconscious of the irony of his effort. "The trickster in the oral tradition," he notes, would "overturn the very printed page on which his name has been printed" ("Trickster Discourse," 34). In many senses, this is precisely Vizenor's effort: as he writes, he challenges the very process of writing; the ideas he expresses "waver on the rim," waiting to be overturned and overturned and overturned again (*The Trickster of Liberty*, xvii). For finally, the place that Vizenor finds on the printed page is an "almost world," a "trickster world" of "performance and creation, rather than a world that is discovered, dependent, and consumed" ("Trickster Discourse," 34–35).[3]

Recognized and reviewed internationally, Vizenor has indeed created a place for his work in the canon of Native American literature. It is in many ways a revolutionary place, since Vizenor's work has to a great extent moved away from the readily recognizable attributes of what is generally classified as Native American literature. By this I do not mean that Vizenor has abandoned the tribal in his writing; rather, he has transplanted it.

While most of the other Native American writers still ground their stories in tribal communities on reservations or in urban settings and deal with the conflicts of their characters as Native American conflicts (as Vizenor did in some of his early work), Vizenor's later characters and stories tend to have internal rather than external tribal connections. For example, most Native American novelists establish a sense of rootedness in their characters partly through a connection with a specific physical (and usually rural) landscape. Novels such as Louise Erdrich's *Love Medicine* create a realistic portrayal of contemporary tribal life, acknowledging the multiple and complicated adaptations or absorptions of mainstream elements into the tribal, but they still maintain an immutable image of place and community. The survival of the various characters stems from their connections to these two core elements. Other contemporary novelists such as Momaday and Welch render the landscape itself as distinctly and fully as they do any character, and it becomes an active entity in their imaginative accounts.

Although we know, through Vizenor's haiku and various descriptions of the woodlands, the power of his own imaginative connection to the landscape, he often chooses to establish tribal connections despite and sometimes through a historic vision of removal or a new sense of rootlessness. His characters are frequently displaced urban dwellers who not only can't, but also don't always want, to go home again. They may have an imaginative rather than an actual connection to place. Having himself experienced how easily actual place can be altered, Vizenor's literary accounts portray a storied "interior landscape" that persists beyond removal and survives physical destruction of place. Not requiring the material manifestations of physical rootedness, his characters seem to achieve another level of connectedness, sometimes intellectual, sometimes imaginary, sometimes by means of "stories in the blood." From Fourth Proude Cedarfair in *Bearheart*, who walks away from four generations of connection to the Red Cedar Reservation to become the leader of a group of wandering pilgrims, to Martin Bear Charme of "Land Fill Meditation," who hitchhikes from Turtle Mountain Reservation in North Dakota to San Francisco, where he becomes a tribal entrepreneur, to Griever, who becomes a cross-cultural trickster in China, the only immutable connections Vizenor's protagonists can afford are interior, just as in his autobiography he himself claims "interior landscapes."[3]

Vizenor's emphasis on the interior connection serves his attempt to universalize his stories, to deliberately extend their significance beyond the mere tribal. For example, in Leslie Silko's *Ceremony*, which has quite rightly been extolled as a novel that opens itself deliberately to encompass the destiny not just of tribal peoples but of all humankind, the plot and setting are identifiably Indian. But in a book like Vizenor's *Griever* the community as well as the physical and political setting are all foreign, made universal by implication. Even the tribal element, trickster consciousness, is identified in concert with a similar tradition of the Chinese Monkey King.

In form, too, Vizenor's work distinguishes itself from the style of many popular Native authors. Much of Native American literature, especially fiction, has received attention for relinquishing conventional chronology as an organizing tool, for the interweaving of tribal stories or myths with the current story, for the humanistic portrayal of other life forms, and for attention to landscape, community, and various aspects of cultural tradition. These traits, which have been seen to distinguish Native American fiction from mainstream fiction, can also be found in Vizenor's writing. But while most of the Native American novels in print are still clearly plot-centered, Vizenor's writing is more idea-centered. Many of his works actually work against a formal plotting. In Vizenor we get "wisps of narrative," with the whole stories scattered in pieces between several of his books.

The standard organizing principles of fiction—cause and effect, conflict and resolution—Vizenor eschews. Although Native American fiction may be disbelieved by readers who do not give credence to the worldview, most tribal writers still present their philosophy through the conventions of a realistic plot line. Vizenor, however, seldom gives his energies to building subtle plot lines. Instead, his plots develop wildly or become a revolutionary vehicle. His characters, too, are drawn boldly, with exaggerated and outlandish qualities, speaking Vizenor's hybrid language and espousing novel beliefs. In these characteristics, his fiction, of course, bears resemblance to freewheeling trickster tales and to the postmodern anti-aesthetic. Alan Velie, in drawing a comparison between Vizenor's *Bearheart* and the postmodern novel, lists four characteristics shared by the two. Each, he says, "ignores established fictional traditions to an extraordinary extent, purposely establishes a limited audience, departs from the illusionist tradition, and represents writing as play." Velie also links Vizenor's *Bearheart* to the tradition of Rabelais and what Bakhtin has termed "fantastic realism." Louis Owens describes the novel as an inversion of the American gothic tradition.[4] What each of these analyses have in common is their recognition of Vizenor's departure from romantic realism.

Most nonhistorical Native American novels relate a story of the healing, initiation or reinitiation, personal growth, or gradual coming to tribal awareness of the protagonist and can therefore be classified as belonging to the tradition of the Bildungsroman. (Although, as William Bevis has rightly noted, the growth of the tribal protagonist usually involves returning home, while the growth of the mainstream protagonist involves leaving home.)[5] Vizenor's prose, although at times following the tradition of the Bildungsroman, resists these standard patterns of a romantic or tragic identity search. Whenever possible he inverts the expected stories. In scenes from *The Trickster of Liberty* ("The Last Lecture on the Edge"), "urban mixedbloods who had moved to the reservation," those Vizenor calls "pretenders to the tribe," take part in an un-naming ceremony, as they give up their pretend Indian names, make "one last telephone call to their past," and drop over the edge of a precipice into "a new wild world" (108). Vizenor's characters go urban, go modern with laser light shows, go off in an ultralight airplane. Vizenor's plots or antiplots find themselves told in epistolary form (*Griever*), as literary nonfiction (*Earthdivers*), as stories within stories about storytelling (*Dead Voices*).

Vizenor's various accounts of the killing of a red squirrel illustrate both the mixed-genre, antiform, intertextual character of his work and the changes his style has undergone over the years. All of the versions describe a scene in which Vizenor shoots a red squirrel and guiltily watches it die. He first passionately recounts the squirrel story in "I Know What You Mean, Erdupps MacChurbb" in 1976. Just over a decade later, he retells it in "Crows Written on the Poplars: Autocritical Autobiographies" (1987), offering some theory on autobiography and a critique of the first account as he does so. He returns to the tale again in his 1990 book-length autobiography, *Interior Landscapes*, in a chapter bearing the title "October 1957: Death Song to a Red Rodent." This version includes critical comments on hunting and the romance of hunting. Finally, he gives the event a fictional rendering in *Dead Voices* in which he is among the other squirrels who witness the killing of their friend. These serial accounts of events model the movement in Vizenor's work, in which ideas exist in the trickster "almost world," always on the verge, never captured, never static.

The story's changing forms also reflect the developments in Vizenor's style and their link to the changes in his life. Although throughout his career Vizenor has been devoted to informing as much as entertaining his reader, his later works incorporate a greater volume of theoretical material and address fewer social and more literary topics. While once he was involved in the politics of the urban reservation, he is now involved in the politics of academics and the university. "Life's different now," he says. "Other people have to write about that [reservation life] now. I'm too far from that" (Interview).

As Vizenor's later writings become more stylistically sophisticated, they place greater demands on his reader and, inevitably, attract a different audience. While his early works such as *The Everlasting Sky* or "I Know What You Mean, Erdupps MacChurbbs" well suited a general audience, more recent writings such as *The Trickster of Liberty* and *Manifest Manners* depend for much of their play on the reader's familiarity with various academic theories or personages, thus limiting their audience. Tom Lynch, for example, criticizes the "density of the jargon" in *Manifest Manners* and wonders if "the valuable insights into issues of Native American identity and survivance might not be rendered inaccessible to many who could benefit from the message."[6]

Indeed, Vizenor's work is not easy by any means, and a reader who follows the writing only on the basic levels of plot and setting miss much of Vizenor's play and brilliance. Readers may find themselves lamenting, as does the narrator in *Dead Voices*, "I was never sure how to hear the stories," or confessing, as he does, "I pretended to understand, but some of the stories were obscure" (10, 9). Nevertheless, to those readers who meet the challenge of Vizenor's writing, he offers new ways to think about reading, writing, speaking, and being.

With his eclectic capacity for fusing the tribal with the nontribal, investing the old with the new, Vizenor performs as tribal wordmaker, confident that through it all "the fine spirit of the Ojibway song has been held in the heart" (*Escorts to White Earth*, introduction). We might say of his work what Vizenor says of haiku: "The printed words . . . are rendered; nothing remains but dreams, oral traditions, the light around our hands, petals, the rain" (*Matsushima*, introduction).

Notes

Introduction

1. "Gerald Vizenor," in Laura Coltelli, *Winged Words: American Indian Writers Speak*, 156.

2. Personal interviews with Gerald Vizenor, 27–29 May 1987; hereafter cited as Interview. This series of interviews was conducted at the University of California at Berkeley, where Gerald Vizenor was then on the faculty. The sessions included both formal questioning and informal discussion. All of the formal interviews were tape-recorded, yielding approximately seven hours of taped material. Quoted passages are from the transcripts of those tapes. Although major subject areas were blocked out for discussion in various sessions, no written questions were prepared. Both questions and answers are thus relatively spontaneous, arising out of the discussion itself. Funding to undertake these interviews was provided by the University of Notre Dame Graduate School through a Zahm Research Travel Grant.

3. Patricia Haseltine discusses the "transformations of the author's voice" in her article "The Voices of Gerald Vizenor: Survival through Transformation," 31.

4. Bowers and Silet, "An Interview with Gerald Vizenor," 45. Maureen Keady also discusses Vizenor's use of contradiction within the text of *The Darkness in Saint Louis Bearheart* and comments, "our desire for resolution . . . is overruled again and again" ("Walking Backwards into the Fourth World: Survival of the Fittest in *Bearheart*," 61).

5. Elaine Jahner discusses creation as an "ongoing process" in Vizenor's writing in "Cultural Shrines Revisited" and in "Heading 'Em Off at the Impasse: Native American Authors Meet the Poststructuralists."

6. Vizenor, "Gerald Vizenor, Ojibway/Chippewa Writer," in *This Song Remembers: Self-Portraits of Native Americans in the Arts*, 168.

7. I offer a brief biographical sketch. For a more detailed account of Vizenor's life, see Vizenor, *Interior Landscapes: Autobiographical Myths and Metaphors*.

8. In the spelling of words with several acceptable forms, I adopt the spelling Vizenor himself uses. Here, for example, I use the "ay" spelling of the tribal designation—Ojibway—as opposed to Ojibwa or Ojibwe. When Vizenor's own spellings vary (as in the case of Anishinaabe/Anishinabe) I use the spelling that he employs in his most recent work (in this case Anishinaabe). Other words I use in this study that are known to have variable spellings include Chippewa (sometimes spelled Chippeway) and Naanabozho (which has several variations in spelling as well as differences in regional pronunciation: Nanabozho, Nanabush, Wenebojo, etc.). In direct quotations, I always follow the spelling of the quoted passage.

For Vizenor the manner in which the tribe is designated has political as well as lexical significance. In many of his works he makes a clear statement about the imposition of white pronunciations and transcriptions on the tribal language. For example, in the book whose very title announces such an imposition—*The People Named the Chippewa*—Vizenor writes, "In the language of the tribal past, the families of the woodland spoke of themselves as the Anishinaabeg until the colonists named them the Ojibway and the Chippewa" (13).

9. *Darkness in Saint Louis Bearheart* was reprinted in 1990 as *Bearheart: The Heirship Chronicles*.

10. Book jacket, *Bearheart: The Heirship Chronicles*.

11. Among the works or excerpts translated, for example, are *Wordarrows* (translated into Italian as *Parolefrecce*), "Reservation Café: The Origins of American Indian Instant Coffee" (translated into French as "Café Reservé, ou les origins du café instanté"), and *Harold of Orange* (translated into German as *Harold of Orange/Harold von Orangen*).

12. Book jacket, *Heirs of Columbus*.

13. A. LaVonne Brown Ruoff's "Woodland Word Warrior: An Introduction to the Works of Gerald Vizenor" and "Gerald Vizenor: Compassionate Trickster" survey Vizenor's writings and are accompanied by an extensive though selective bibliography of his works. Louis Owens discusses Vizenor's first three novels, his use of the mixedblood as mediator, and various critical connections in his chapter entitled "Ecstatic Strategies: Gerald Vizenor's Trickster Narratives," in

Other Destinies: Understanding the American Indian Novel. A. Robert Lee gives an overview of Vizenor's works and methods in his introduction to *Shadow Distance: A Gerald Vizenor Reader*, and James Ruppert offers a reading of *Bearheart* in his chapter entitled "Mythic Verism" in *Mediation in Contemporary Native American Fiction*.

14. Jahner discusses connections between Vizenor's work and Derrida's concept of the "trace" in "Heading 'Em Off."

15. Ruoff, Jahner, Owens, and Haseltine all discuss Vizenor's use of the trickster, as does Alan Velie in his chapter entitled "Beyond the Novel Chippewa-style: Gerald Vizenor's Post-Modern Fiction," in *Four American Indian Literary Masters: N. Scott Momaday, James Welch, Leslie Marmon Silko, and Gerald Vizenor*; Franchot Ballinger in "Sacred Reversals: Trickster in Gerald Vizenor's *Earthdivers: Tribal Narratives on Mixed Descent*"; and Robert Silberman in "Gerald Vizenor and *Harold of Orange*: From Word Cinemas to Real Cinema."

Chapter 1. Intersections with the Oral Tradition

1. Vizenor employs the neologism "word cinemas" to connote the visual and performative quality he feels is essential in tribal telling. The phrase becomes the title for a short story and his descriptive characterization for certain pieces of his own work. In the introductory commentary to the story "Word Cinemas" as it appears in *Book Forum*, for example, he writes of "the satirical word cinemas in my book *Four Skin* [an unpublished novel] from which these pages are taken" (389); and in his introduction to *Summer in the Spring*, he says of the pieces in the collection: "The stories in this book are a written voice, new word cinemas from oral tradition" (14–15).

2. The differences between orality and textuality, the multidimensional quality of oral tribal literature, and the problems of translation have been given considerable critical discussion. See, for example: Brian Swann, ed., *Smoothing the Ground: Essays on Native American Oral Literature*; Brian Swann and Arnold Krupat, eds., *Recovering the Word: Essays on Native American Literature*; and Walter J. Ong, *The Presence of the Word* and *Orality and Literacy: The Technologizing of the Word*.

3. Bowers and Silet, "An Interview with Gerald Vizenor," 49.

4. In discussing tribal literature, distinctions are frequently made between oral literary genres: sacred and secular; myth, folktale, legend; and so on. However, because Vizenor in his own work does not make a point of distinguishing between the classes, in this study I use the terms *story, tale, myth, legend,* and so on in their least restrictive sense.

Vizenor coined "wordmaker" to draw a parallel between the literary artist and the "arrowmaker" of an N. Scott Momaday story. The "arrowmaker" of Momaday's tale is "preeminently the man made of words" for whom "language represented the only chance for survival." Vizenor quotes Momaday's story in the preface to *Wordarrows*, where he also introduces the epithet "wordmaker" (vi–viii). Both, he claims, "survive in the word wars with sacred memories" while others "separate themselves in wordless and eventless social and political categories" (viii).

5. Vizenor writes frequently of "terminal creeds" and "terminal believers." In "I Know What You Mean, Erdupps MacChurbbs: Autobiographical Myths and Metaphors," for example, he defines "terminal believers" as "those believing in only one vision of the world" (96). When asked about the relationship of this term to Eric Hoffer's "true believer," Vizenor acknowledges that Hoffer's book "had real impact" on him. However, he sees Hoffer's idea as more of a "political true believer" while he thinks about the concept more broadly (Interview).

6. Haseltine suggests that Vizenor is recounting a dream vision experience when he describes his encounter with Baragga in "I Know What You Mean, Erdupps MacChurbbs" ("Voices" 36). The significance and duration of the dream vision experience in tribal life can be seen in the well known as-told-to biography *Black Elk Speaks* by John G. Neihardt. For discussion of the significance of the dream as it relates specifically to the Ojibway see, for example, Frances Densmore, *Chippewa Customs*.

7. See also Jahner, "Heading 'Em Off."

8. Ruoff, *American Indian Literatures: An Introduction, Bibliographic Review, and Selected Bibliography*, 5; Allen, *Studies in American Indian Literature: Critical Essays and Course Designs*, 33; Swann, *Smoothing the Ground*, xi; Simon Ortiz, "You Were Real, the White Radical Said to Me," 44.

9. To speak of "Native American tradition," tribal beliefs, and so on, is, of course, to make generalizations. There are hundreds of individual Native American tribes, each with its own unique system of beliefs and customs. At the same time, scholars recognize that the various groups have in common not only philosophical ideas but also a history of similar encounters with the U.S. government, which has brought about closer connections between them with the passing of time. Today many elements contribute to a sense of unity or pan-Indian feeling that cuts across tribal distinctions.

10. S. Ortiz, "Always the Stories: A Brief History and Thoughts on My Writing," 57.

11. Astrov, ed., *The Winged Serpent: American Indian Prose and Poetry*, 19.

12. Momaday, *The Way to Rainy Mountain*, (1969), 33; *House Made of Dawn*, 91.

13. Silko, *Ceremony*, 1.

14. Allen, *The Woman Who Owned the Shadows*, 2.

15. Allen, *Studies in American Indian Literature*, 37.

16. Silko, *Ceremony*, 1.

17. Ruoff, *American Indian Literatures*, 7.

18. Silko, *Ceremony*, 141, 145.

19. Ruoff, *American Indian Literatures*, 7.

20. Astrov, *American Indian Prose and Poetry*, 36; Momaday, *House Made of Dawn*, 57.

21. Momaday, *House Made of Dawn*, 180–81.

22. Henry Rowe Schoolcraft, *Algic Researches*, as quoted in A. Grove Day, *The Sky Clears: Poetry of the American Indians*, 146. Frances Densmore, *Chippewa Music* 1:47, 115.

23. Momaday, *House Made of Dawn*, 16.

24. Witherspoon, *Language and Art in the Navajo Universe*, 16; Evers and Molina, *Yaqui Deer Songs/Maso Bwikam: A Native American Poetry*, 7, 18.

25. This statement appears in "Spacious Treeline in Words" from *Earthdivers* (176) and in "Land Fill Meditation" from *Words in the Blood: Contemporary Indian Writers of North and South America*, ed. Jamake Highwater, 137. A slightly altered version of the statement appears in the story "Landfill Meditation" from the collection by that same name (99). Here the parallel phrase to the quoted section reads, "rituals in the oral tradition, from the sound of creation, the wisps of visions on the wind."

26. Allen, "The Sacred Hoop: A Contemporary Perspective," 4.

27. S. Ortiz, "Always the Stories," 57.

28. Momaday, *House Made of Dawn*, 88.

29. S. Ortiz, *Song, Poetry, and Language: Expression and Perception*, 9.

30. Momaday, "The Man Made of Words," 55; "Native American Attitudes to the Environment," 81, 84.

31. Toelkin, "Seeing with a Native Eye: How Many Sheep Will It Hold?" in *Seeing With a Native Eye: Essays on Native American Religion*, 24; Schubnell, *N. Scott Momaday: The Cultural and Literary Background*, 65.

32. Scholars including Astrov, Allen, and Lincoln comment on this dual plane of vision. Astrov, for example, writes, "To the Hopi the phenomena of what we would call the objective side of the world are intimately interlocked with those of the subjective side of it. . . . The 'inner' world is apt to dominate over the 'outer' world" (*Winged Serpent*, 8); and Lincoln speaks of "correspondences between inner and outer states of being" (*Native American Renaissance*, 138). "American Indian thought," Allen explains, does not "draw a hard and fast line between what is material and what is spiritual, for it regards the two as different

expressions of the same reality, as though life has twin manifestations that are mutually interchangeable and, in many instances, virtually identical aspects of a reality that is essentially more spirit than matter or, more correctly, that manifests its spirit in a tangible way" ("Sacred Hoop," 225).

33. Toelken and Scott, "Poetic Retranslation and the 'Pretty Languages' of Yellowman," 110.

34. Ong, *The Interfaces of the Word: Studies in the Evolution of Consciousness and Culture*, 276; Ong, *Orality and Literacy*, 74; Toelken and Scott, "Poetic Retranslations," 110.

35. See, for example, Bakhtin, *The Dialogic Imagination: Four Essays* and *Speech Genres and Other Late Essays*.

36. Bruchac, "Follow the Trickroutes: An Interview with Gerald Vizenor," 301.

37. Ong, *Orality and Literacy*, 75. Ong also makes distinctions between the printed text and handwritten manuscripts. Again in *Orality and Literacy*, for example, he writes: "By contrast [with the printed text], manuscripts, with their glosses or marginal comments . . . were in dialogue with the world outside of their own borders. They remained closer to the give-and-take of oral expression" (132).

38. Ibid., 72.

39. Ong, *Interfaces of the Word*, 312; Jahner, "Heading 'Em Off," 2.

40. Ong, *Orality and Literacy*, 167.

41. Sledge, "Oral Tradition in Kingston's China Men," 147; Ong, *Orality and Literacy*, 31–77.

42. Velie, *Four American Indian Literary Masters*, 144.

43. Ramsey, *Reading the Fire: Essays in the Traditional Indian Literatures of the Far West*, 186–87. Underhill describes the encounter in *Papago Woman*, 51.

44. Ramsey, *Reading the Fire*, 186–87.

45. Lame Deer and Erdoes, *Lame Deer: Seeker of Visions*, 97; Smith quoted in Lincoln, *Native American Renaissance*, 40; Standiford, "Worlds Made of Dawn: Characteristic Image and Incident in Native American Imaginative Literature," 185–86, 188; Lincoln, *Native American Renaissance*, 49.

46. Krupat, *For Those Who Come After: A Study of Native American Autobiography*, especially 1–27, and "Post-Structuralism and Oral Literature," 113–28; Jahner, "Allies in the Word Wars: Vizenor's Uses of Contemporary Critical Theory," 64–69.

47. Ramsey, *Reading the Fire*, 181–82; Jahner, "Heading 'Em Off," 1.

48. For a discussion of these connections, see, for example, Jahner, "Heading 'Em Off" and "Allies in the Word Wars." In the discussion of reader-response criticism that follows, I acknowledge a debt to the following works: Terry Eagleton, *Literary Theory: An Introduction*; Umberto Eco, *The Role of Reader:*

Explorations in the Semiotics of Texts; Ihab Hassan, *The Postmodern Turn: Essays in Postmodern Theory and Culture*; David Lodge, ed., *Twentieth-Century Literary Criticism: A Reader*; and Jane P. Tompkins, ed., *Reader-Response Criticism: From Formalism to Post-Structuralism*.

49. Eagleton, *Literary Theory*, 7.

50. Iser, "The Reading Process: A Phenomenological Approach" in Tompkins, *Reader-Response Criticism*, 50–51.

51. I draw from the following works in my discussion of the methods of the "open" text: Chris Anderson, *Style as Argument: Contemporary American Nonfiction*; William Empson, *Seven Types of Ambiguity*; Frederick R. Karl, *American Fictions, 1940–1980: A Comprehensive History and Critical Evaluation*; and Tompkins, *Reader-Response Criticism*.

52. Eagleton, *Literary Theory*, 76–77.

53. Hassan, *The Postmodern Turn*, 91.

54. Eagleton, *Literary Theory*, 138.

Chapter 2. Surviving the Word Wars

1. Bowers and Silet, "An Interview with Gerald Vizenor," 48.

2. Lincoln, *Native American Renaissance*, 184.

3. Owens, *Other Destinies*, 231; Lee, Introduction to *Shadow Distance*, xiv.

4. Ruoff, "Gerald Vizenor: Compassionate Trickster," 73.

5. Ainsworth, "History and the Imagination: Gerald Vizenor's *The People Named the Chippewa*," 54; Silko, *Ceremony*, 133.

6. Ruoff, "Gerald Vizenor: Compassionate Trickster," 73.

7. Said, *Orientalism*, 3.

8. Pearce, *Savagism and Civilization: A Study of the Indian and the American Mind*, 200.

9. "Marlene American Horse," 38–46. The surname Vizenor uses is likely a historical allusion to the Oglala Sioux chief American Horse, who fought with Sitting Bull.

10. Quoted in Vizenor, "Rattling Hail Ceremonial: Cultural Word Wars Downtown on the Reservation," 134, which has also appeared in two other versions: "Rattling Hail," in *Landfill Meditation*, 151, and "Rattling Hail Ceremonial," in *Wordarrows*, 22. The full quotation is as follows: "Good words will not give my people good health and stop them from dying. . . . I am tired of talk that comes to nothing. It makes my heart sick when I remember all the good words and all the broken promises. There has been too much talking by men who had no right to talk."

11. Toelkin, "Seeing with a Native Eye: How Many Sheep Will It Hold?", 15.

12. This is the most oft quoted form of Pratt's original statement. The statement itself has also been given in various longer versions, such as the following, from Sharon O'Brien, *American Indian Tribal Governments*: "We accept the watchword, let us by patient effort kill the Indian in him and save the man" (76).

13. Keady, "Walking Backwards into the Fourth World," 62.

14. A similar account appears in the story "Landfill Meditation" (*Landfill Meditation*, 107–15).

15. Owens, Afterword to *Bearheart: The Heirship Chronicles*, 249.

16. Quoted in Vizenor, *The Everlasting Sky*, 21.

17. Drinnon, *Facing West: The Metaphysics of Indian-Hating and Empire Building*; Slotkin, *Regeneration through Violence: The Mythology of the American Frontier, 1600–1860*. Slotkin claims, for example, that the colonists' negative depiction of Native Americans grew out of their own need to define themselves positively or to justify their own actions. "In opposing Indian culture," he says, "the Puritan symbolically affirmed his Englishness" (22); and "representatives of social, religious, and political factions" used Indian war tales to "justify their particular conceptions of the truth" (23).

18. Berkhofer, *The White Man's Indian: Images of the American Indian from Columbus to the Present*, 20. Among the other works that offer a discussion of Native American identity are Leslie A. Fiedler, *The Return of the Vanishing American*; Gretchen M. Bataille and Charles L. P. Silet, eds., *The Pretend Indians: Images of Native Americans in the Movies*; Raymond William Stedman, *Shadows of the Indian: Stereotypes in American Culture*; and Frederick E. Hoxie, ed., *Indians in American History: An Introduction*.

19. Vizenor draws the term *simulation* from Jean Baudrillard's *Simulacres et Simulation* and *hyperreal* from Umberto Eco's *Travels in Hyperreality*.

20. Ainsworth, "History and the Imagination: Gerald Vizenor's *The People Named the Chippewa*," 52; Jahner, "Heading 'Em Off," 6.

21. In the following discussion, page numbers refer to the *Manifest Manners* text unless otherwise noted. I play here on the title of the tribal newspaper *Indian Country Today*, which is published by Native American Publishing in Rapid City, South Dakota.

22. The notion of an "absolute fake" Vizenor borrows from Umberto Eco, and the characterization of a "hyperreal" as arising from a model without "origin or reality," from Jean Baudrillard (see note 19 above).

23. Lee, Introduction to *Shadow Distance*, xi.

24. "Socioacupuncture," 180–91. *Trickster of Liberty*, 43–50. "Socioacupuncture" also appears in a slightly different form in *Crossbloods*, 83–97. Unless noted

otherwise, page numbers in the following discussion refer to the version in *The American Indian and the Problem of History.*

25. Barthes, *Camera Lucida: Reflections on Photography*; John Berger and Jean Mohr, *Another Way of Telling*; Sontag, *On Photography.*

26. In addition to "Graduation with Ishi" and the two versions of "Socioacupuncture," other sources of Vizenor's discussion of Ishi include "Ishi Obscura," in *Manifest Manners*, 126–37; "Manifest Manners"; "Ishi Bares His Chest: Tribal Simulations and Survivance"; and *Ishi and the Wood Ducks: Postindian Trickster Comedies.*

27. Karl Kroeber also gave his support to the effort to have a hall named after Ishi. The speeches by Vizenor and others given on the dedication of the interior court are published in *News from Native California* 7.3 (Summer 1993): 38–41.

28. Sidney quoted in Julie Cruikshank, *Life Lived Like a Story: Life Stories of Three Yukon Native Elders*, 36.

29. This story has appeared in several versions. I use the text from *Words in the Blood*, 136–47.

30. Vizenor's use of the name Bear Charme and his frequent use of bear characters or transformations from human to bear and bear to human have tribal as well as personal significance. Bear is totemic in Anishinaabeg culture, bear being one of the principle clans of the tribe. The bear is also associated with spiritual power in the *midéwiwin* or Grand Medicine Society. Vizenor also speaks of the way tribal storytellers understood the humanlike qualities of bear, and he quotes A. Irving Hallowell's *Bear Ceremonialism in the Northern Hemisphere* on this point in *Earthdivers* (145). His own experience in the Imperial National Forest in Hokkaido, Japan, involved living in unusually close association with black bears for several months. Finally, in this story particularly, Vizenor plays on bears' habit of grazing in garbage dumps.

31. In both books Vizenor identifies Beaulieu as the stand-in for himself. He calls Clement Beaulieu the "created name for the author who appears in several narratives" (*Wordarrows*, x; *Earthdivers*, xviii).

32. Silko, *Ceremony*, 273.

33. Bowers and Silet, "An Interview with Gerald Vizenor," 48.

Chapter 3. The Wordmaker: "Subverting the Strategies of Containment"

1. Ziff, *Writing in the New Nation*, 155, 173, as quoted in Vizenor, "The Ruins of Representation," *Manifest Manners: Postindian Warriors of Survivance*, 8, 77.

2. Niranjana, *Siting Translation*, 3.

3. Owens, *Other Destinies*, 6.

4. Silberman, "Gerald Vizenor and *Harold of Orange*: From Word Cinemas to Real Cinema," 14.

5. This phrase is Vizenor's, from "Trickster Discourse: Comic and Tragic Themes in Native American Literature," 35.

6. Jahner, "Cultural Shrines Revisited," 25.

7. Lincoln, *Native American Renaissance*, 25. The issues of translation have been addressed by Vizenor throughout his work, but particularly in *The People Named the Chippewa*, *Crossbloods*, and *Manifest Manners*. Many other scholars have also explored the problems of translation. See, for example, Brian Swann, ed., *On the Translation of Native American Literatures*, and the essays by Dennis Tedlock and Jeffrey Huntsman in *Smoothing the Ground: Essays on Native American Oral Literatures*. For a discussion of translation and colonialism, see, for example, Ashcroft, Griffiths, and Tiffin, *The Empire Writes Back: Theory and Practice in Post Colonial Literatures*.

8. Krupat discusses the way translations arise partly out of an unintentional comparison with the dominant models with which the translators are familiar. See "On the Translation of Native American Song and Story: A Theorized History," and *The Voice in the Margin: Native American Literature and the Canon*.

9. Bowers and Silet, "An Interview with Gerald Vizenor," 49.

10. Owens, *Other Destinies*, 13.

11. Emma LaRocque, "Preface: Here Are Our Voices—Who Will Hear?," xx–xxi.

12. S. Ortiz, Preface to *A Good Journey*, 9; Larry J. Evers, "A Conversation with N. Scott Momaday," 21.

13. Both the notion of language and performance imply for Vizenor the active participation of speaker/writer and listener/reader; therefore, the metaphor of shadow becomes another way of explaining the notion of discourse if we recognize that discourse involves much more than an exchange of words.

14. Mailer, *The Armies of the Night: History As a Novel: The Novel As History*, 14.

15. Owens, *Other Destinies*, 13; Schubnell, *N. Scott Momaday*, 183.

16. Silko, *Ceremony*, 258; Waters, *The Man Who Killed the Deer*, 18–19.

17. S. Ortiz, "Always the Stories: A Brief History and Thoughts on My Writing," 66.

18. Standiford, "Worlds Made of Dawn: Characteristic Image and Incident in Native American Imaginative Literature," 175; Martin, "An Introduction aboard the Fidèle"; Drinnon, "The Metaphysics of Dancing Tribes," in *The American Indian and the Problem of History*, 111; Ziff, *Writing in the New Nation*, as quoted in Vizenor, *Manifest Manners*, 8.

19. Deloria, Foreword to *New and Old Voices of Wah'kon-tah: Contemporary Native American Poetry*, ix–x.

20. Owens, "Mixedblood Metaphors: Identity in Contemporary Native American Fiction."

21. Jones, *That Art of Difference: "Documentary-Collage" and English-Canadian Writing*, 7, 14–18.

22. Momaday quoted in Schubnell, *N. Scott Momaday*, 185; Forster, *Aspects of the Novel*, 63; Lopez, "Landscape and Narrative," 71.

23. See especially "Anthropological and Historical Inventions" (27–31) and pp. 60–61 on Copway. Vizenor's use of the word "invention" in this section is linked to Roy Wagner's *The Invention of Culture*, which he quotes.

24. Acknowledgement of oral telling as an acceptable form and personal remembrance as an acceptable source is implied in such works as Evers, ed., *The South Corner of Time: hopi navajo papgo yaqui tribal literature*; Nabokov, *Native American Testimony: A Chronicle of Indian-White Relations from Prophecy to the Present*; and Hinton and Watahomigie, eds., *Spirit Mountain*

25. Ainsworth, "History and Imagination," 52–53.

26. Cruikshank, *Life Lived Like a Story: Life Stories of Three Yukon Native Elders*, 347.

27. Momaday, "The Man Made of Words," 56–57; Cruikshank, *Life Lived Like a Story*, ix.

28. Momaday, *The Way to Rainy Mountain*, 4.

29. Note the title of one version of Schoolcraft's report: *Expedition to Lake Itasca: The Discovery of the Source of the Mississippi*. An example of the texts that acknowledge Schoolcraft as discoverer is Harold Hickerson, *The Chippewa and Their Neighbors: A Study in Ethnohistory*. Hickerson writes, "In 1831 Schoolcraft led an expedition to discover the main source of the Mississippi, which turned out to be Lake Itasca, generally accepted as the main source today" (98).

30. A. Ortiz, "Indian/White Relations: A View from the Other Side of the 'Frontier,'" 11.

31. Will Rosco, Review of *The Heirs of Columbus* by Gerald Vizenor, 11.

32. Ibid., 11.

33. I use Louis Owens's phrase here. See "Acts of Recovery: The American Indian Novel in the 80's."

34. Elliot Emory, ed., "The Journal of the First Voyage of Christopher Columbus," in *American Literature: A Prentice Hall Anthology*, vol. 1, 33–38.

35. Among the works that take up the issues of autobiographical writing is Olney, ed., *Autobiography: Essays Theoretical and Critical*.

36. Krupat, *For Those Who Come After: A Study of Native American Autobiography*, 29.

37. Krupat and Swann, *I Tell You Now*, ix; Wong, *Sending My Heart Back Across the Years*.

38. Many scholars have discussed the formal models of autobiography and the ways in which Native life stories were made to fit these models. See, for example, Krupat, *For Those Who Come After* and *The Voice in the Margin*; Bataille and Sands, *American Indian Women: Telling Their Lives*; and Brumble, *American Indian Autobiography*.

39. The passage quoted here is from *Manifest Manners* (95) and "Ruins of Representations" (156–57). Vizenor employs part of the same statement in "Crows Written on the Poplars" (107).

40. Krupat, "Trickster's Lives: The Autobiographies of Gerald Vizenor."

41. Lee, Introduction to *Shadow Distance*, xv.

42. Bell, "Almost a Story," 193, 187.

43. Cruikshank, *Life Lived Like a Story*, 14–15.

Chapter 4. Multiple Traditions in Haiku

1. Glauber, Review of *Summer in the Spring*, 39.

2. See, for example, B. H. Chamberlain, *Japanese Poetry*; Donald Keene, *Japanese Literature: An Introduction for Western Readers*; D. T. Suzuki, *Zen and Japanese Culture*; Kenneth Yasuda, *The Japanese Haiku: Its Essential Nature, History, and Possibilities in English, with Selected Examples*.

3. Vizenor offers explanatory notes for many of the songs, some of which include quotations and pieces of information offered in Densmore's original.

4. Frost, Review of *Chippewa Music*, 255.

5. Austin, Introduction to *The Path on the Rainbow: An Anthology of Songs and Chants from the Indians of North America*, rpt. in *Literature of the American Indians: Views and Interpretations*, 267; Astrov, Introduction to *The Winged Serpent*, 16; Day, *The Sky Clears: Poetry of the American Indians*, 32.

6. Vizenor accepts and bases his own reexpressions on the work of Densmore. Note, for example, how close is the language between versions of one dream song, the second version of which is Vizenor's: "as my eyes search / the prairie / I feel the summer in the spring" and "as my eyes / look across the prairie / I feel the summer in the spring." In one of his dream song collections Vizenor describes Densmore as "one of the most sensitive musicologists and ethnologists working with the anishinaabeg" (*Summer in Spring*, 19). He has spoken "in praise of Densmore," calling her work "brilliant and honest" and describing her efforts to somehow record not only the songs themselves but the musical notations and the song pictures as well: "No one," he says, "has done a work as honest with such dedication as hers. She recorded, transcribed, transliterated and translated" (Interview). If the accuracy of Densmore's work is challenged (as it is in Evers and Molina's *Yaqui Deer Songs*), then Vizenor's

"reexpressions," of course, become suspect as well. Even if the translations are not sound word for word, however, certain key characteristics do surface, and the intentions and practice of creating dream songs can themselves be compared to the intentions and practices of haiku art.

7. Castro, *Interpreting the Indian: Twentieth-Century Poets and the Native American*, 22.

8. Rexroth, "American Indian Songs: The United States Bureau of Ethnology Collection," 283.

9. Castro, *Interpreting the Indian*, 23.

10. Bowers and Silet, "An Interview with Gerald Vizenor," 49.

11. Krupat, "Post-Structuralism and Oral Tradition," 118, 124–25, 122–23.

12. Rexroth, "American Indian Songs," 282; Ruoff, *American Indian Literatures*, 19; Kroeber, "Deconstructionist Criticism and American Indian Literature," 72; Castro, *Interpreting the Indian*, 24.

13. Densmore, *Chippewa Music* 1:16.

14. Fletcher, Introduction to *A Pepper Pod*, ix–x.

15. Quoted in Yasuda, *The Japanese Haiku*, 12–13.

16. Densmore, *Chippewa Music* 1:118, 126; 2:37.

17. Evers and Molina, *Yaqui Deer Songs/Maso Bwikam: A Native American Poetry*, 47, 40.

18. Austin, *American Indian Poetry*, 270; Evers and Molina, *Yaqui Deer Songs*, 40.

19. Suzuki, *Zen and Japanese Culture*, 219–20.

20. Evers and Molina, *Yaqui Deer Songs*, 37.

21. Britton, Introduction to *A Haiku Journey: Basho's "Narrow Road to a Far Province,"* 17.

22. Yasuda, *The Japanese Haiku*, 44.

23. Suzuki, *Zen in Japanese Culture*, 5, 36, 360, 220. For a discussion of the similarity between Suzuki's use of the phrase "dead words" and Vizenor's own "dead voices" from the novel of that title, see Chapter 6.

24. Brumble, *American Indian Autobiography*, 45.

25. Evers and Molina, *Yaqui Deer Songs*, 18.

26. Yasuda, *The Japanese Haiku*, 7; Astrov, Introduction to *The Winged Serpent*, 15–16.

27. Underhill, *Papago Woman*, 51.

28. Suzuki, *Zen in Japanese Culture*, 257, 24.

29. Keene, *Japanese Literature*, 40.

30. The movement in this haiku can be compared to that in the poem recognized by many as the one that gave birth to the present school of haiku. One translation of the poem, by the seventeenth-century master Basho, reads:

"The old pond, ah! / A frog jumps in: / The water's sound." The dynamics of this poem as analyzed by both Suzuki (*Zen and Japanese Culture*, 227–29, 238–41) and Keene (*Japanese Literature*, 38–39) include a collision between the tranquillity of the ancient pond (standing for the "eternal and the constant") and the disruptive sound of the loud splash of water (standing for "the momentary"). The imaginative experience of the collision then results in an awareness of the point of intersection (of the eternal and the momentary) "on the other side of eternity, where timeless time is," and thus leads to an understanding of the unity of the two worlds—the "sensual" and the "supersensual" (*Zen and Japanese Culture*, 241).

31. Griffin, *Woman and Nature: The Roaring Inside Her*, 190–91; Evers and Molina, *Yaqui Deer Songs*, 44, 47.

32. Suzuki, *Zen and Japanese Culture*, 242–43.

33. Matthias Schubnell, in *N. Scott Momaday: The Cultural and Literary Background*, talks about Momaday's idea of racial memory and the various terms he employs to describe it: "Momaday uses several terms to describe the extension of individual memory into anteriority: 'blood memory' or 'blood recollection,' 'whole memory,' 'memory of the blood,' and 'racial memory.' They all describe a verbal dimension of reality which perpetuates cultural identity" (54). Vizenor, however, says, "I think there is something going on there, too, but I would rather go for a larger collective unconscious. . . . I had a time with that—[the] racial unconscious. I think we can draw more immediate, closer environmental experience which is racial, but I'm less about it [race] than I am about an intersection in the world" (Interview).

34. Dewey, *Art as Experience*, 89.

35. Suzuki, for example, comments: "The images thus held up and arranged in a haiku may not be at all intelligible to those whose minds have not been fully trained to read the meanings conveyed therein" (*Zen and Japanese Culture*, 243). Vizenor notes how important a sense of place can be in the rendering of haiku and notes how the natural and seasonal qualities vary with location. The haiku images, he says, "set up possibility," and he compares them to the "naming of a town." The images reveal "the place, the time, the relationship so we can understand." For example, "if I say winter in Minnesota, you know there's a connection visually and by experience" (Interview).

Many others have taken up this idea of the place-specific quality of primal knowledge. For example, in *The American Rhythm: Studies and Reexpressions of American Indian Songs*, Mary Austin advances the idea of the "landscape line," which acknowledges a concrete connection between environment and literary rhythm and form, and James Ruppert uses the term "geographical determinism" to describe a similar relationship in "Discovering America: Mary Austin and Imagism." In his essay "Landscape and Narrative," from *Crossing Open Ground* (1989), Barry Lopez claims, "The shape of the individual mind is affected by land as it is by genes" (65).

36. Quoted in Yasuda, *The Japanese Haiku*, 44.

37. Babcock, "'A Tolerated Margin of Mess,'" 180.

38. Suzuki, *Zen in Japanese Culture*, 24.

39. Ibid., 349.

Chapter 5. Trickster Signatures

1. Among the works that offer some discussion of the trickster-transformer are William Bright, "The Natural History of Old Man Coyote"; A. LaVonne Ruoff, "The Survival of Tradition: American Indian Oral and Written Narratives"; Jarold Ramsey, "Coyote and Friends: An Experiment in Interpretive Bricolage"; Barre Toelken, "Ma'i Joldloshi: Legendary Styles and Navajo Myth"; Barbara Babcock, "'A Tolerated Margin of Mess': The Trickster and His Tales Reconsidered"; and Mac Linscott Ricketts, "The North American Trickster."

2. See, for example, Babcock, "'A Tolerated Margin of Mess,'" especially 167–79, and Paul Radin, *The Trickster: A Study in American Indian Mythology*.

3. Kenneth Lincoln, *Indi'n Humor: Bicultural Play in Native America*. Lincoln's vehement critique of Vizenor's work is in a section entitled "Trickster Slippage" (152–62). Among the other elements of Vizenor's work with which Lincoln finds fault are his self-conscious and sometimes self-referential wordplay, his use of sex and violence, and his recycling of characters and incidents from one work to another. About *Bearheart*, for example, he writes, "This fiction of a sado-masochist America, then, serves up dissonant Trickster jokes—cheap puns, degrading sex, random violence, and a clichéd journey to uncertain ends" (156).

4. Lincoln, *Native American Renaissance*, 122; Babcock, "'A Tolerated Margin of Mess,'" 163.

5. Vizenor's theoretical works on the trickster likewise emphasize this point.

6. Toelkin, "Ma'i Joldloshi," 203.

7. Toelkin, Foreword to *Giving Birth to Thunder, Sleeping With His Daughter*, xii; Ramsey, *Reading the Fire*, 29.

8. Ibid., 26.

9. Ibid., 28.

10. Radin, *Trickster*, xxiv, 168.

11. Jung, "On the Psychology of the Trickster Figure," 207.

12. Vizenor is also critical of Victor Barnouw's *Wisconsin Chippewa Myths and Tales and Their Relation to Chippewa Life* and of Andrew Wiget's comments on

trickster in *Native American Literature*. He says, for example, that Wiget "bears the worst of colonial historicism in this interpretation of trickster figuration in tribal literature" (*Manifest Manners*, 96, and "Ruins of Representation," 146–47).

13. Radin does acknowledge that "no generation understands him [trickster] fully but no generation can do without him," and that "he represents not only the undifferentiated and distant past, but likewise the undifferentiated present within every individual" (*Trickster*, 168). However, in the process of differentiating between the "original" trickster cycle and plot and the stories he collected in the earlier 1900s, Radin implies that changes and additions tainted the original.

14. Jung, "On the Psychology of the Trickster Figure," 200–201.

15. Wiget, Review of *Narrative Chance*, 478.

16. Owens, *Other Destinies*, 235.

17. Boyarin, "Europe's Indian, America's Jew: Modiano and Vizenor," 26.

18. See, for example, "Trickster Discourse: Comic Holotropes and Language Games."

19. Babcock, "'A Tolerated Margin of Mess,'" 162–63.

20. Ibid., 179–81.

21. Jaskoski, Review of *The Heirs of Columbus*, 82; Ramsey, *Reading the Fire*, 79; Owens, *Other Destinies*, 234–35.

22. Elaine Jahner has commented on Vizenor's awareness of "how writing is a specific kind of mythic 'breakthrough into performance'" in "Heading 'Em Off at the Impasse"; Velie, "The Trickster Novel," 136.

23. Babcock, "'A Tolerated Margin of Mess,'" 181; Turner, "Betwixt and Between: The Liminal Period in Rites de Passage," in *The Forest of Symbols: Aspects of Ndembu Ritual* (Ithaca: Cornell University Press, 1967), 106, as quoted in Babcock, "'A Tolerated Margin of Mess,'" 182.

24. Jahner, "Heading 'Em Off," 6.

25. Gerald Vizenor, *Harold of Orange*, film (30 min.), dir. Richard Weise (Minnesota Film-in-the-Cities, 1983). Screenplay in *Shadow Distance*, 297–333 (quotation from 333). In the following discussion of *Harold of Orange*, I refer to the actual film, to the text of the screenplay as published in *Shadow Distance*, and to the original thirty-seven-page manuscript version of the screenplay. Parenthetical references identify the source of the quoted material.

26. Babcock, "'A Tolerated Margin of Mess,'" 181.

27. Ibid.

28. Ibid.

29. Ibid., 158.

30. This particular scene, absent in the original script, was added to the film

version while it was being shot at the Sun Dance Institute, and a version of it is included in the published screenplay.

31. Buffy Sainte-Marie, "Trickster," song from *Harold of Orange*.

32. Louis Owens makes an important distinction between notions of territory (unoccupied space) and frontier (place of contact), on which I build here ("Mixedblood Metaphors: Identity in Contemporary Native American Fiction").

33. Ruppert, "Mediation and Multiple Narrative in Contemporary Native American Fiction," 213 (Ruppert's *Mediation in Contemporary Native American Fiction* explores these same ideas in greater depth); Ashcroft, Griffiths, and Tiffen, *The Empire Writes Back*, 195.

34. Ruppert, "Mediation and Multiple Narrative," 210; Ascroft, Griffiths, and Tiffen, 110.

35. Owens, *Other Destinies*, 243.

36. In her discussion on marginality in "'A Tolerated Margin of Mess,'" Babcock distinguishes between such aspects of marginality as volition and nonvolition, permanent and temporary, type and phase. I build on her discussion here.

37. In *Other Destinies*, for example, Owens writes: "Gerald Vizenor goes still farther [than Leslie Silko in *Ceremony*] in his celebration of mixedbloods. . . . Vizenor rejects entirely the conventional posture of mourning for the hapless mixedblood trapped between two worlds" (26–27), and "Vizenor is the first American Indian author to find 'crossbloods' a cause for joyous celebration" (254). In *Four American Indian Literary Masters*, Velie notes, "Vizenor . . . tries to celebrate the unique status of the mixed-bloods—to reverse the prejudice that has plagued them, to make a hero of the halfbreed" (138).

38. Owens, *Other Destinies*, 5.

39. Ashcroft, Griffiths, and Tiffen, *The Empire Writes Back*, 81; Owens, *Other Destinies*, 11. For further discussion of the danger to tribal oral traditions see, for example, Jana Sequoya, "How (!) is an Indian?: A Contest of Stories," in *New Voices in Native American Literary Criticism*, ed. Arnold Krupat (Washington, D.C.: Smithsonian Institution Press, 1993), 453–73.

Chapter 6. Reanimating the Dead Voices: Strategies of a Revolutionary Style

1. Bowers and Silet, "An Interview with Gerald Vizenor," 45.

2. The term "postindian turns," which Vizenor uses in *Manifest Manners* (63), is a twist on Richard Rorty's and Ihab Hassan's use of the phrase "the postmodern turn." See Rorty, *The Linguistic Turn: Recent Essays in Philosophical Method*, and Hassan, *The Postmodern Turn: Essays in Postmodern Theory and*

Culture. The phrase "consumer mentality of the arts" is from my 1987 interview with Vizenor.

3. Vizenor notes that this insight came from the British novelist and social critic John Berger, who co-authored *Another Way of Telling* with Jean Mohr.

4. Iser, "The Reading Process," 65, 60.

5. Empson, *Seven Types of Ambiguity,* 1, 5–6; Eagleton, *Literary Theory,* 52.

6. Anderson, *Style As Argument;* Karl, *American Fictions, 1940–1980,* 384; Jahner, "Heading 'Em Off at the Impasse," 23.

7. Anderson, *Style As Argument,* 5.

8. Empson, *Seven Types of Ambiguity,* 155.

9. Iser, "The Reading Process," 55.

10. Ramsey, *Reading the Fire,* 194.

11. Anderson, *Style As Argument,* 134.

12. Iser, "The Reading Process," 58.

13. Some critics have noted how the role enacted here by Griever has troubling similarities to the "savior" role or superior stance taken by colonizers in their relations with Native Americans and Native lifestyles.

14. Eco, "The Poetics of the Open Work," in *The Role of the Reader,* 51–53.

15. *The American Heritage Dictionary of the English Language* (Boston: Houghton Mifflin, 1980), 775.

16. Iser, "The Reading Process," 54; Pousseur quoted in Eco, *The Role of the Reader,* 55.

17. In *anishinabe nagamon* Vizenor writes, "The *anishinabe*—the original people of the woodland—believe they were given wisdom and life color from the sun reflecting on the sacred shell during this long migration" (9). William Warren, in *History of the Ojibway People,* one of the sources for Vizenor's work, quotes from a speech made at a Midéwiwin ceremony about the shell: "The great Megis (seashell) showed itself above the surface of the great water, and the rays of the sun for a long period were reflected from its glossy back. It gave the warmth and light to the An-ish-in-aub-ag (red race)" (78).

18. Geok-lin Lim, "Twelve Asian American Writers," 240.

19. Fenollosa, *The Chinese Written Character As a Medium for Poetry,* 31. For a discussion of Fenollosa's ideas, especially as Pound uses them in his own theories regarding "luminous details," see Michael Bernstein, *The Tale of the Tribe: Ezra Pound and the Modern Verse Epic,* esp. 36–43. If we entertain the possibility of a connection between Vizenor's use of *luminous* and that of Pound or Fenollosa, the resulting implications are massive and entail, for example, the critical discussions regarding the relationships between, on the one hand, the ideogram, the haiku, and the embedding technique of Native American picto-

graphs and poetry, and on the other hand, the imagist and vorticist movements of modern poetry. (Some of these connections were previously mentioned in Chapter 4).

20. Joseph Bruchac, "Follow the Trickroutes: An Interview with Gerald Vizenor," 301.

21. Eagleton, *Literary Theory*, 125.

22. Babcock uses this phrase in "'A Tolerated Margin of Mess,'" 166.

23. Bruchac, "Follow the Trickroutes," 306.

24. Andrew Connors discusses this pronoun switching by Vizenor in an unpublished paper, "Gerald Vizenor's *Griever*: American Indian Literature Comes of Age."

25. Information about the fate of the *Bearheart* manuscript comes from my 1987 interview with Vizenor and from subsequent conversations with the author. Owens's 1990 afterword to the second edition also reports the losses of the manuscript and describes Owens's students' protests against the work (247–48).

26. Lincoln, *Indi'n Humor*, 156, 158.

27. Eagleton, *Literary Theory*, 41.

28. Owens, Afterword, 247–48.

29. Lincoln, *Native American Renaissance*, 34.

30. Tom Lynch, "Politely Practicing Manifest Destiny"; Kathy Whitson, Review of *Dead Voices: Natural Agonies in the New World* and *Summer in the Spring: Anishinaabe Lyric Poems and Stories*, 132.

31. Campbell, *The Inner Reaches of Outer Space: Metaphor As Myth and As Religion*, 20, 21, 31.

32. Jahner, "Heading 'Em Off," 8.

33. As Ruoff notes in "American Indian Literatures: Introduction and Bibliography," *American Studies International* 24.2 (1986): 2–52, earthdiver myths are "common throughout North America, except in the extreme North, Northeast, and Southwest, and are also widely distributed outside North America" (5). In the Ojibway tribal myth the world is covered with water, and Naanabozho asks various creatures to dive beneath the water to retrieve some mud with which to create a new earth. The muskrat succeeds in bringing back a small amount of earth. From this Naanabozho makes a small island (referred to in some versions of the story as "Turtle Island"). Vizenor quotes from one version of the earthdiver story in *The People Named the Chippewa*.

34. Vizenor has spoken of his first reading of Wolfe's work as a "profound reading experience": "I randomly found a copy of Thomas Wolfe . . . a volume entitled *A Stone, a Leaf, a Door*. It was a collection of his prose pieces, put into kind of a free verse. It was an average-length book . . . two hundred to two

hundred and fifty pages. And I was so transported by the power of his language and imagination that I read the whole book through, standing at the shelf for several hours. It was extraordinary" (Interview). Examples of the many connections with Vizenor's other works include "summer in the spring" (88), an echo of his reexpression of an Ojibway dream song and the title he gives to three editions of his collection of reexpressions; "small pox and the rivers are dead" (132), an echo of a short story title; and "the leaves are down" (132), an echo of a haiku line.

35. Suzuki, *Zen and Japanese Culture*, 7–8.

36. Vološinov, *Marxism and the Philosophy of Language*, 73, 102, 103, 118.

37. Ong, *Orality and Literacy*, 117, 161.

38. Zebroski, "The English Department and Social Class," 82–83.

39. Hartsock, "Rethinking Modernism: Minority vs. Majority Theories," 204.

40. Iser, "The Reading Process," 63.

Conclusion. The Almost World: Finding a Place on the Printed Page

1. Anishinaabemowin was not Vizenor's childhood language, although he was exposed to words from the tribal language through his paternal relatives. As an adult he studied the Ojibway language on his own and through the language program at Bemidji State University.

2. This phrase is from "Ice Tricksters," in *Landfill Meditation*, where Vizenor writes: "The almost world is a better world, a sweeter dream world than the world we are taught to understand in school." Things in the story are "almost" but never quite what words say, and the word "almost" is "used to stretch the truth like a tribal trickster" (24).

3. Barry Lopez's discussion of "external" and "internal" landscape, the relationship between the two, and the way they can be brought together in story, in "Landscape and Narrative," seems helpful in understanding the embedded landscape of much of Vizenor's work.

4. Velie, "Vizenor: Post-Modern Fiction," in *Four American Indian Literary Masters*, 135 (Velie bases his identification of these characteristics on an article by Phillip Stevick, "Scherezade runs out of plots, goes on talking; the king puzzled, listens: An essay on the new fiction" *Triquarterly* 26 [Winter 1973]: 332–62); Velie, "The Trickster Novel," 129; Owens, " 'Grinning Aboriginal Demons.' "

5. Bevis, "Native American Novels: Homing In," in *Recovering the Word: Essays on Native American Literature*, 580–620.

6. Lynch, "Politely Practicing Manifest Destiny."

Works by Gerald Vizenor
A Selected Bibliography

Books as Author

anishinabe adisokan: Tales of the People. Minneapolis: Nodin Press, 1970.

anishinabe nagamon: Songs of the People. Minneapolis: Nodin Press, 1965.

Beaulieu and Vizenor Families: Genealogies. Minneapolis: privately published, 1983.

Crossbloods: Bone Courts, Bingo, and Other Reports. Minneapolis: University of Minnesota Press, 1990.

Darkness in Saint Louis Bearheart. St. Paul, Minn.: Truck Press, 1978. Reprinted as *Bearheart: The Heirship Chronicles*. Minneapolis: University of Minnesota Press, 1990.

Dead Voices: Natural Agonies in the New World. Norman: University of Oklahoma Press, 1992.

Earthdivers: Tribal Narratives on Mixed Descent. Minneapolis: University of Minnesota Press, 1981.

Empty Swings: Haiku in English. Minneapolis: Nodin Press, 1967.

Escorts to White Earth, 1868–1968: 100 Years on a Reservation. Minneapolis: Four Winds, 1968.

The Everlasting Sky: New Voices from the People Named the Chippewa. New York: Crowell-Collier Press, 1972.

Griever: An American Monkey King in China. Normal: Illinois State University/ Fiction Collective, 1987.

The Heirs of Columbus. Hanover, N.H.: Wesleyan University Press/University Press of New England, 1991.

Interior Landscapes: Autobiographical Myths and Metaphors. Minneapolis: University of Minnesota Press, 1990.

Landfill Meditation: Crossblood Stories. Hanover, N.H.: Wesleyan University Press/University Press of New England, 1991.

Manifest Manners: Postindian Warriors of Survivance. Hanover, N.H.: Wesleyan University Press/University Press of New England, 1994.

Matsushima: Pine Islands. Minneapolis: Nodin Press, 1984.

The People Named the Chippewa: Narrative Histories. Minneapolis: University of Minnesota Press, 1984.

Raising the Moon Vines: Original Haiku in English. Minneapolis: Nodin Press, 1964.

Seventeen Chirps: Haiku in English. Minneapolis: Nodin Press, 1964.

Shadow Distance: A Gerald Vizenor Reader. Hanover, N.H.: Wesleyan University Press/University Press of New England, 1994.

Slight Abrasions: A Dialogue in Haiku. With Jerome Downes. Minneapolis: Nodin Press, 1966.

Summer in the Spring: Ojibwe Lyric Poems and Tribal Stories. Minneapolis: Nodin Press, 1981. A revised edition of materials earlier published in *Summer in the Spring* (1965), *anishinabe adisokan* (1970), and *anishinabe nagamon* (1970). Reprinted as *Summer in the Spring: Anishinaabe Lyric Poems and Stories*, new ed., Norman: University of Oklahoma Press, 1993.

Thomas James White Hawk. Mound, Minn.: Four Winds, 1968.

Tribal Scenes and Ceremonies. Minneapolis: Nodin Press, 1976. New edition. University of Minnesota Press, 1990.

The Trickster of Liberty: Tribal Heirs to a Wild Baronage. Minneapolis: University of Minnesota Press, 1988.

Two Wings the Butterfly: Haiku Poems in English. St. Cloud, Minn.: privately published, 1962.

Wordarrows: Indians and Whites in the New Fur Trade. Minneapolis: University of Minnesota Press, 1978. Italian translation: *Parolefrecce*. Translated by Maria Vittoria D'Amico. In literature series Indianamericana, edited by Laura Coltelli. University of Pisa, 1992.

Books as Editor

Narrative Chance: Postmodern Discourse on Native American Indian Literatures. Albuquerque: University of New Mexico Press, 1989. Reprint. Norman: University of Oklahoma Press, 1993.

Native American Literature: A Brief Introduction and Anthology. New York: HarperCollins, 1995.

Touchwood: A Collection of Ojibway Prose. New York: New Rivers Press, 1987.

Excerpts

Bearheart. (Excerpts.) In *Stand in Good Relations to the Earth,* translated and edited by Alexandre Vaschenko, 162–73. Moscow: Raduga, 1983.

"Bound Feet." (From *Griever,* 13–18.) *Fiction International* 17.1 (Spring 1987): 4–8. Reprinted in *Before Columbus Foundation Fiction Anthology,* edited by Ishmael Reed, Kathryn Trueblood, and Shawn Wong, 654–58. New York: Norton, 1992.

"Casino Coups." (From *Manifest Manners,* 138–48.) *Wicazo Sa Review* 9.2 (Fall 1993): 80–84. Reprinted in *Shadow Distance.* 210–18.

Heirs of Columbus. (Excerpts.) *Paint Brush: A Journal of Contemporary Multicultural Literature.* Special issue: *The World of N. Scott Momaday,* edited by Richard Fleck. 11 (Autumn 1994): 29–30.

"Holosexual Clown." (From *Griever,* 19–26.) In *Before Columbus Foundation Fiction Anthology,* edited by Ishmael Reed, Kathryn Trueblood, and Shawn Wong, 658–65. New York: Norton, 1992.

"Measuring My Blood." (From *Interior Landscapes,* 26–33). In *Shadow Distance,* 7–13. Also in *Native American Literature,* 68–74.

"Pink Flamingos." (From *Interior Landscapes,* 101–13.) *Caliban* 7 (Winter 1989): 140–49.

"Postmodern Discourse on Native American Literature." (From *Narrative Chance,* ix–xiii.) *Halcyon* 12 (1990): 43–48.

Short Fiction

"Almost a Whole Trickster." In *A Gathering of Flowers,* edited by Joyce Carol Thomas, 3–20. New York: Harper and Row, 1990. Reprinted as "Ice Tricksters" in *Landfill Meditation,* 22–34.

"Almost Browne: The Twice Told Tribal Trickster." In *Listening to Ourselves: More Stories from "The Sound of Writing,"* edited by Alan Cheuse and Caroline Marshall, 233–41. Doubleday/Anchor Books, 1994.

"Bad Breath." In *An Illuminated History of the Future,* edited by Curtis White, 135–64. Normal: Illinois State University/Fiction Collective Two, 1989. Reprinted in *Landfill Meditation,* 68–97.

"The Baron of Patronia." In *Talking Leaves: Contemporary Native American Short Stories,* edited by Craig Lesley, 284–93. New York: Dell Publishing, 1991. Reprinted in *The Trickster of Liberty,* 3–19.

"China Browne." In *Talking Leaves: Contemporary Native American Short Stories*, edited by Craig Lesley, 294–303. New York: Dell, 1991. Reprinted in *The Trickster of Liberty*, 21–42.

"Episodes in Mythic Verism, from *Monsignor Missalwait's Interstate*." In *The New Native American Novel: Works in Progress*, edited by Mary Dougherty Bartlett, 109–26. Albuquerque: University of New Mexico Press, 1986. Reprinted as "Interstate Reservation" in *Landfill Meditation*, 116–35.

"Feral Lasers." *Caliban* 6 (Fall 1989): 16–23. Reprinted in *Landfill Meditation*, 11–21.

"Four Skin." *Tamaqua* 2 (Winter–Spring 1991): 89–104. Reprinted as "Four Skin Documents" in *Landfill Meditation*, 162–79.

"Land Fill Meditation." *Minneapolis Star Saturday Magazine* 10 February 1979: 8–12. Reprinted in *Words in the Blood: Contemporary Indian Writers of North and South America*, edited by Jamake Highwater, 136–47. New York: New American Library, 1984; and in *Landfill Meditation*, 98–115.

"The Last Lecture." In *American Indian Literature*, edited by Alan Velie, 339–47. Norman: University of Oklahoma Press, 1991.

"Luminous Thighs." In *The Lightning Within*, edited by Alan Velie, 67–89. Norman: University of Oklahoma Press, 1991.

"Luminous Thighs: Mythic Tropisms." *Genre* 18.2 (Summer 1985): 131–49. Reprinted in *Landfill Meditation*, 180–201.

"MacChurbbs and the Celibate Juicer: Winter Quarter Lecture Notes." *Metropolis Magazine* (Minneapolis/St. Paul), 15 February 1977: 27. Reprinted in revised version as "Fruit Juice and Tribal Trickeries" in *Wordarrows*, 75–81.

"Migration Tricks from Tribalness: Five Sorties." *Minnesota Monthly* January 1978: 8–9.

"The Moccasin Game." In *Earth Song, Sky Spirit: Short Stories of the Contemporary Native American Experience*, edited by Clifford E. Trafzer, 37–62. New York: Doubleday, 1992.

"Moccasin Games." *Caliban* 9 (Spring 1990): 96–109. Reprinted in revised version in *Without Discovery*, edited by Ray Gonzales, 73–89. Broken Moon Press, 1992.

"Monte Cassino Curiosa: Heart Dancers at the Headwaters." *Caliban* 14 (1994): 60–70.

"Oshkiwiigan: Heartlines on the Trickster Express." *Religion and Literature* 26.1 (Spring 1994): 89–106. Reprinted as "Heartlines" in *Native American Literature*, 142–57.

"Paraday at the Berkeley Chicken Center." *Metropolis Magazine* 12 Apr. 1977: 23. Reprinted in revised version as "Paraday Chicken Pluck" in *Earthdivers*, 95–104.

"The Psychotaxidermist." *Minneapolis Star Saturday Magazine* 29 July 1978: 8–11. Reprinted in *The Minnesota Experience*, edited by Jean Ervin, 220–28. Minneapolis: Adams, 1979. Also in *Words in the Blood: Contemporary Indian Writers of North and South America*, edited by Jamake Highwater, 124–31. New York: New American Library, 1984. Also in *Landfill Meditation*, 136–46.

"Rattling Hail Ceremonial." *Minnesota Star Saturday Magazine* 2 April 1978: 8–9. Reprinted in *Words in the Blood: Contemporary Indian Writers of North and South America*, edited by Jamake Highwater, 131–36. New York: New American Library, 1984. Also in *Landfill Meditation*, 147–54.

"Reservation Café: The Origins of American Indian Instant Coffee." In *Earth Power Coming: Short Fiction in Native American Literature*, edited by Simon J. Ortiz: 31–36. Tsaile, Ariz.: Navajo Community College Press, 1983. Reprinted as "Crossblood Coffee" in *Landfill Meditation*, 155–61. Revised version of "Anishinabica: Instant Tribal Coffee." *Minnesota Star*, 1981. French translation: "Café Reservé ou les origins du café instante." Translated by Manuel Van Thienen. *Sur le dos de la tortue, revue bilingue de littérature amerindienne*, 1991.

"Reversal of Fortunes: Tribalism in the Nick of Time." *Caliban* 13 (1993): 22–28. Reprinted in *Shadow Distance*, 219–26.

"Shadows at La Pointe." In *Touchwood: A Collection of Ojibway Prose*. Many Minnesota Project no. 3, pp. 120–37. St. Paul, Minn.: New Rivers, 1987. Reprinted from *The People Named the Chippewa*, 37–55.

"Smallpox and the River Are Dead." *Minneapolis Tribune Sunday Picture Magazine*, 30 December 1979: 12.

"Stone Trickster." *Northeast Indian Quarterly* 8 (Fall 1991): 26–27.

"The Tragic Wisdom of Salamanders." *Caliban* 12 (1993): 16–27. Reprinted in *Sacred Trusts: Essays on Stewardship and Responsibility*, edited by Michael Katakis: 161–76. San Francisco: Mercury House, 1993. Reprinted in condensed version in *Bear Essentials* 3 (Summer 1994): 46–51. Reprinted in *Shadow Distance*, 194–209.

"Tribal Trickster Dissolves: White 'Word' Piles with a Red Man's Brew." *Minneapolis Star* 31 August 1981: A4.

"Trickster Photography: Simulations in the Ethnographic Present." *Exposure* 29.1 (Fall 1993): 4–5.

"White Noise." In *White Noise, The Fellin Sisters, The Man of Sorrows*, by Gerald Vizenor, Lon Otto, and Jonis Agee, 1–13. St. Paul, Minn.: Fodder, 1983.

"Wings on the Santa Maria." In *Avante-Pop: Fiction for a Daydream Nation*, edited by Larry McCaffery, 199–206. Boulder, Colo.: Black Ice Books, 1993.

"Word Cinemas." *Book Forum*. Special Issue: *American Indians Today: Thought, Literature, Art,* edited by Elaine Jahner. 5.3 (Summer 1981): 389–95. Reprinted in revised version as "Four Skin," *Tamaqua* 2 (Winter 1991): 89–104. Reprinted as "Four Skin Documents" in *Landfill Meditation,* 162–179.

Autobiographical Essays

"Crows Written on the Poplars: Autocritical Autobiographies." In *I Tell You Now: Autobiographical Essays by Native American Writers,* edited by Arnold Krupat and Brian Swann, 99–110. Lincoln: University of Nebraska Press, 1987.

"Gerald Vizenor, Ojibway/Chippewa Writer." In *This Song Remembers: Self-Portraits of Native Americans in the Arts,* edited by Jane B. Katz, 163–69. Boston: Houghton Mifflin, 1980.

"I Know What You Mean, Erdupps MacChurbbs: Autobiographical Myths and Metaphors." In *Growing Up in Minnesota: Ten Writers Remember Their Childhoods,* edited by Chester Anderson, 79–111. Minneapolis: University of Minnesota Press, 1976.

"July 1947: Many Point Camp." In *Inheriting the Land,* edited by Mark Vinz and Thom Tammaro, 313–18. University of Minnesota Press, 1993.

Poetry

An American Indian Anthology, compiled by Benet Tvedten, 46–48. Marvin, N.D.: Blue Cloud Abbey, 1971.

L'arbe a paroles. Special issue: *14 poetes amerindiens contemporains,* translated by Manuel Van Thienen. Four haiku and three poems in French translation. *Identités wallonie* 65 (Brussels, Autumn 1989): 122–25.

Chariton Review 5 (1979): 67.

The Clouds Threw This Light: Contemporary Native American Poetry, edited by Phillip Foss, 317–20. Santa Fe: Institute of American Indian Arts Press, 1983.

Dakota Territory 6 (1973–74): 28–31.

American Indian Poets, translated and edited by Alexandre Vaschenko. Eight poems in Russian translation, 51–57 Moscow: Moladaja Gvardija, 1983.

From the Belly of the Shark, edited by Walter Lowenfels, 69–70. New York: Vintage Books, 1973.

The Haiku Anthology, edited by Cor van den Hevel, 200–203. New York: Doubleday, 1974.

Harper's Anthology of 20th-Century Native American Poetry, edited by Duane Niatum, 71–74. New York: Harper and Row, 1988.

"An Introduction to Haiku." Sixteen poems and a critical introduction. *Neeuropa* (Spring–Summer 1991-92): 63-67.

"Our Land: Anishinaabe." Haiku. Photographs by Bjorn Sletto. *Native Peoples* (Spring 1993): 32-35.

The Pursuit of Poetry, edited by Louis Untermeyer, 205-06. New York: Simon and Schuster, 1970.

Songs from This Earth on Turtle's Back: Contemporary American Indian Poetry, edited by Joseph Bruchac, 261-66. Greenfield Center, N.Y.: Greenfield Review Press, 1983.

Voices of the Rainbow, edited by Kenneth Rosen, 31-45. New York: Viking Press, 1975.

Water Striders. Haiku. Porter Broadside Series. Santa Cruz, Calif.: Moving Parts Press, 1989.

Films, Screenplays, and Scripts

Gerald Vizenor. A fifty-minute film from the "Native American Novelists" series. Produced by RTSI (Swiss Television). Released for U.S. distribution in 1994. Distributed by Films for the Humanities, Princeton, N.J.

Harold of Orange. Film directed by Richard Weise. Minnesota Film-in-the-Cities, 1983. Screenplay in *Shadow Distance*, 297-333.

Harold of Orange/Harold von Orangen. Translated by Wolfgang Hochbruck. Osnabrueck Bi-Lingual Editions of Marginalized Authors. Eddignen, Germany: Edition Claus Iselee, 1994.

Ishi and the Wood Ducks: Postindian Trickster Comedies. Stage play. In *Native American Literature*, 299-336.

The Moccasin Games. Radio play in German translation. Berlin: Sender Feiers, 1992.

Wortlichtspiele. Scenes from *Harold of Orange* in German translation. *Chelsea Hotel* 1 (Eggingen, Germany, 1992).

Essays and Works of Mixed Genre

"Bone Courts: The Rights and Narrative Representation of Tribal Bones." *American Indian Quarterly* 10.4 (1986): 319-31. Reprinted and revised as "Bone Courts: The Natural Rights of Tribal Remains" in *The Interrupted Life*, 58-67. New York: Museum of Contemporary Art, 1991. Reprinted as "Bone Courts: The Natural Rights of Tribal Bones" in *Crossbloods*, 62-82.

"Buffalo Bill: An Emblem of Ersatz History." *Minneapolis Tribune* 29 November 1981: A19.

"Brixton: A New Circus of Proud People." *Minneapolis Tribune* 31 January 1982: A15.

"Christopher Columbus: Lost Havens in the Ruins of Representations." *American Indian Quarterly* 16.4 (Fall 1992): 521–32.

"Confrontation or Negotiation." In *Native American Testimony: A Chronicle of Indian-White Relations from Prophesy to the Present, 1492–1992,* edited by Peter Nabokov, 376–80. New York: Viking Penguin, 1991.

"The Envoy to Haiku." *Chicago Review* 39.3 (1993): 55–62.

"Dennis Banks: What Sort of Hero?" *Minneapolis Tribune* 22 July 1978: A4.

"Gerald Vizenor." In *The Writer's Notebook,* edited by Howard Junker, 219–33. New York: HarperCollins, 1995.

"Gambling on Sovereignty." *American Indian Quarterly* 16.3 (Summer 1992): 411–13.

"Heirs of Columbus." *Fiction International* 20 (Fall 1991): 182–92. This volume reprinted as *Looking Glass,* edited by Clifford Trafzer. San Diego State University Press, 1991.

"How Sly Davis Sees It." *Twin Citian* 10 (October 1967): 60–62.

"Indian Alcoholics Are Individuals, Not White Mice." *Minneapolis Tribune* 23 April 1982: A15.

"Indian Manikins with a Few References." *Minneapolis Tribune* 5 September 1981: A10.

"Introduction." *Genre* 25.4 (Winter 1992): 315–19.

"Ishi Bares His Chest: Tribal Simulations and Survivance." In *Partial Recall: Photographs of Native North Americans,* edited by Lucy R. Lippard, 65–71. New York: New Press, 1992.

"Job Corps Center at Lydick Lake: For Some a Wager, for Others a Chance." *Twin Citian* 9 (August 1966): 15–21.

"Laurel Hole In The Day." *On the Reservation* 14.3 (Spring 1986): 30–32. Reprinted in *Touchwood: A Collection of Ojibway Prose,* 138–41. Revised version from *Wordarrows,* 47–53.

"Manifest Manners: The Long Gaze of Christopher Columbus." *Boundary 2* 19.2 (Fall 1992): 223–35.

"Mystic Warrior Speaks with Tongue Forked and a Vision Flawed." *Minneapolis Star and Tribune* 18 May 1984: C16.

"Native American Dissolve." *Oshkaabewis Native Journal* 1.1 (1990): 63–65.

"Native American Indian Identies: Autoinscriptions and the Cultures of Names." *Genre* 25.4 (Winter 1992): 431–40.

"Native American Indian Literature: Critical Metaphors of the Ghost Dance." *World Literature Today* 66.2 (Spring 1992): 223–27.

"1966: Plymouth Avenue Is Going to Burn." *Twin Citian* 9 (October 1966): 20–21.

"The Ojibway." *Twin Citian* 8.10 (May 1966): 18–19.

"The Power of Names." Article on the naming of Ishi Court at the University of California, Berkeley. *News From Native California* 7.3 (Summer 1993): 38–41.

"Preserving Trivial Tattle in California." *Minneapolis Tribune* 5 February 1978: A13.

"The Ruins of Representations: Shadow Survivance and the Literature of Dominance." *American Indian Quarterly* 17.1 (Winter 1993): 7–30. Reprinted in *An Other Tongue*, edited by Alfred Arteaga, 139–67. Durham, N.C.: Duke University Press, 1994.

"Socioacupuncture: Mythic Reversals and the Striptease in Four Scenes." In *The American Indian and the Problem of History*, edited by Calvin Martin, 180–91. New York: Oxford University Press, 1987. Reprinted in *Out There: Marginalization and Contemporary Cultures*, 411–19. New York: New Museum of Contemporary Art/MIT Press, 1990.

"'This Is Good for the People': Indian Education and Senator Mondale at Rough Rock." *Twin Citian* (July 1969): 17–20.

"Thomas James White Hawk: Wrap-Up?" *New Twin Citian* 1.1 (Jan. 1970): 39–44.

"Tribal People and the Poetic Image: Visions of Eyes and Hands." In *American Indian Art: Form and Tradition*, 15–22. Minneapolis: Walker Art Center, 1972.

"Trickster Discourse." *Wicazo Sa Review* 5.1 (Spring 1989): 2–7.

"Trickster Discourse." *American Indian Quarterly* 16.3 (Summer 1990): 277–87.

"Trickster Discourse: Comic and Tragic Themes in Native American Literature." In *"Buried Roots and Indestructible Seeds": The Survival of American Indian Life in Story, History, and Spirit*, edited by Mark Lindquist and Martin Zanger, 33–41. Madison: Wisconsin Humanities Council, 1993. New edition. University of Wisconsin Press, 1994.

"Trickster Discourse: Comic Holotropes and Language Games." In *Narrative Chance*, 187–211.

"The Urban Indian." *Twin Citian* 8 (June 1966): 13.

"Wampum to Pictures of Presidents." In *Different Shores: Perspectives on Race and Ethnicity in America*, edited by Ronald Takaki, 126–28. Oxford University Press, 1987.

"We Rarely Turn Anyone Down." *Twin Citian* 6 (October 1969): 35–38.

"Why Must Thomas White Hawk Die?" *Twin Citian* 10 (June 1968): 17–32.

Works Cited

Ainsworth, Linda. "History and Imagination: Gerald Vizenor's *The People Named the Chippewa*." *American Indian Quarterly* 9.1 (Winter 1985): 52–53.

Allen, Paula Gunn. *Grandmothers of the Light: A Medicine Woman's Sourcebook*. Boston: Beacon Press, 1991.

———. "The Sacred Hoop: A Contemporary Perspective." In *Studies in American Indian Literature: Critical Essays and Course Designs*, edited by Paula Gunn Allen, 4–22. New York: Modern Language Association Press, 1983.

———. *The Sacred Hoop: Recovering the Feminine in American Indian Traditions*. Boston: Beacon Press, 1986.

———, ed. *Studies in American Indian Literature: Critical Essays and Course Designs*. New York: Modern Language Association Press, 1983.

———. *The Woman Who Owned the Shadows*. San Francisco: Spinsters, 1983.

Anderson, Chris. *Style As Argument: Contemporary American Nonfiction*. Carbondale: Southern Illinois University Press, 1987.

Ashcroft, Bill, Gareth Griffiths, and Helen Tiffin. *The Empire Writes Back: Theory and Practice in Post-Colonial Literatures*. New York: Routledge, 1989.

Astrov, Margot, ed. *The Winged Serpent*. New York: John Day Company, 1946. Reprint. *American Indian Prose and Poetry*. New York: Capricorn Books, 1962. Reprint. *The Winged Serpent: American Indian Prose and Poetry*. Boston: Beacon Press, 1992.

Austin, Mary. *The American Rhythm: Studies and Reexpressions of Amerindian Songs*. 1923. Reprint. New York: Cooper Square, 1970.

———. Introduction to *The Path on the Rainbow: An Anthology of Songs and Chants from the Indians of North America*. 1918. Reprinted in *Literature of the American Indians: Views and Interpretations. A Gathering of Memories, Symbolic Contexts, and Literary Criticism*, edited by Abraham Chapman, 266–75. Reprint. *American Indian Poetry: An Anthology of Songs and Chants*. New York: New American Library, 1972.

———. Review of *Dawn Boy* by Edna Lou Walton. *Saturday Review of Literature* 10 (April 1924).

Babcock, Barbara. " 'A Tolerated Margin of Mess': The Trickster and His Tales Reconsidered." In *Critical Essays on Native American Literature*, edited by Andrew Wiget, 153–85. Boston: G. K. Hall, 1985.

Ballinger, Franchot. "Sacred Reversals: Trickster in Gerald Vizenor's *Earthdivers: Tribal Narratives on Mixed Descent*." *American Indian Quarterly* 9.1 (Winter 1985): 55–59.

Bakhtin, Mikhail. *The Dialogic Imagination: Four Essays*. Translated by Caryl Emerson and Michael Holquist. Austin: University of Texas Press, 1981.

———. *Speech Genres and Other Late Essays*. Translated by Vern W. McGee. Austin: University of Texas Press, 1986.

Barnouw, Victor. *Wisconsin Chippewa Myths and Tales and Their Relation to Chippewa Life*. Madison: University of Wisconsin Press, 1977.

Barthes, Roland. *Camera Lucida: Reflections on Photography*. New York: Hill and Wang, 1981.

Bataille, Gretchen M., and Kathleen Mullen Sands. *American Indian Women: Telling Their Lives*. Lincoln: University of Nebraska Press, 1984.

Bataille, Gretchen M., Charles L. P. Silet, eds. *The Pretend Indians: Images of Native Americans in the Movies*. Ames: Iowa State University Press, 1980.

Baudrillard, Jean. *Simulacres et simulation*. Paris: Galiée, 1981.

Bell, Betty Louise. "Almost the Whole Truth: Gerald Vizenor's Shadow Working and Native American Autobiography." *A/B Auto/Biography* 7.2 (Fall 1992): 180–95.

Berger, John, and Jean Mohr. *Another Way of Telling*. New York: Pantheon Books, 1982.

Berkhofer, Robert, Jr. *The White Man's Indian: Images of the American Indian from Columbus to the Present*. New York: Vintage Books, 1978.

Bernstein, Michael. *The Tale of the Tribe: Ezra Pound and the Modern Verse Epic*. Princeton, N.J.: Princeton University Press, 1980.

Bevis, William. "Native American Novels: Homing In." In *Recovering the Word: Essays on Native American Literature*, edited by Brian Swann and Arnold Krupat, 580–620. Berkeley and Los Angeles: University of California Press, 1987. Reprinted in *Critical Perspectives on Native American Literature*, edited by Richard F. Fleck, 15–45. Washinton, D.C.: Three Continents Press, 1993.

Blaeser, Kimberly M. Personal interview with Gerald Vizenor. Berkeley, California, 27–29, May 1987.

Bowers, Neal, and Charles L. P. Silet. "An Interview with Gerald Vizenor." *Melus* 8.1 (1981): 41–49.

Boyarin, Jonathan. "Europe's Indian, American's Jew: Modiano and Vizenor." In *Storm from Paradise: The Politics of Jewish Memory*, 9–31. Minneapolis: University of Minnesota Press, 1992.

Bright, William. "The Natural History of Old Man Coyote." In *Recovering the Word: Essays on Native American Literature*, edited by Brian Swann and Arnold Krupat, 339–87. Berkeley and Los Angeles: University of California Press, 1987.

Britton, Dorothy. Introduction to *A Haiku Journey: Basho's "Narrow Road to a Far Province."* Tokyo and New York: Kodansha International, 1980.

Bruchac, Joseph. "Follow the Trickroutes: An Interview with Gerald Vizenor." In *Survival This Way: Interviews with American Indian Poets*, 287–310. Tucson: University of Arizona Press, 1987.

Brumble, H. David, III. *American Indian Autobiography*. Berkeley and Los Angeles: University of California Press, 1988.

Campbell, Joseph. *The Inner Reaches of Outer Space: Metaphor As Myth and As Religion*. New York: Harper and Row, 1988.

Capps, Walter Holden, ed. *Seeing with a Native Eye: Essays on Native American Religion*. New York: Harper & Row, 1976.

Castro, Michael. *Interpreting the Indian: Twentieth-Century Poets and the Native American*. Albuquerque: University of New Mexico Press, 1983.

Chamberlain, B. H. *Japanese Poetry*. London: John Murray, 1910.

Churchill, Ward. *Fantasies of the Master Race: Literature, Cinema and the Colonization of American Indians*. Monroe, Me.: Common Courage Press, 1992.

Coltelli, Laura. "Gerald Vizenor: The Trickster Heirs of Columbus." Interview. *Native American Literature Forum* (Pisa, Italy: University of Pisa) 2–3 (1990–91): 101–16.

———. *Winged Words: American Indian Writers Speak*. Lincoln: University of Nebraska Press, 1990.

Cruikshank, Julie. *Life Lived Like a Story: Life Stories of Three Yukon Native Elders.* In collaboration with Angela Sidney, Kitty Smith and Annie Ned. Lincoln: University of Nebraska Press, 1990.

Day, A. Grove. *The Sky Clears: Poetry of the American Indians.* 1951. Reprint. Lincoln: University of Nebraska Press, 1964.

Deloria, Vine, Jr. Foreword to *New and Old Voices of Wah'kon-tah: Contemporary Native American Poetry,* edited by Robert K. Dodge and Joseph B. McCullough, ix–x. New York: International, 1985.

———. *God Is Red.* New York: Dell, 1973.

Densmore, Frances. *Chippewa Customs.* 1929. Reprint. N.p.: Minnesota Historical Society Press, 1979.

———. *Chippewa Music.* Vol 1. Bureau of American Ethnology Bulletin no. 45. Washington, D.C.: Smithsonian Institute, 1910. Reprint. New York: Da Capo Press, 1972.

———. *Chippewa Music.* Vol. 2. Bureau of American Ethnology Bulletin no. 53. Washington, D.C.: Smithsonian Institute, 1913. Reprint. New York, Da Capo Press, 1972.

Dewey, John. *Art As Experience.* New York: Mentor, Balch, 1934.

Drinnon, Richard. *Facing West: The Metaphysics of Indian-Hating and Empire-Building.* Minneapolis: University of Minnesota Press, 1980.

———. "The Metaphysics of Dancing Tribes." In *The American Indian and the Problem of History,* edited by Calvin Martin, 106–13. New York: Oxford University Press, 1987.

Dundes, Alan. "Earth-Diver: Creation of the Mythopoeic Male." In *Sacred Narrative: Readings in the Theory of Myth,* edited by Alan Dundes, 27–94. Berkeley and Los Angeles: University of California Press, 1984.

Eagleton, Terry. *Literary Theory: An Introduction.* Minneapolis: University of Minnesota Press, 1983.

Eco, Umberto. *The Role of Reader: Explorations in the Semiotics of Texts.* Bloomington: Indiana University Press, 1984.

———. *Travels in Hyperreality.* Translated by William Weaver. San Diego: Harcourt, Brace, Jovanovich, 1990.

Elliot, Emory, ed. "The Journal of the First Voyage of Christopher Columbus." In *American Literature: A Prentice Hall Anthology* 1.33–38. Englewood Cliffs, N.J.: Prentice Hall, 1991.

Empson, William. *Seven Types of Ambiguity.* 1947. Reprint. New York: New Directions, 1966.

Erdoes, Richard, and John (Fire) Lame Deer. *Lame Deer: Seeker of Visions.* New York: Simon and Schuster, 1972.

Erdrich, Louise. *Love Medicine*. New York: Holt, Rinehart, and Winston, 1984.

Evers, Larry J. "A Conversation with N. Scott Momaday." *Sun Tracks: An American Indian Literary Magazine* 2.2 (1976): 21.

———, ed. *The South Corner of Time: hopi navajo papgo yaqui tribal literature*. Tucson: University of Arizona Press, 1983.

Evers, Larry J., and Felipe S. Molina. *Yaqui Deer Songs/Maso Bwikam: A Native American Poetry*. Tucson: Sun Tracks/University of Arizona Press, 1990.

Fenollosa, Ernest. *The Chinese Written Character As a Medium for Poetry*. 1918. Reprinted in *The Poetics of the New American Poetry*, edited by Donald Allen and Warren Tallman. New York: Grove Press, 1973.

Fiedler, Leslie A. *The Return of the Vanishing American*. New York: Stein and Day, 1969.

Fletcher, John Gould. Introduction to *A Pepper Pod* by Kenneth Yasuda. New York: Knopf, 1947.

Forster, E. M. *Aspects of the Novel*. 1927. Reprint. New York: Harcourt Brace, 1955.

Geok-lin Lim, Shirley. "Twelve Asian American Writers." In *Redefining American Literary History*, edited by A. LaVonne Brown Ruoff and Jerry W. Ward Jr., 237–50. New York: Modern Language Association of America, 1990.

Glauber, Robert. Review of *Summer in the Spring* by Gerald Vizenor. *Beloit Poetry Journal* 16.2 (1965–66): 39.

Griffin, Susan. *Woman and Nature: The Roaring inside Her*. New York: Harper and Row, 1978.

Hale, Janet Campbell. *The Jailing of Cecilia Capture*. New York: Random House, 1985.

Hartsock, Nancy. "Rethinking Modernism: Minority vs. Majority Theories." *Cultural Critique* 7 (1987): 187–206.

Haseltine, Patricia. "The Voices of Gerald Vizenor: Survival through Transformation." *American Indian Quarterly* 9.1 (Winter 1985): 31.

Hassan, Ihab. *The Postmodern Turn: Essays in Postmodern Theory and Culture*. Columbus: Ohio State University Press, 1987.

Hickerson, Harold. *The Chippewa and Their Neighbors: A Study in Ethnohistory*. New York: Holt, 1970.

Hinton, Leanne, and Lucille J. Watahomigie, eds. *Spirit Mountain: An Anthology of Yuman Story and Song*. Tucson: University of Arizona Press, 1984.

Hogan, Linda. *Mean Spirit*. New York: Atheneum, 1990.

Hoxie, Frederick E. *Indians in American History: An Introduction*. Arlington Heights, Ill.: Harlan Davidson, 1988.

Iser, Wolfgang. "The Reading Process: A Phenomenological Approach." In *Reader-Response Criticism: From Formalism to Post-Structuralism*, edited by Jane P. Tompkins, 50–69. Baltimore: John Hopkins University Press, 1980.

Jahner, Elaine. "Allies in the Word Wars: Vizenor's Uses of Contemporary Critical Theory." *Studies in American Indian Literatures* 9.2 (1985): 64–69.

———. "Cultural Shrines Revisited." *American Indian Quarterly* 9.1 (Winter 1985): 25.

———. "Heading 'Em Off at the Impasse: Native American Authors Meet the Poststructuralists." Unpublished essay.

———. "Trickster Discourse: Comic and Tragic Themes in Native American Literature." In *"Buried Roots and Indestructible Seeds": The Survival of American Indian Life in Story, History, and Spirit*, edited by Mark Lindquist and Martin Zanger, 33–41. New edition, 67–83. Madison: Wisconsin Humanities Council, 1993.

Jaskoski, Helen. Review of *The Heirs of Columbus* by Gerald Vizenor. *Studies in American Indian Literatures* 4.2 (Spring 1992): 79–82.

Jones, Manina. *That Art of Difference: "Documentary-Collage" and English-Canadian Writing*. University of Toronto Press, 1993.

Jung, Carl Gustav. "On the Psychology of the Trickster Figure." In *The Trickster: A Study in American Indian Mythology*, edited by Paul Radin, 193–211. New York: Schocken Books, 1976.

Karl, Frederick R. *American Fictions, 1940–1980: A Comprehensive History and Critical Evaluation*. New York: Harper and Row, 1983.

Katz, Jane B. *This Song Remembers: Self-Portraits of Native Americans in the Arts*. Boston: Houghton Mifflin, 1980.

Keady, Maureen. "Walking Backwards into the Fourth World: Survival of the Fittest in *Bearheart*." *American Indian Quarterly* 9.1 (Winter 1985): 61.

Keene, Donald. *Japanese Literature: An Introduction for Western Readers*. New York: Grove Press, 1955.

Kroeber, Karl. "Deconstructionist Criticism and American Indian Literature." *Boundary* 2 7 (1979): 72–87.

———. "1492–1992: American Indian Persistence and Resurgence." *Boundary* 2 19.3 (Fall 1992): 231.

Krupat, Arnold. *For Those Who Come After: A Study of Native American Autobiography*. Berkeley and Los Angeles: University of California Press, 1985.

———. "On the Translation of Native American Song and Story: A Theorized History." In *On the Translation of Native American Literature*, edited by Brian Swann, 3–32. Washington, D.C.: Smithsonian Institution Press, 1992.

──────. "Post-Structuralism and Oral Tradition." In *Recovering the Word: Essays on Native American Literature*, edited by Brian Swann and Arnold Krupat, 113–28. Berkeley and Los Angeles: University of California Press, 1987.

──────. "Trickster's Lives: The Autobiographies of Gerald Vizenor." Paper presented at the annual meeting of the Modern Language Association, Toronto, 1993.

──────. *The Voice in the Margin: Native American Literature and the Canon*. Berkeley and Los Angeles: University of California Press, 1989.

Krupat, Arnold, and Brian Swann, eds. *I Tell You Now: Autobiographical Essays by Native American Writers*. Lincoln: University of Nebraska Press, 1987.

──────. *Recovering the Word: Essays on Native American Literature*. Berkeley and Los Angeles: University of California Press, 1987.

LaRocque, Emma. "Preface: Here Are Our Voices—Who Will Hear?" In *Writing the Circle: Native Women of Western Canada*, xx–xxi. Edmonton, Alberta: NeWest, 1990.

Larson, Charles. *American Indian Fiction*. Albuquerque: University of New Mexico Press, 1978.

Lee, A. Robert. Introduction to *Shadow Distance: A Gerald Vizenor Reader*. Hanover, N.H.: Wesleyan University Press/University Press of New England, 1994.

Lincoln, Kenneth. *Indi'n Humor: Bicultural Play in Native America*. New York: Oxford University Press, 1993.

──────. *Native American Renaissance*. Berkeley and Los Angeles: University of California Press, 1983.

Lodge, David, ed. *Twentieth-Century Literary Criticism: A Reader*. London: Longman Group, 1972.

Lopez, Barry. *Giving Birth to Thunder, Sleeping with His Daughter: Coyote Builds North America*. Kansas City: Sheed/Andrews and McNeel, 1977.

──────. "Landscape and Narrative." In *Crossing Open Ground*. New York: Vintage Books, 1989.

Lynch, Tom. "Politely Practicing Manifest Destiny." Review of *Manifest Manners* by Gerald Vizenor. *San Francisco Chronicle* 15 May 1994.

Mailer, Norman. *The Armies of the Night: History As a Novel, the Novel As History*. New York: New American Library, 1968.

Martin, Calvin, ed. "An Introduction aboard the Fidèle." In *The American Indian and the Problem of History*. New York: Oxford University Press, 1987.

Momaday, N. Scott. *House Made of Dawn*. New York: Signet/New American Library, 1966.

──────. "The Man Made of Words." In *Indian Voices: The First Convocation of American Indian Scholars*, 55. San Francisco: Indian Historian Press, 1970.

———. "Native American Attitudes to the Environment." In *Seeing with a Native Eye*, edited by Walter Holden Capps, 79–85. New York: Harper and Row, 1976.

———. *The Way to Rainy Mountain*. Albuquerque: University of New Mexico Press, 1969.

———. "The Writing of Nonfiction Prose." A discussion at the Library of Congress, Washington, January 1974. In *Teaching Creative Writing*, 26–64. Washington, D.C.: Government Printing Office, 1974.

Nabokov, Peter. *Native American Testimony: A Chronicle of Indian-White Relations from Prophecy to the Present, 1492–1992*. New York: Viking Penguin, 1991.

Neihardt, John G. *Black Elk Speaks*. 1932. Reprint. Lincoln: University of Nebraska Press, 1961.

Niranjana, Tejaswini. *Siting Translation*. Berkeley and Los Angeles: University of California Press, 1992.

O'Brien, Sharon. *American Indian Tribal Governments*. Norman: University of Oklahoma Press, 1989.

Olney, James. *Autobiography: Essays Theoretical and Critical*. Princeton, N.J.: Princeton University Press, 1980.

Ong, Walter J. *The Interfaces of the Word: Studies in the Evolution of Consciousness and Culture*. Ithaca, N.Y.: Cornell University Press, 1977.

———. *Orality and Literacy: The Technologizing of the Word*. London: Methuen, 1982.

———. *The Presence of the Word*. New Haven, Conn.: Yale University Press, 1967.

Ortiz, Alfonso. "Indian/White Relations: A View from the Other Side of the 'Frontier.'" In *Indians in American History: An Introduction*, edited by Frederick E. Hoxie, 1–16. Arlington Heights, Ill.: Harlan Davidson, 1988.

Ortiz, Simon. "Always the Stories: A Brief History and Thoughts on My Writing." In *Coyote Was Here: Essays on Contemporary Native American Literary and Political Mobilization*, edited by Bo Schöler, 57–69. Aarhus, Denmark: SEKLOS/University of Aarhus, 1984.

———. "Fight Back: For the Sake of the People, for the Sake of the Land." *INAD Journal* (University of New Mexico) 1.1 (1980).

———. *A Good Journey*. Tucson: Sun Tracks/University of Arizona Press, 1977.

———. *Song, Poetry, and Language: Expression and Perception*. Tsaile, Ariz.: Navajo Community College Press, 1977.

———. "You Were Real, The White Radical Said to Me." In *Fightin': New and Collected Stories*. Chicago: Thunder's Mouth Press, 1969.

Owens, Louis. "Acts of Recovery: The American Indian Novel in the 80's." *Western American Literature* 22.1 (1987): 53–57.

——. Afterword to *Bearheart: The Heirship Chronicles* by Gerald Vizenor. Minneapolis: University of Minnesota Press, 1990.

——. "'Grinning Aboriginal Demons': Gerald Vizenor's *Bearheart* and the Indian's Escape from Gothic." In *Frontier Gothic: Terror and Wonder at the Frontier in American Literature*, edited by Joanne B. Karpinski, David Mogen, and Scott P. Sanders, 71–83. Rutherford, N.J.: Fairleigh Dickinson University Press, 1993.

——. "Mixedblood Metaphors: Identity in Contemporary Native American Fiction." Program for Faculty Renewal Workshop on American Indian Identity, Santa Fe, N.M., February 1993.

——. *Other Destinies: Understanding the American Indian Novel*. Norman: University of Oklahoma Press, 1992.

——. *Wolfsong*. Albuquerque: West End Press, 1991.

Radin, Paul. *The Trickster: A Study in American Indian Mythology*. New York: Schocken Books, 1972.

Ramsey, Jarold. *Reading the Fire: Essays in the Traditional Indian Literatures of the Far West*. Lincoln: University of Nebraska Press, 1983.

Rexroth, Kenneth. "American Indian Songs: The United States Bureau of Ethnology Collection." Reprinted in *Literature of the American Indians: Views and Interpretations: A Gathering of Indian Memories, Symbolic Contexts, and Literary Criticism*, edited by Abraham Chapman, 278–91. New York: New American Library, 1961.

Ricketts, Mac Linscott. "The North American Trickster." *History of Religions* 5 (1966): 327–50.

Rorty, Richard, ed. *The Linguistic Turn: Recent Essays in Philosophical Method*. Chicago: University of Chicago Press, 1967.

Rosco, Will. Review of *The Heirs of Columbus* by Gerald Vizenor. *San Francisco Chronicle* 4 August 1991: 1, 11.

Ruoff, A. LaVonne Brown. *American Indian Literatures: An Introduction, Bibliographic Review, and Selected Bibliography*. New York: Modern Language Association of America, 1990.

——. "American Indian Literatures: Introduction and Bibliography." *American Studies International* 24.2 (1986): 2–52.

——. "Gerald Vizenor: Compassionate Trickster." *American Indian Quarterly* 9.1 (Winter 1985): 67–73. Reprinted in *Studies in American Indian Literatures* 9.2 (Spring 1985): 52–63.

——. "Old Traditions and New Forms." In *Studies in American Indian Literature: Critical Essays and Course Designs*, edited by Paula Gunn Allen, 147–68. New York: Modern Language Association Press, 1983.

———. "The Survival of Tradition: American Indian Oral and Written Narratives". *Massachusetts Review* 27 (1986): 274–93.

———. "Woodland Word Warrior: An Introduction to the Works of Gerald Vizenor." *Melus* 13.1, 2 (Spring–Summer 1986): 13–43.

Ruppert, James. "Discovering America: Mary Austin and Imagism." In *Studies in American Indian Literature: Critical Essays and Course Designs*, edited by Paula Gunn Allen, 243–58. New York: Modern Language Association of America, 1983.

———. "Mediation and Multiple Narrative in Contemporary Native American Fiction." *Texas Studies in Literature and Language* 28.1 (1986): 209–225.

———. *Mediation in Contemporary Native American Fiction*. Norman: University of Oklahoma Press, 1995.

Said, Edward. *Orientalism*. New York: Pantheon Books, 1978.

Sandburg, Carl. Review of *Chippewa Music* by Frances Desnmore. *Poetry: A Magazine of Verse* 9 (February 1917): 245–55.

Schoolcraft, Henry Rowe. *Expedition to Lake Itasca; The Discovery of the Source of the Mississippi*. In collected reports edited by Philip P. Mason.

Schubnell, Matthias. *N. Scott Momaday: The Cultural and Literary Background*. Norman: University of Oklahoma Press, 1985.

Silberman, Robert. "Gerald Vizenor and *Harold of Orange*: From Word Cinemas to Real Cinema." *American Indian Quarterly* 9.1 (Winter 1985): 14.

Silko, Leslie M. *Ceremony*. New York: Viking Press, 1977.

Sledge, Linda Ching. "Oral Tradition in Kingston's *China Men*." In *Redefining American Literary History*, edited by A. LaVonne Brown Ruoff and Jerry W. Ward Jr., 142–54. New York: Modern Language Association of America, 1990.

Slotkin, Richard. *Regeneration through Violence: The Mythology of the American Frontier, 1600–1860*. Middletown, Conn.: Wesleyan University Press, 1973.

Sontag, Susan. *On Photography*. New York: Farrar, Straus, and Giroux, 1977.

Standiford, Lester. "Worlds Made of Dawn: Characteristic Image and Incident in Native American Imaginative Literature." In *Three American Literatures: Essays in Chicano, Native American, and Asian-American Literature for Teachers of American Literature*, edited by Houston A. Baker, Jr., 168–96. New York: Modern Language Association of America, 1982.

Stedmand, Raymond William. *Shadows of the Indian: Stereotypes in American Culture*. Norman: University of Oklahoma Press, 1982.

Suzuki, Daisetz T. *Zen and Japanese Culture*. Princeton, N.J.: Princeton University Press, 1959.

Swann, Brian. Introduction to *Harper's Anthology of 20th Century Native American Poetry*, edited by Duane Niatum. San Francisco: Harper and Row, 1988.

—. *On the Translation of Native American Literatures*. Washington, D.C.: Smithsonian Institution Press, 1992.

—, ed. *Smoothing the Ground: Essays on Native American Oral Literature*. Berkeley and Los Angeles: University of California Press, 1983.

Toelken, Barre. Foreword to *Giving Birth to Thunder, Sleeping with His Daughter: Coyote Builds North America*, by Barry Lopez. Kansas City: Sheed/Andrews and McNeel, 1977.

—. "Ma'i Joldloshi: Legendary Styles and Navajo Myth." In *American Folk Legend*, edited by Wayland Hand, 203-11. Berkeley and Los Angeles: University of California Press, 1971.

—. "Seeing with a Native Eye: How Many Sheep Will It Hold?" In *Seeing with a Native Eye: Essays on Native American Religion*, edited by Walter Holden Capps, 9-24. New York: Harper and Row, 1976.

Toelken, Barre, and Tacheeni Scott, "Poetic Retranslations and the 'Pretty Languages' of Yellowman." In *Traditional Literatures of the American Indian: Texts and Interpretations*, edited by Karl Kroeber, 65-116. Lincoln: University of Nebraska Press, 1981.

Tompkins, Jane P., ed. *Reader-Response Criticism: From Formalism to Post-Structuralism*. Baltimore: John Hopkins University Press, 1980.

Turner, Victor. "Betwixt and Between: The Liminal Period in Rites de Passage." In *The Forest of Symbols: Aspects of Ndembu Ritual*, edited by V. W. Turner. Ithaca, N.Y.: Cornell University Press, 1967.

Underhill, Ruth Murray. *The Autobiography of a Papago Woman*. Memoirs of the American Anthropological Association, vol. 46. 1936. Reprint. *Papago Woman*. 1979. Reprint. Prospect Heights, Ill.: Waveland Press, 1985.

Velie, Alan. *Four American Indian Literary Masters: N. Scott Momaday, James Welch, Leslie Marmon Silko, and Gerald Vizenor*. Norman: University of Oklahoma Press, 1982.

—. "The Trickster Novel." In *Narrative Chance: Postmodern Discourse on Native American Literatures*, edited by Gerald Vizenor, 121-39. Albuquerque: University of New Mexico Press, 1989. Reprint. Norman: University of Oklahoma Press, 1993.

Vološinov, V. N. *Marxism and the Philosophy of Language*. Cambridge, Mass.: Harvard University Press, 1973.

Wagner, Roy. *The Invention of Culture*. Chicago: University of Chicago Press, 1975.

Warren, William W. *History of the Ojibway People*. 1885. Reprint. St. Paul: Minnesota Historical Society Press, 1984.

Waters, Frank. *The Man Who Killed the Deer*. 1941. Reprint. New York: Pocket Books, 1971.

Welch, James. *Winter in the Blood*. New York: Harper and Row, 1974. Reprint. New York: Penguin Books, 1986.

Whitson, Kathy. Review of *Dead Voices: Natural Agonies in the New World* and *Summer in the Spring: Anishinaabe Lyric Poems and Stories* by Gerald Vizenor. *Studies in Short Fiction* (Spring 1994): 130–32.

Wiget, Andrew. Review of *Narrative Chance: Postmodern Discourse on Native American Indian Literatures*, edited by Gerald Vizenor. *Modern Philology* (May 1991): 476–79.

Witherspoon, Gary. *Language and Art in the Navajo Universe*. Ann Arbor: University of Michigan Press, 1977.

Wong, Hertha. *Sending My Heart Back Across the Years: Tradition and Innovation in Native American Autobiography*. New York: Oxford University Press, 1992.

Yasuda, Kenneth. *The Japanese Haiku: Its Essential Nature, History, and Possibilities in English, with Selected Examples*. Rutland, Vt.: Tuttle, 1957.

Zebroski, James Thomas. "The English Department and Social Class: Resisting Writing." In *The Right to Literacy*, edited by Andrea A. Lunsford, Helene Moglen, and James Slevin, 81–87. New York: Modern Language Association of America, 1990.

Ziff, Larzer. *Writing in the New Nation*. New Haven, Conn.: Yale University Press, 1991.

Zinsser, William, ed. *Inventing the Truth: The Art and Craft of Memoir*. Boston: Houghton Mifflin, 1987.

Index

Ideological colonization, Martin's notion of, 83

"I Know What You Mean, Erdupps MacChurbbs," 49, 59, 101, 106, 147, 180–81, 203, 204

Imagination, 4, 26, 179; freeing of, 146; and history, 86, 87, 91, 92, 95, 96; luminosity and, 175, 176; minimalism and, 32; new ghost dance literature, 196; of non-Indians, 53, 54; truth of, 89

Imagism, 111, 112, 114

Indeterminacy. *See* Ambiguity and indeterminacy

Indian, as label, 53, 56

Indians. *See* Native Americans

Inner Reaches of Outer Space, The: Metaphor as Myth and as Religion (Campbell), 188

Inner words, Vološinov's notion of, 193

Interior landscapes, 201

Interior Landscapes: Autobiographical Myths and Metaphors, 9, 11, 30, 63, 71, 99, 101–106, 157; squirrel story, retelling of, 203; trickster, 137; White Hawk, Thomas James, 45

Interview scenes, in Vizenor's works, 30

Intuition, 26

Invented Indian, 41, 49, 52, 53–63, 158, 163; in *Harold of Orange*, 151

Inventing the Truth (Zinsser), 100

Invention, in non-tribal writing of history, 87

Ironmoccasin, Novena Mae (character), 187

Iser, Wolfgang, 10, 35, 166, 168, 172, 176, 196

Ishi, 40, 57, 58–59

I Tell You Now (Krupat and Swann), 100

Jackson, Barbara, 86

Jahner, Elaine, 30, 33, 34, 54, 63, 74, 146, 167, 189, 190, 206n.5, 220n.22

Jailing of Cecilia Capture, The (Hale), 158

Japanese culture: arts, Suzuki's analysis of, 116, 118, 120; Vizenor's exposure to, 6, 109. *See also* Haiku

Japanese Literature (Keene), 218n.30

Jaskoski, Helen, 145

Jefferson, Thomas, 56

Jones, Manina, 86

Jones, Mark, 173

Joseph, Chief, 43

Journalism, 7; and shadow stories, 78–82, 95

Jung, Carl, 140, 141

Ka Ka Geesick, John, 172, 173

Karl, Frederick, 167

Keady, Maureen, 50, 205n.4

Keene, Donald, 117, 121, 218n.30

"Keeping the Family Together," 64

Kitschymen, 61

Klamath, 137

Kroeber, Karl, 58, 111, 112, 114

Krupat, Arnold, 16, 33, 74, 100, 101, 113

Lake Forest College, Ill., 8

Lakota, 137

Lame Deer, John (Fire), 32, 72

Lame Deer: Seeker of Visions (Lame Deer), 32, 72

"Land Fill Meditation," 67, 148, 201

Landfill Meditation: Crossblood Stories, 9, 11, 18, 21, 136, 159, 178

Land rights, 39

"Landscape and Narrative" (Lopez), 224n.3

Landscape line, Austin's notion of, 218n.35

Language: alive quality of, 28; appropriate use of, 20, 29; code transgression, 184, 185; and community, 27–28, 29; dead, 191; as dialogic relationship, 193; and experience, 191; limits of, 167, 168; metaphor, use of, 187–90; of mixedbloods, 159, 160; power of, 19, 179; relational contexts of, 27; of social services, 44; tribal cultures' reverence for, 17; and tribal survival, 39; in Vizenor's trickster stories, 143; white and Indian understandings of, 65; and worldview, 165

Minnesota, University of, 6, 9
Mixedbloods, 5, 8, 139, 155–61, 163, 174; earthdiver metaphor, 189–90; survivors, 67, 68; trickster as metaphor for, 138; urban, 203
"Moccasin Game, The," 105
Modernism, 36
Modoc, 137
Molina, Felipe, 24, 111, 112, 115, 116, 117, 119, 122, 216n.6
Momaday, N. Scott, 3, 9, 10, 16, 53, 91, 200; imagination, role of, 26; mixedbloods, 158; perception and reception, in oral tradition, 24–25; racial memory, 127, 218n.33; silence, necessity of, 21; sound, function of, 22; speculation, notion of, 86; storytelling, 70, 90; word, power of, 18; writings in oral tradition, 76–77
Monkey King (character), 177
Monologic writing style, 195, 196
Morrison, Eliza, 92
"Mother Earth Man and Paradise Flies," 23, 169
Motion pictures, 56
Myth, 188; in autobiographical writings, 100, 102, 104, 105; and history, 90, 91; as social charter, 144, 150; transformative powers of, 82

N. Scott Momaday: The Cultural and Literary Background (Schubnell), 218n.33
Naanabozho, 9, 30, 69, 90, 105, 136, 137, 138, 142, 144, 148, 194
"Naanabozho and the Gambler," 137
Names: proper use of, in tribal cultures, 20; of Vizenor's characters, 170
Narrative Chance: Postmodern Discourse on Native American Literatures, 10
"Native American Attitudes to the Environment" (Momaday), 26
Native American languages, tension between English and, 73, 74
Native American literature, 200, 201–202; autobiographical form, 100, 104; in

English, 75–76; history in, 84–85. *See also* Oral tradition
Native American Literature (Wiget), 220n.12
Native Americans: historical accounts of, 83–84; invented Indian, 41, 53–63; misrepresentations of, 72–73; oral tradition, 17–28; primal memory, 127; response to histories, 84; survival, 38, 39, 40, 63–71; worldview, 26
"Natural Tilts," 22
Nature: communication with, in Yaqui deer songs, 119; participation in, in Vizenor's poetry, 125
Navajo, 137, 138; healing rituals, 44; language, relational contexts of, 27; speech and song, 24
Nebraska, University of: Native American Prose Award, 9
Negotiation, Vizenor's concept of, 62
Neihardt, John G., 84, 190
New earthdivers, 40
New ghost dance literature, 75, 107, 196
New people of the woodland. *See* Oshki anishinabe
Newton, Kingsley (character), 149
Niranjana, Tejaswini, 77
Noble savage, image of, 53, 59, 152
Nonlinguistic sound, 22–23
"Now Day Indi'ns," 38, 41

"October 1957: Death Song to a Red Rodent," 203
Ojibway, 10, 16, 64; creation story, 191, 194; dish game, 192; trickster, 137
"Ojibway, The," 112, 119
Ojibway dream songs, 204; Vizenor's haiku and, 6, 108–115; Vizenor's transcriptions, 130–33
Oklahoma, University of, 9
Ong, Walter J., 10, 11, 17, 27–31, 191, 193
"On the Psychology of the Trickster Figure" (Jung), 140
Opened closure, Ong's concept of, 30
Open texts, 13, 34, 35, 113, 119, 166, 175, 176, 179; Vizenor's haiku, 121, 126

Oral history, 88
Orality and Literacy (Ong), 30–31, 191
Oral tradition, 17, 29, 30, 31; allusiveness
    of, 27, 29, 120; and autobiographical
    form, 100; closure, lack of, in stories,
    170; community and, 27; dialogic
    quality of, 27, 28, 29; emphasis on,
    in *Dead Voices*, 192; and haiku, 119;
    historical significance of, 87; and
    identity, 159; liberating power of, 3;
    listener response in, 117; perception
    and reception in, 24–26; and spiritual
    realm, 24; survival and, 39, 65, 69,
    70; translation, 15–16, 74, 113; visual
    thinking in, 65–66; Vizenor's efforts
    to write in, 29–30, 115, 156, 199; words
    in, 18, 21, 24; and written literature,
    11, 12, 15–16, 73–74, 76, 160, 193
Orientalism (Said), 42
Origin, Native American understanding
    of, 18–19
Ortiz, Alfonso, 95
Ortiz, Simon, 15, 16, 17, 24, 25, 76, 82, 84
Oshki anishinabe, 7, 25, 40, 55, 64, 65,
    66
Osuga, Seki. *See* Otsuji
Other Destinies (Owens), 73
Otsuji, 115, 128
Owens, Louis, 39, 73, 75, 80, 159;
    Bearheart, analysis of, 186, 202;
    mixedbloods, 157, 158; terminal
    creeds, 52; territory and frontier,
    distinction between, 85; tricksters,
    136, 143, 145

Papago, 32, 120
"Paraday at the Berkeley Chicken
    Center," 105
Parkman, Francis, 56
Path on the Rainbow, The (Austin), 111
Pearce, Roy Harvey, 42
PEN Oakland Book Award, 9
*People Named the Chippewa, The: Narrative
    Histories*, 72, 83, 84, 86, 87, 88, 90,
    200, 206n.8; invented Indian, 7, 8,
    30, 51, 54, 55, 59, 62; juxtapositions,

172; trickster, 105, 142, 143; words,
    power of, 17
Perception. *See* Listener participation;
    Reader-response aesthetics
Peripatetic mouth warriors, 62
Personality, and historiography, 88
Photography, 57–58, 59
Pictorial writing style, 195, 196
Pierz, Francis, 92
Place, sense of, 85, 90, 200–201, 218n.35
Planes of vision, dual, 26, 209n.32
Play, 4
Plot, in Vizenor's writing, 202
Pocahontas, 96, 97
"Poetics of the Open Work, The"
    (Eco), 175
Poetry: purpose of, 71. *See also* Haiku
Political intent: in cultural word wars,
    42; Vizenor's revolutionary intentions,
    164–65, 185, 194–97
Pope, Saxton, 58
Post-colonial culture, hybridization of,
    155–56
Postindian, 56, 57, 63
Postindian turns, 165
Postindian warriors, 11, 40, 41, 57, 147,
    148, 196; survivance, 68, 157
"Postindian Warriors" (essay), 61
Postmodernism, 36, 37, 145, 165, 202
Poststructuralism, 36, 37, 143, 146
"Post-Structuralism and Oral
    Literature" (Krupat), 33
Pound, Ezra, 178
Pousseur, Henri, 176
Pratt, Richard, 46
Pretenders to the tribe, 203
Primal memory, 127
Projection, trickster tales' function as,
    144

Rabelais, François, 202
Racial memory, Momaday's notion of,
    127, 218n.33
Racism: and cultural schizophrenia,
    46; in cultural word wars, 42
Radical particularity, 168, 170, 171, 172

Radin, Paul, 138, 140, 141, 142, 219n.2
Radio talk show segments, in Vizenor's
    works, 30
Raising the Moon Vines, 6, 124, 129
Ramsey, Jarold, 32, 33–34, 139, 140, 145
Reader-response aesthetics, 12, 13, 14,
    27, 34, 164, 165, 196, 197; ambiguity
    and, 166–72, 179; code transgression
    and, 186; education of audience,
    179–82; haiku, 117–21; intertextual
    dialogue, in *Dead Voices*, 190;
    liberation from dead voices, 193;
    minimalism and, 32; narrative
    history, 82, 89; open work and, 175,
    176; silence as technique of, 22;
    song poems, 120, 133; theories of,
    10, 34–37; trickster tales, 137, 141,
    143, 144, 145; Vizenor's autobio-
    graphical texts, 102, 103; Vizenor's
    haiku, 125–27; Vizenor's prose,
    29–30, 82, 134, 135; Vizenor's
    translations, 113. *See also* Listener
    participation
Reading the Fire (Ramsey), 32
Reagan, Ronald, 97
Reception. *See* Listener participation;
    Reader-response aesthetics
Reed, Ishmael, 10
Reexpression and reimagination: of
    Native traditions, 74–75, 113; of
    Ojibway dream songs, 6–7, 130–33, 178
*Regeneration through Violence: The
    Mythology of the American Frontier,
    1600–1860* (Slotkin), 84
Reluming the past, Vizenor's notion of
    history as, 86
Remains, tribal. *See* Tribal artifacts and
    remains
"Rethinking Modernism: Minority *vs.*
    Majority Theories" (Hartsock), 195
"Reversals of Fortune," 86
Revolutionary intentions, Vizenor's,
    164–65, 185, 194–97
Rexroth, Kenneth, 111, 112, 114, 116
Rhetoric of gaps, 168–73
Rhetoric of process, 168, 179–82

Riel, Louis, 99
Romantic Indian stereotype, 53, 54, 55,
    59, 61
Roscoe, Will, 95, 96
"Ruins of Representation, The: Shadow
    Survivance and the Literature of
    Dominance," 73, 74, 75, 77, 82, 106, 107
Ruoff, A. LaVonne, 17, 19, 20, 40, 41, 11
Ruppert, James, 111, 155, 156, 218n.35

Sacred, the, in trickster literature, 146
"Sacred Hoop, The: A Contemporary
    Perspective" (Allen), 24
*Sacred Hoop, The: Recovering the
    Feminine in American Indian Traditions*
    (Allen), 173
Said, Edward, 42
St. Paul, Minn., 7
Salish, 137
Samana (character), 96, 98
Sandburg, Carl, 111
Sand Creek Massacre, 80, 81, 95
"Sand Creek Survivors," 11, 77–82
Satire, 178, 194; *Harold of Orange*, 151,
    152; of trickster tales, 144, 151
Satori, in Zen philosophy. *See*
    Enlightenment
Savagism and Civilization (Pearce), 42
Savala, Refugio, 116
Schoolcraft, Henry Rowe, 86, 92–93
Schubnell, Matthias, 26, 80, 218n.33
"Seeing with a Native Eye" (Toelken),
    26
Self-image, cultural word wars and, 43
Self-victimization, 48–52
Seventeen Chirps: Haiku in English, 6,
    121, 128, 130, 133
Seven Types of Ambiguity (Empson), 166
Sex, Vizenor's graphic descriptions of,
    184, 185, 186
Shadow Distance, 9, 149–53
Shadow reality, 12; in autobiographica
    texts, 103, 106, 107; in historical
    accounts, 82, 86, 88, 94–95; in
    journalism, 78–82
"Shadows at La Pointe," 11, 88–90, 92–9

Wolfe, Thomas, 190–91
Wolfsong (Owens), 158
Woman and Nature: The Roaring Inside Her (Griffin), 122
Woman Who Owned the Shadows, The (Allen), 19, 158
Wong, Hertha, 100
Wordarrows: Indians and Whites in the New Fur Trade, 7, 11, 16, 18, 30, 79, 101; ambiguity and indeterminacy, 169; cultural word wars, 39, 40, 42, 43; language and formation of community, 27; language use, commentary on, 20–21; sound, use of, 23; survivance, 64, 67–71; terminal believers, 49; tricksters, 148; White Hawk, Thomas James, 45, 46, 48
Word cinemas, 15, 66, 76
"Word Cinemas" (essay), 182
Wordmakers, 16, 17, 79, 204
Words, 160; as dead voices, 21; and experiential reality, 192; inadequacy of, and use of metaphor, 188, 189; living and dead, 118, 193; as origin, 18–19; power of, 17–18, 20, 29, 44, 178, 179; as rituals, 24; use of, 20, 21; Vizenor's coining of, 183; in Zen and haiku, 118
Word wars. *See* Cultural word wars
World, origin of, 19
Worldview, nontribal, 47, 165
Worldview, tribal, 26, 47, 51; of Anishinaabeg, 87; and autobio-graphical form, 100; humankind as part of nature, 128; and Vizenor's haiku, 115, 126
Wounded Knee Massacre, 81, 84
Writing of Disaster, The (Blanchot), 190
Writing styles: and social structure, 194, 195, 196
Writing the Circle: Native Women of Western Canada (LaRocque), 76
Written texts: artifice of written language, 13; basic styles, Vološinov's notion of, 195; Native, in English, 75–76; and oral traditions, 15–16, 73–74, 76, 160, 193; subversion of, 161
Written word, Ong's notion of, 28, 30

Yaba Gezi (character), 177
Yaqui: deer songs, 115–16, 119; listener response, to talking stick story, 117; supernatural world of, 122
Yaqui Deer Songs (Evers and Molina), 24, 216n.6
Yasuda, Kenneth, 117, 118, 119

Zebroski, James Thomas, 194, 195
Zen and Japanese Culture (Suzuki), 191, 218n.30, 218n.35
Zen philosophy, 125, 128, 193; haiku and, 110, 115, 116, 118, 122
Ziff, Larzer, 73, 83–84
Zinsser, William, 100
Zoubek, Philip, 45